AF606980

Ruth Asawa Life’s Work

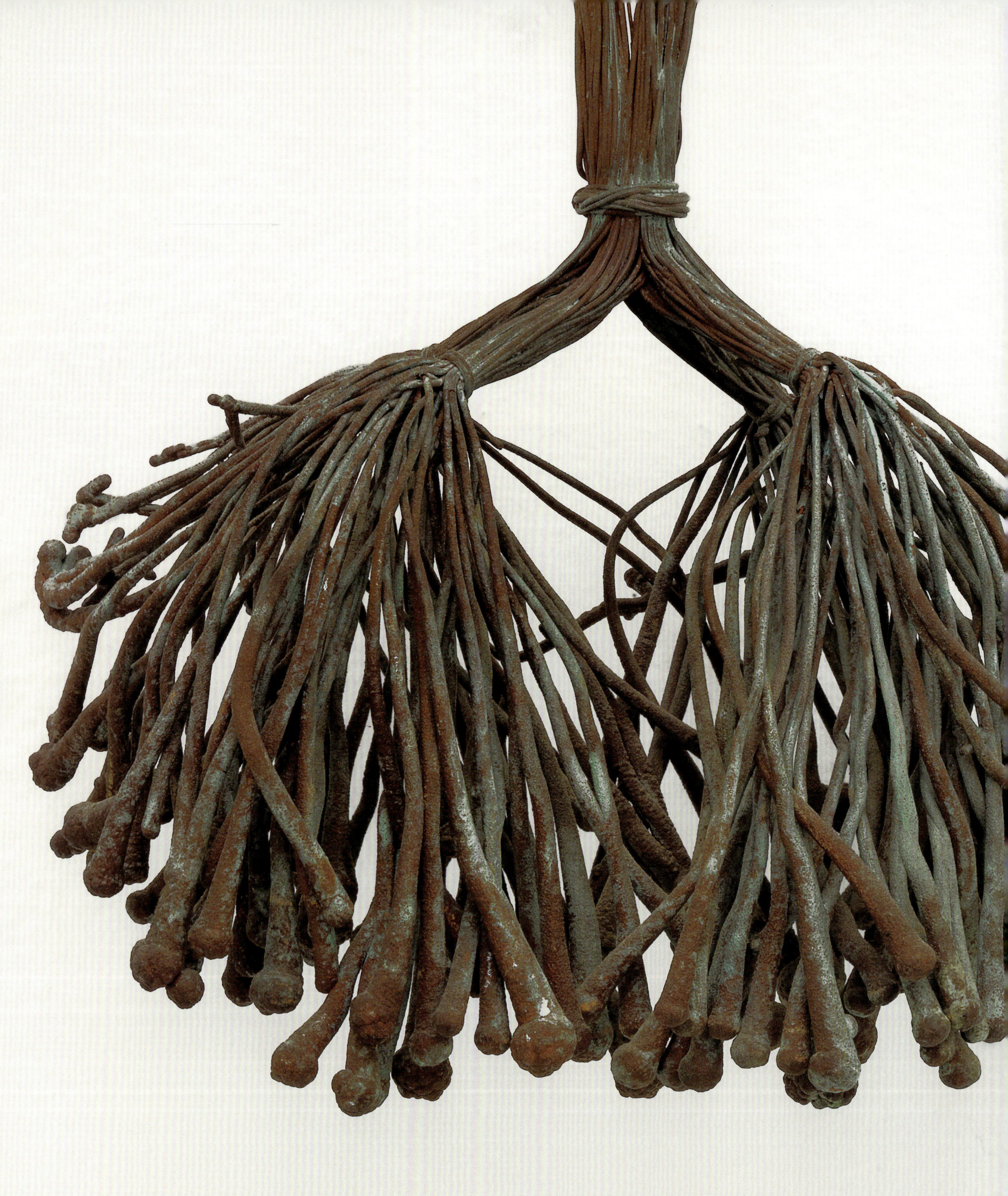

Ruth Asawa Life's Work

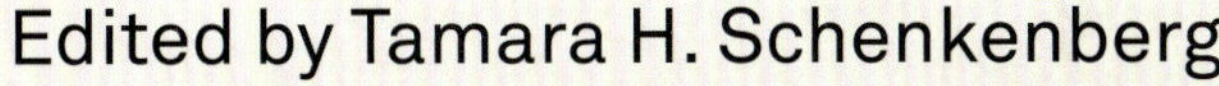
Edited by Tamara H. Schenkenberg

Essays by Aruna D'Souza, Helen Molesworth, and Tamara H. Schenkenberg

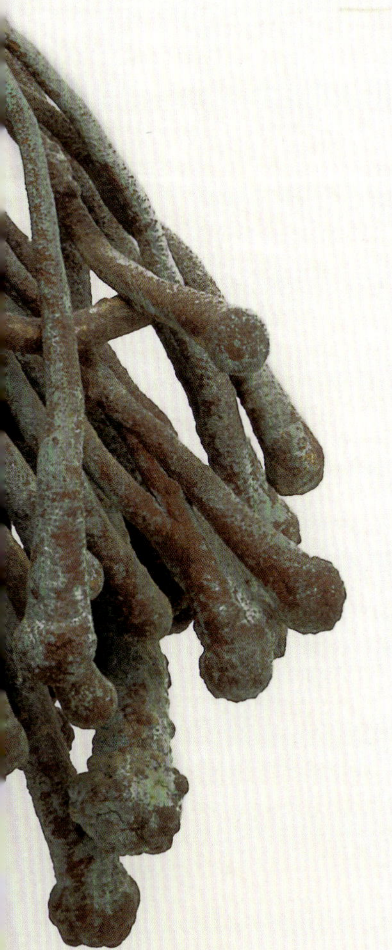

Pulitzer Arts Foundation
In association with Yale University Press, New Haven and London

This book is published on the occasion of the exhibition

Ruth Asawa: Life's Work

Organized by Tamara H. Schenkenberg,
Curator, Pulitzer Arts Foundation

Pulitzer Arts Foundation
September 14, 2018–February 16, 2019

Published by
Pulitzer Arts Foundation
3716 Washington Boulevard
St. Louis, MO 63108
pulitzerarts.org

Published in association with
Yale University Press
302 Temple Street
P.O. Box 209040
New Haven, CT 06520-9040
yalebooks.com

Produced by
Lucia | Marquand, Seattle
luciamarquand.com

Editors: Donna Wingate and Marc Joseph Berg
Publication Coordinator: Brittny Koskela
Research assistant: Heather Alexis Smith
Proofreader: Jane Hyun
Designers: Rita Jules and Miko McGinty
Typesetter: Tina Henderson
Color management: iocolor, Seattle
Printed and bound in Italy by Graphicom

Second printing, 2021

Library of Congress Cataloging-in-Publication Data

Names: Schenkenberg, Tamara H., editor. | D'Souza, Aruna. | Molesworth, Helen Anne. | Asawa, Ruth. Works. Selections. | Pulitzer Arts Foundation, organizer, host institution.
Title: Ruth Asawa : life's work / edited by Tamara Schenkenberg ; essays by Aruna D'Souza, Helen Molesworth, and Tamara H. Schenkenberg.
Description: St. Louis, MO : Pulitzer Arts Foundation ; New Haven, CT : in association with Yale University Press, 2019. | Published on the occasion of the exhibition held Sept. 14, 2018–Feb. 16, 2019, Pulitzer Arts Foundation, Saint Louis, Missouri. | Includes bibliographical references and index.
Identifiers: LCCN 2018044957 | ISBN 9780300242690 (hardback)
Subjects: LCSH: Asawa, Ruth—Exhibitions. | Asawa, Ruth—Criticism and interpretation. | BISAC: ART / Individual Artists / Monographs. | ART / History / Contemporary (1945–). | ART / Collections, Catalogs, Exhibitions / General.
Classification: LCC NB237.A82 A4 2018 | DDC 730.92—dc23
LC record available at https://lccn.loc.gov/2018044957

Front cover: Ruth Asawa, 1957. Photo by Imogen Cunningham, © Imogen Cunningham Trust.

Frontispiece: *Untitled* (S.059, Wall-Mounted Electroplated Tied-Wire, Center-Tied, Four-Branched Form Based on Nature) (detail), ca. 1963. Electroplated copper wire, 7⅝ × 8 × 4 inches (19.4 × 20.3 × 10.2 cm). © Estate of Ruth Asawa. Courtesy the Estate of Ruth Asawa and David Zwirner. Photo by Alise O'Brien Photography, © Pulitzer Arts Foundation and Alise O'Brien Photography

Back cover: Installation view of *Ruth Asawa: Life's Work*. Photo by Alise O'Brien Photography, © Pulitzer Arts Foundation and Alise O'Brien Photography

All unidentified installation views are from the exhibition *Ruth Asawa: Life's Work*, Pulitzer Arts Foundation, St. Louis September 14, 2018–February 16, 2019. Photos by Alise O'Brien Photography, © Pulitzer Arts Foundation and Alise O'Brien Photography

Contents

Director's Foreword

Cara Starke

For Ruth Asawa, art and life were inseparable. From her days as a student at Black Mountain College to her advocacy for arts education in San Francisco public schools, art and daily life were entwined. Perhaps this is best exemplified by her studio, a dynamic space actively used for both work and dialogue with her community, situated in the home she shared with her husband, architect Albert Lanier, and their six children. Although Asawa's influence was widespread, until very recently she remained underrepresented in museums outside of her native California.

It is the Pulitzer Arts Foundation's great privilege to present the first museum exhibition of Asawa's work beyond the West Coast, and this accompanying publication. I would like to thank Pulitzer Arts Foundation Curator Tamara H. Schenkenberg for her clarity of vision, impeccable planning, and deep sensitivity to how one best experiences Asawa's work, qualities that were reinforced by her sincere commitment to the artist's vision and legacy. I would also like to thank Aruna D'Souza and Helen Molesworth for the thought-provoking and insightful essays. Their texts are important contributions to the growing scholarly literature about this remarkable artist.

Many individuals and museums made this exhibition possible by generously lending works from their collections, some of which have never before been exhibited: Executive Director Jeff Arnal of the Black Mountain College Museum + Arts Center; Susan Sayre Batton, Oshman Executive Director of the San José Museum of Art; Dr. Neal Benezra, Helen and Charles Schwab Director of the San Francisco Museum of Modern Art; Executive Director and Chief Diversity and Inclusion Officer Rod Bigelow at the Crystal Bridges Museum of American Art; Chuck and Kathy Harper; Mrs. Philip A. Hassel; Max Hollein, Former Director and CEO of the Fine Arts Museums of San Francisco; Chris Houston; Holly Johnson and Parker Harris; Director Glenn D. Lowry at the Museum of Modern Art, New York; Diana Nelson and John Atwater; William and Joan Roth; the Snyder Family Living Trust; Martha Tedeschi, Elizabeth and John Moors Cabot Director of the Harvard Art Museums; Director Gary Tinterow of the Museum of Fine Arts, Houston; Alice and Tom Tisch; Adam D. Weinberg, Alice Pratt Brown Director of the Whitney Museum of American Art; David Zwirner for facilitating loans; and those lenders who wish to remain anonymous.

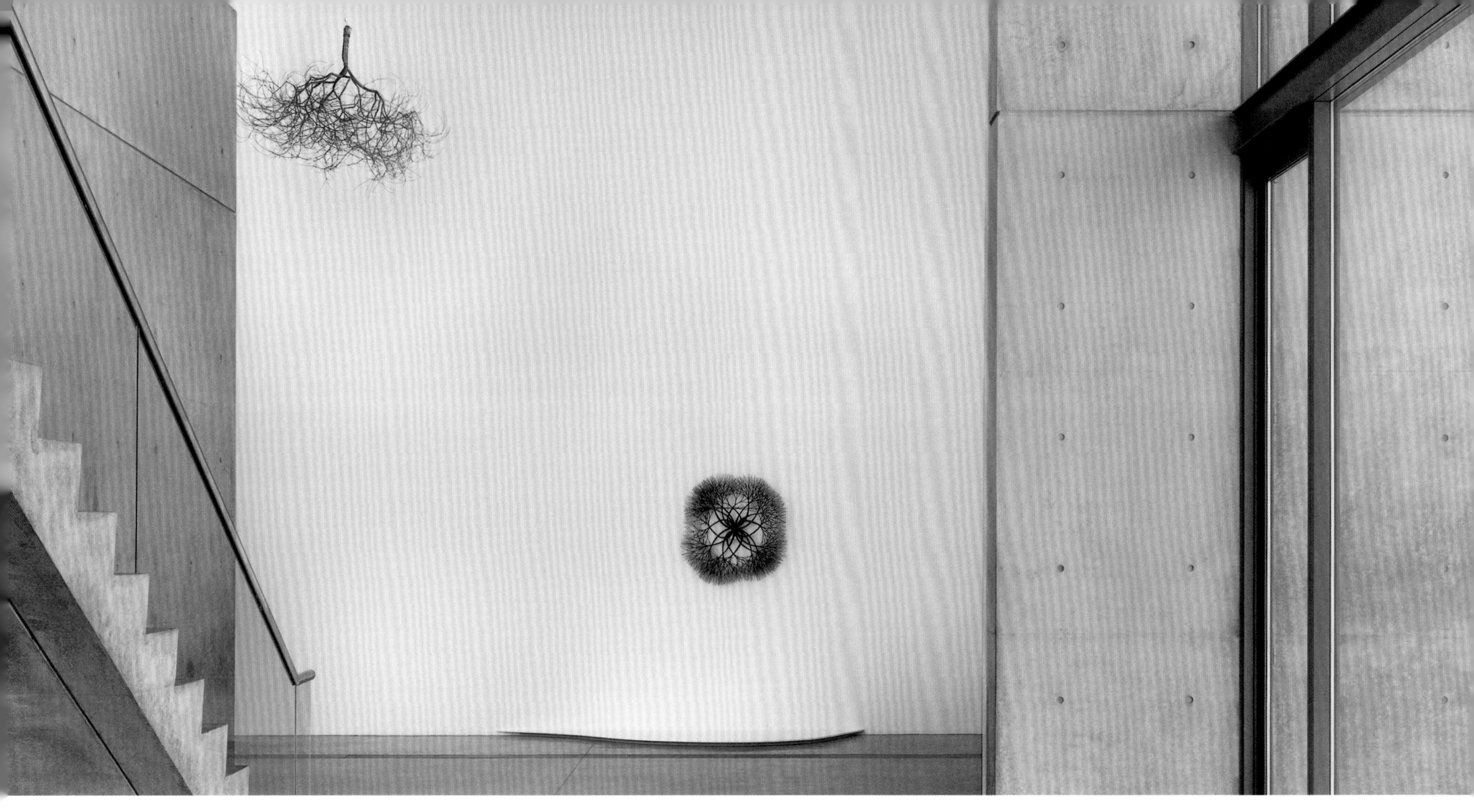

I also thank Jonathan Laib, Director at David Zwirner, whose steadfast commitment to Asawa has been integral to advancing the artist's legacy, and whose understanding of Asawa's work has been invaluable throughout the development of this exhibition.

I extend my warmest gratitude to Ruth Asawa's extraordinary family, who wholeheartedly supported this project and opened their hearts and homes to us. Our most sincere thanks go to Asawa's children Aiko Cuneo and Addie Lanier, who graciously assisted our team at many stages, as well as Hudson, Paul, and Xavier Lanier, who provided us with important insights into their mother's work. I also thank dancer Emma Lanier for choreographing and performing a thoughtful work inspired by her grandmother at the opening of the exhibition.

For their support and assistance I additionally acknowledge Timothy Anglin Burgard, Ednah Root Curator in Charge of American Art Department at the Fine Arts Museums of San Francisco; Laura Edelman, Assistant to Jonathan Laib at David Zwirner; the Imogen Cunningham Trust; Jaime Schwartz, Associate Director of Research and Exhibitions at David Zwirner; the Stanford University Libraries' Special Collections department, which granted access to Asawa's archive; Miko McGinty and Rita Jules, for their beautiful and intelligent book design; Donna Wingate and Marc Joseph Berg, who edited this catalogue; and Leah Finger and Meghann Ney at Lucia|Marquand, who provided vital production coordination.

The Pulitzer's extraordinary staff played an important role in realizing this exhibition. I am grateful to Curatorial Assistant Heather Alexis Smith for her invaluable help at all stages of the project. I recognize Registrar Natalie M. Foster, Lead Preparator Steve Gibbs, Assistant Registrar Brittny Koskela, Director of Exhibition Design and Installation Shane Simmons, Curatorial Administrative Assistant Neena Wang, and Assistant Curator Stephanie Weissberg, along with the dedicated colleagues in our Communications, Public Programs and Engagement, and Visitor Services departments. Finally, I offer my gratitude to Board Chair Emily Rauh Pulitzer and to all members of the Pulitzer's Board of Trustees. Their generosity of spirit, enthusiasm, and guidance allow us to realize projects of this magnitude.

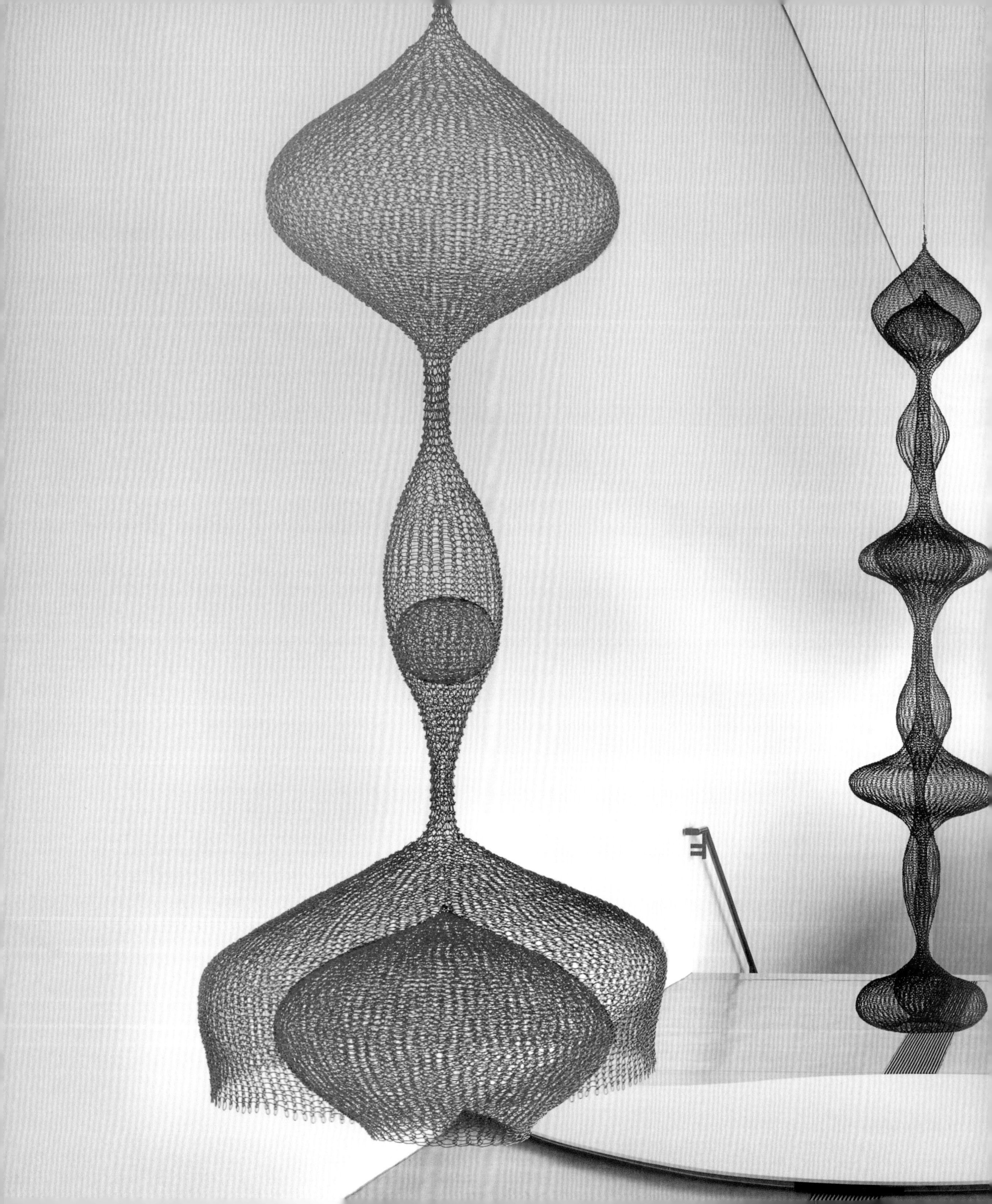

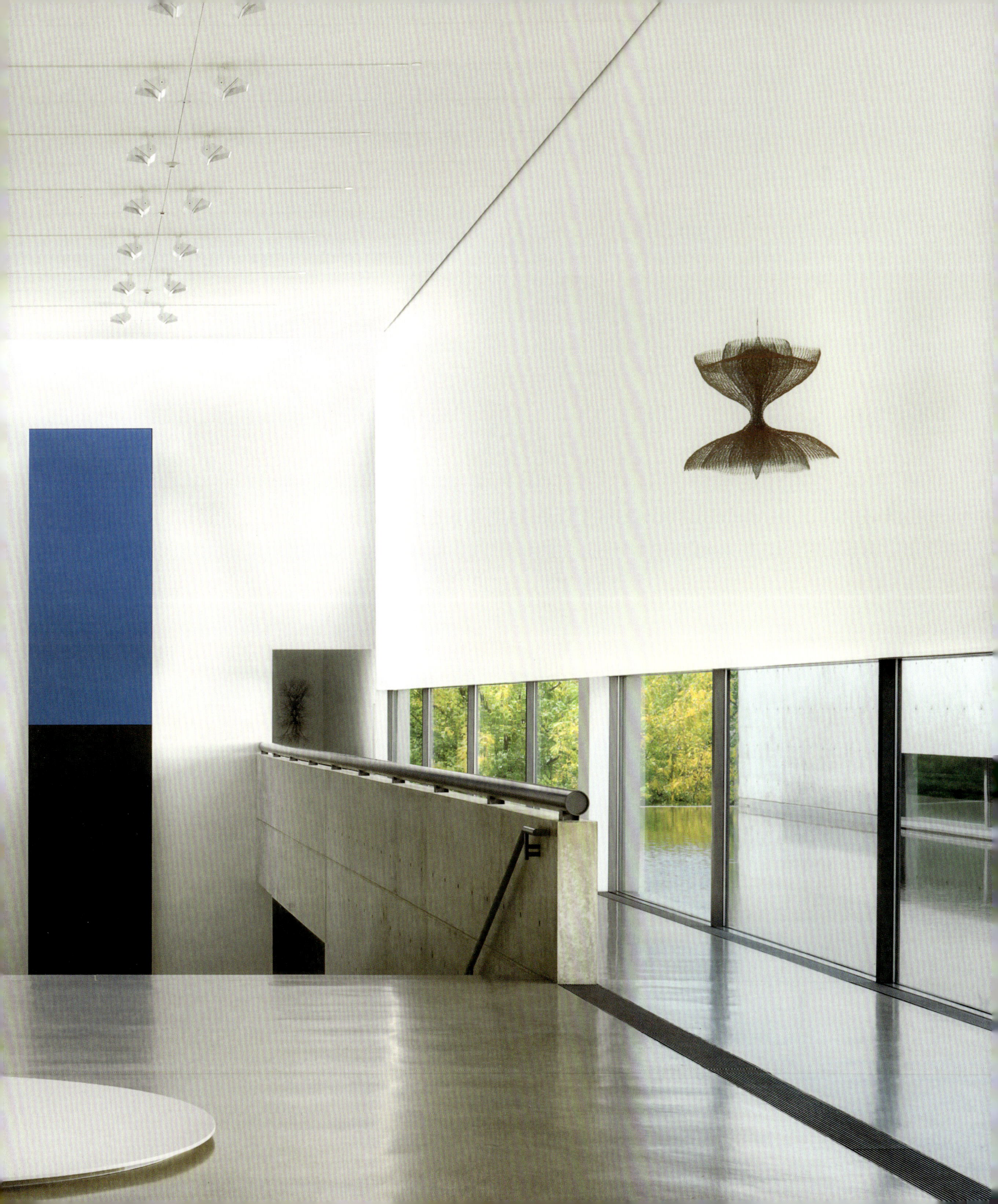

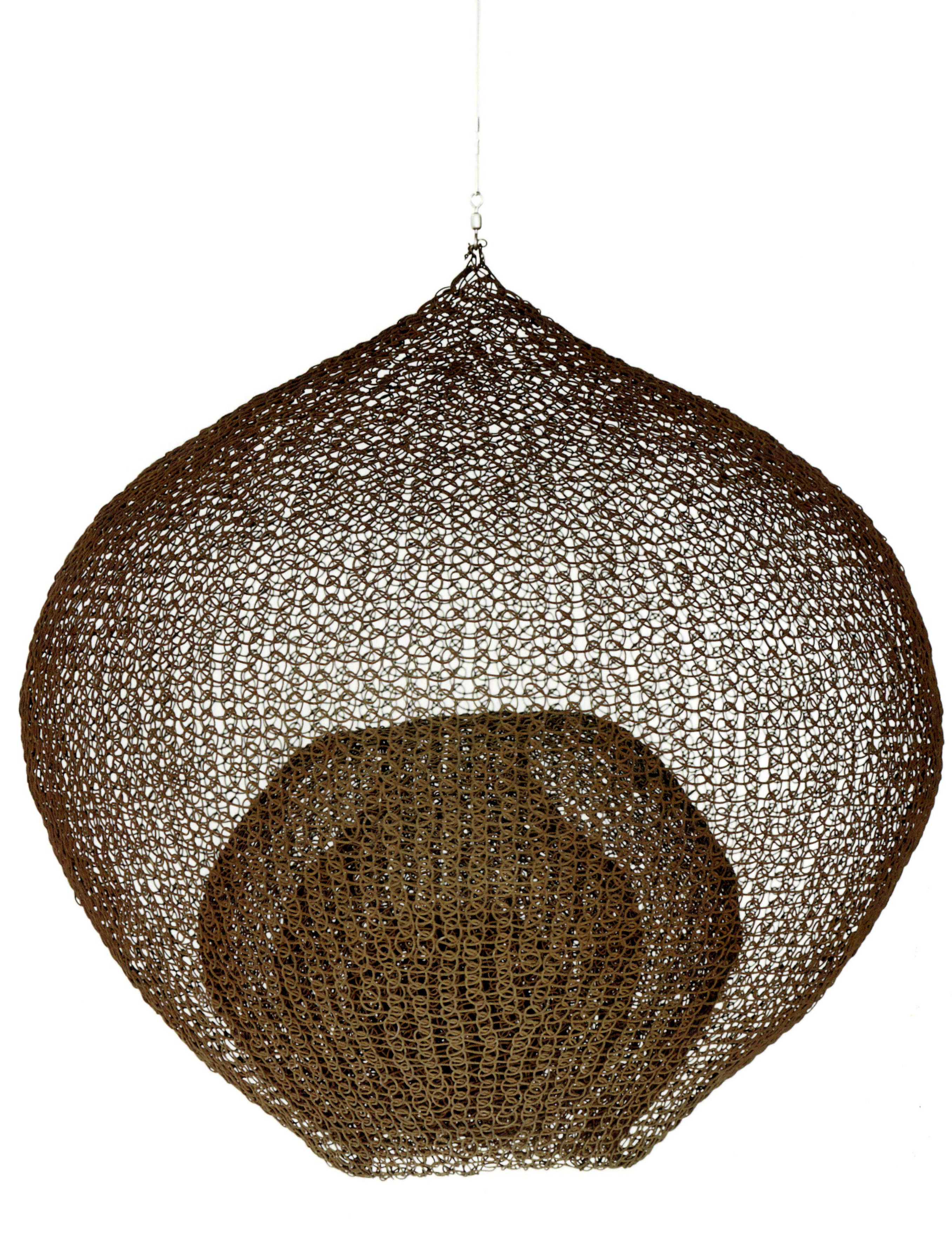

Untitled (S.095, Hanging Single-Lobed, Six-Layered Continuous Form within a Form), ca. 1952. Iron wire, 15½ × 17 × 17 inches (39.4 × 43.2 × 43.2 cm)

Life's Work

Tamara H. Schenkenberg

Learning is cumulative, which comes from experiences with many people with different viewpoints and techniques. Techniques are simple to learn. Digesting them and making something that represents you will take a lifetime. Learn to draw, build, work with materials. Above everything be curious, learn all you can, and take a lifetime doing it.

—Ruth Asawa

From the time she began working in the early 1940s, Ruth Asawa was a consummate artist. Largely underrecognized outside the San Francisco Bay Area, where she lived for over six decades, Asawa is now best known for innovative sculptures in wire, her signature material. Over the course of her prolific career, she continually developed new techniques and processes for working with wire, each one inspiring new directions in her work.

Asawa first hit upon a key idea and a new method for one of those technical achievements in the early 1950s. She excitedly described this breakthrough and the potential it held for the development of her sculpture in her application for a Guggenheim Fellowship, hoping to secure financial support as she worked to further develop it.[1] Asawa visualized this "continuous form within a form" in a drawing featuring a sculpture composed of six graduating spheres [fig. 1, top right]. The descriptive title referred to the way she started the work from within—beginning with the innermost, or the smallest, sphere—and then progressed outward, to create a series of overlapping spheres in a continuous surface, with no disruption from beginning to end. Asawa considered this technique one of her most important innovations, and the six-layered sculpture depicted in this drawing—her most unique construction by far—was made sometime around 1952: *Untitled* (S.095) [p. 10]. Although the Guggenheim passed her over for the fellowship, Asawa continued to realize this form, employing extraordinary skill and precision to create a number of original and intricate works.

This early and pivotal technical achievement greatly advanced a line of thinking that Asawa elaborated into varied formal applications and with increasing complexity. In order to trace the evolution of Asawa's sculpture across decades and multiple periods of development, it is instructive to examine the contexts from which her groundbreaking work emerged, including her early years growing up on a farm; her studies at Black Mountain

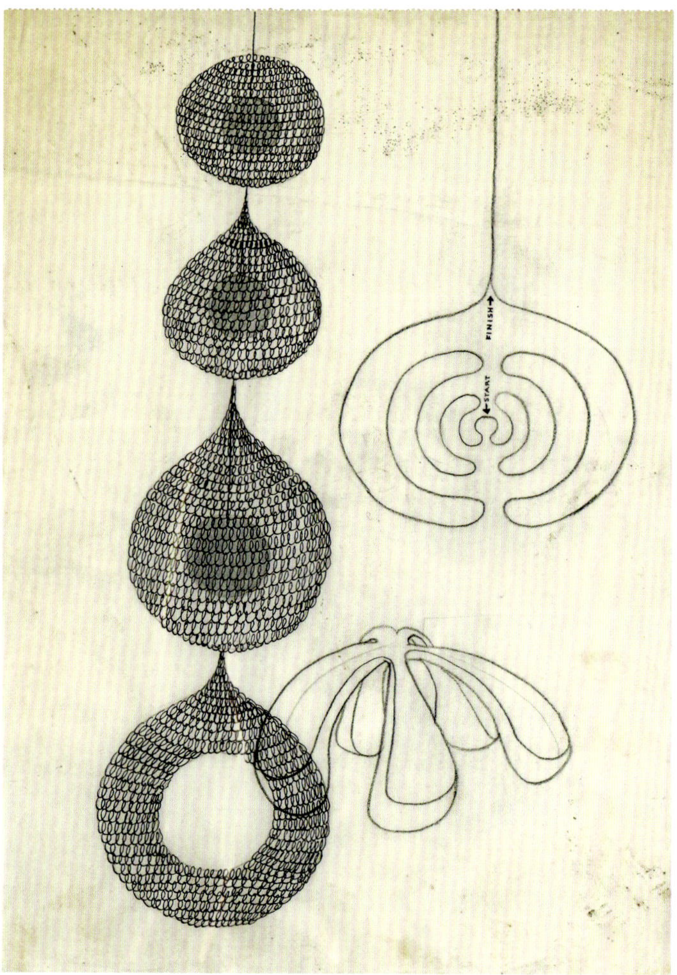

Fig. 1. Ruth Asawa Papers, 1952. Department of Special Collections and University Archives, Stanford University Libraries, box 129, folder 1

College; and her family life—all of which she cited as essential to her truly remarkable artistic practice.

•

During the early 1960s, Asawa and her family spent summers in the community of Guerneville, in the Russian River area of Sonoma County, just north of San Francisco. The rough-and-tumble acreage Asawa and her husband, the architect Albert Lanier, purchased had once housed a ranch, though a flood during the prior decade had wiped out that enterprise. The property included a barn-like structure with aluminum siding, a nearby shed, an underground spring, and large redwood trees in a canyon. The artist was determined to use this rural site to teach her six children hard work, so six days a week during three summers, while the three youngest played in the fields, Asawa and her three older children picked apples for eight hours a day. The children earned money to buy their school clothes in the fall.

Asawa and Lanier's ideas about art making and family were consistently fused with actual labor. In the summer of 1961, Asawa worked with her children to carve a pair of oversized redwood entry doors for the family's San Francisco home [fig. 2]. While Asawa did most of the work, including using white chalk to draw a series of wave-like patterns (a moving spiral line she called "the meander"), the three older children helped with the carving and burnishing. Adam, who was about five years old at the time and obsessed with bees, carved "bee holes" in the doors. Once an area was chiseled, the family used a small torch to burn the rough edges smooth. Then, with a wire brush, they removed most of the charred surface debris. This darkening technique raised the grain and softened the splintery edges.[2]

By the time the doors were installed at the family home, Asawa had spent just over a decade in San Francisco. Before moving there in 1949, she studied for three years at Black Mountain College, a small art school in rural North Carolina that became an unlikely epicenter for multidisciplinary learning, whose distinguished faculty and alumni accomplished nothing short of charting the course for postwar American art. The Bay Area was appealing to Asawa and fellow student Lanier, then her fiancé, for at least two reasons: a friend had informed them that in San Francisco, a multicourse Italian dinner and a bottle of red wine could be had for seventy-five cents; and especially, in the months leading up to their arrival, California had legalized interracial marriage (Asawa was Asian American and Lanier was Caucasian American).[3]

It was immediately after this period, in the 1950s and '60s, that Asawa began her lifelong project, most notably her innovative wire sculptures, advancing her art practice while simultaneously raising their children. She also cofounded the Alvarado School Arts Workshop in 1968, whose main goal was to bring working artists in various disciplines into public schools to teach on an ongoing basis. This initiative, which eventually developed into an artist-in-residence program across fifty San Francisco public schools, launched Asawa's longstanding involvement in arts advocacy, a facet of her career that she further propagated by serving on numerous commissions and boards. It was also in

1968 that Asawa installed her first public sculpture, in Ghirardelli Square [see p. 31, fig. 15]; other such public installations would soon follow, expanding yet another sphere of her artistic engagement.

Two ambitious retrospectives of Asawa's work were organized by major museums in San Francisco, in 1973 and 2006. Prior to these, Asawa exhibited her work sporadically, though steadily, predominantly in California. Only recently—after Jonathan Laib organized two exhibitions at Christie's (the first, in 2013, was the artist's first showing in New York in over fifty years)—has greater national attention been paid to Asawa's extraordinary career, bringing with it growing representation in museum collections across the country.

Reevaluation of Asawa's work has thus occurred, and falls into three broad categories. One tends toward the biographical, and has helped flesh out various episodes in her remarkable life: as a child born in 1926 to a Japanese immigrant farming family in Southern California; as a prisoner, along with her family, during the US internment of Japanese and Japanese American citizens and residents after the attack on Pearl Harbor between 1942 and 1945; as a student at Black Mountain College, training with pioneering modernists, such as Josef and Anni Albers, Buckminster Fuller, and Merce Cunningham; and finally, as an artist and arts advocate who worked for over five decades in San Francisco until her death in 2013, at the age of eighty-seven.[4] Scholars have also reexamined the early reception of her work, highlighting her various identities—as a person of Japanese heritage, as a woman, wife, and mother—often at the expense of carefully considering her art or, alternately, situating it in the context of craft-based practices rather than sculpture.[5]

Contemporary scholarship has also raised questions about the recent positioning of Asawa as a forgotten "bohemian gamine,"[6] without recognizing her many public commissions and influential work in San Francisco public schools, a reductive view that minimizes her great accomplishments as a whole.[7] This image, buttressed by certain of the more stylized pictures taken by Asawa's friend and pioneering photographer Imogen Cunningham, have created an impression of the artist as chic and cool, possessing a certain mystique. In these photographs, Asawa, as directed by Cunningham, peers alluringly from behind her sculptures, her lips painted bright red. In some images she even poses with the work, which drapes sensually

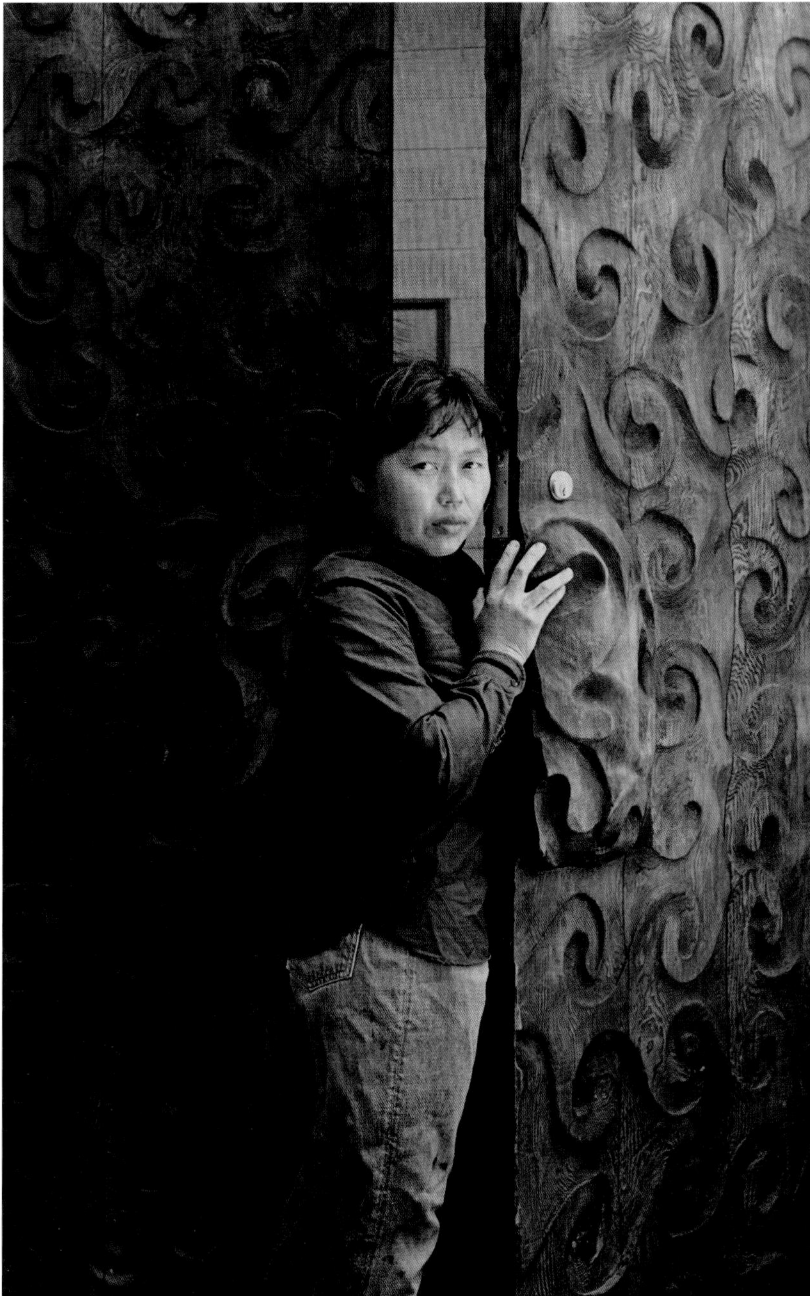

Fig. 2. Ruth Asawa at the front door to her Noe Valley home, San Francisco, 1963. Photo by Imogen Cunningham

around her body [fig. 3]. This portrayal as a fashionable Beat-era heroine stands in stark contrast with the hard-working artist, who preferred more utilitarian attire. Many contemporaneous photographs show Asawa dressed in a pair of jeans, an old dress shirt, and well-worn sneakers [fig. 4]. These images of the artist at work align more closely with the story of a woman who involved her family with labor and art making, expressed in part through their summer activities. It is also especially via the artist's own words that the romantic notion of Asawa, adrift in her own inner world, is quickly dispelled. If we closely read statements she made during the course of her long career, another portrait comes into view: that of Asawa as a dedicated maker, deeply committed to performing acts of labor as a catalyst for both artistic innovation and personal growth and fulfilment.

Speaking about her teachers at Black Mountain College, Asawa said, "They taught me that there is no separation between studying, performing the daily chores of living, and creating one's own work. . . . Through them I came to understand the total commitment required to be an artist."[8] Seen through this lens, we begin to understand how the notion of work can situate Asawa's unique and highly individualized practice and unite her multifaceted roles as artist, mother, wife, and community member.

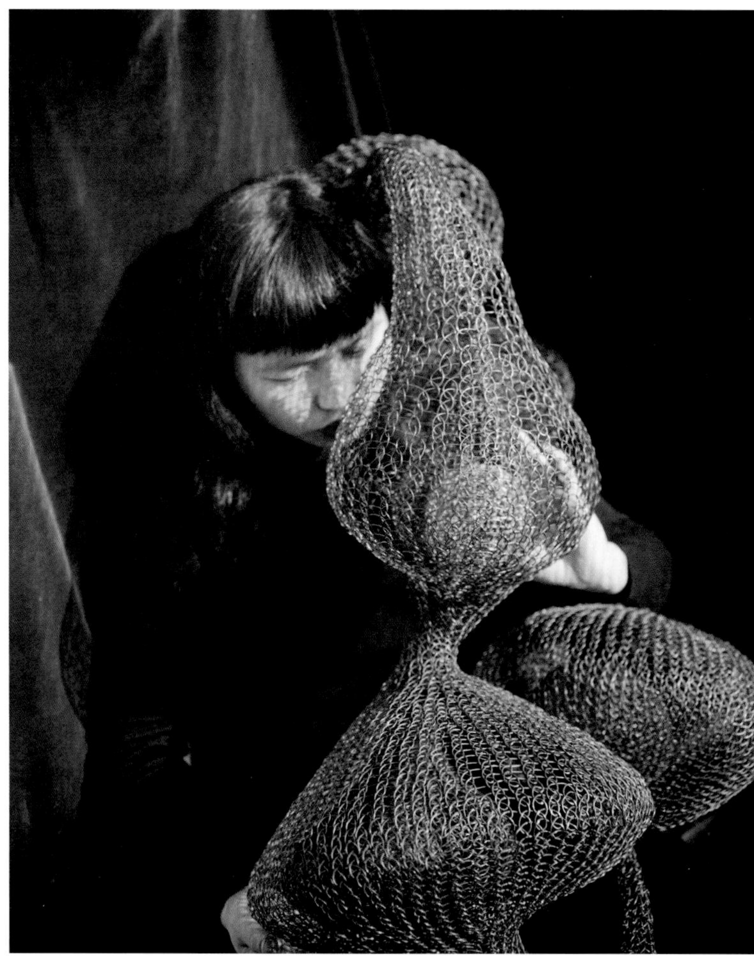

Fig. 3. Ruth Asawa, 1951. Photo by Imogen Cunningham

•

Ruth Asawa's lifelong experiments in form were based on the self-imposed material limitation of working predominantly with industrial wire. By the mid-1990s, after more than five decades of this specific aspect of her practice, she continued to express enthusiasm over the "endless possibilities" that wire could afford.[9] Wire was ubiquitous on her parents' farm, and she was deeply familiar with it from a young age. "I used to unwind the wire tags that labeled the crates of vegetables and took the fine brass and steel wires and braided and twisted them together to make bracelets, rings, and figures."[10] Wire as a material in fine art was not exalted and was largely free of symbolic associations. This would have resonated with Asawa's training under Josef Albers, whom she considered her principal teacher at Black Mountain College; her first course of study with him, Basic Color and Design, in 1946, was transformative. "Another world opened up for me," she later said.[11] In that class, Asawa was particularly inspired by the

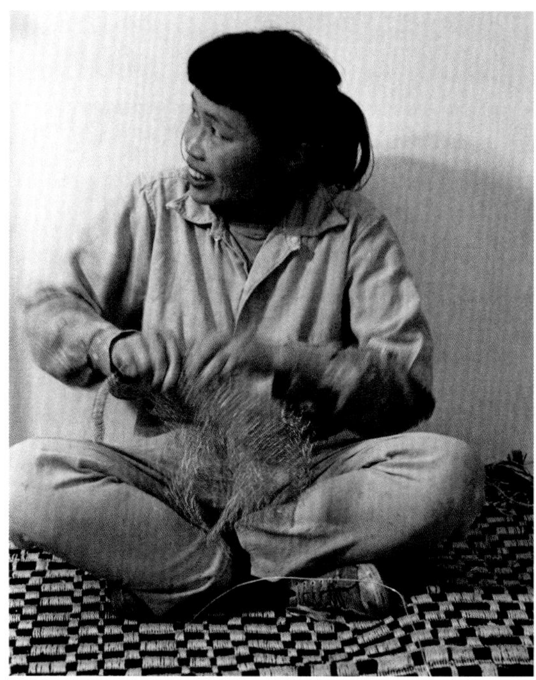

Fig. 4. Asawa looping wire, ca. 1956. Photo by Paul Hassel

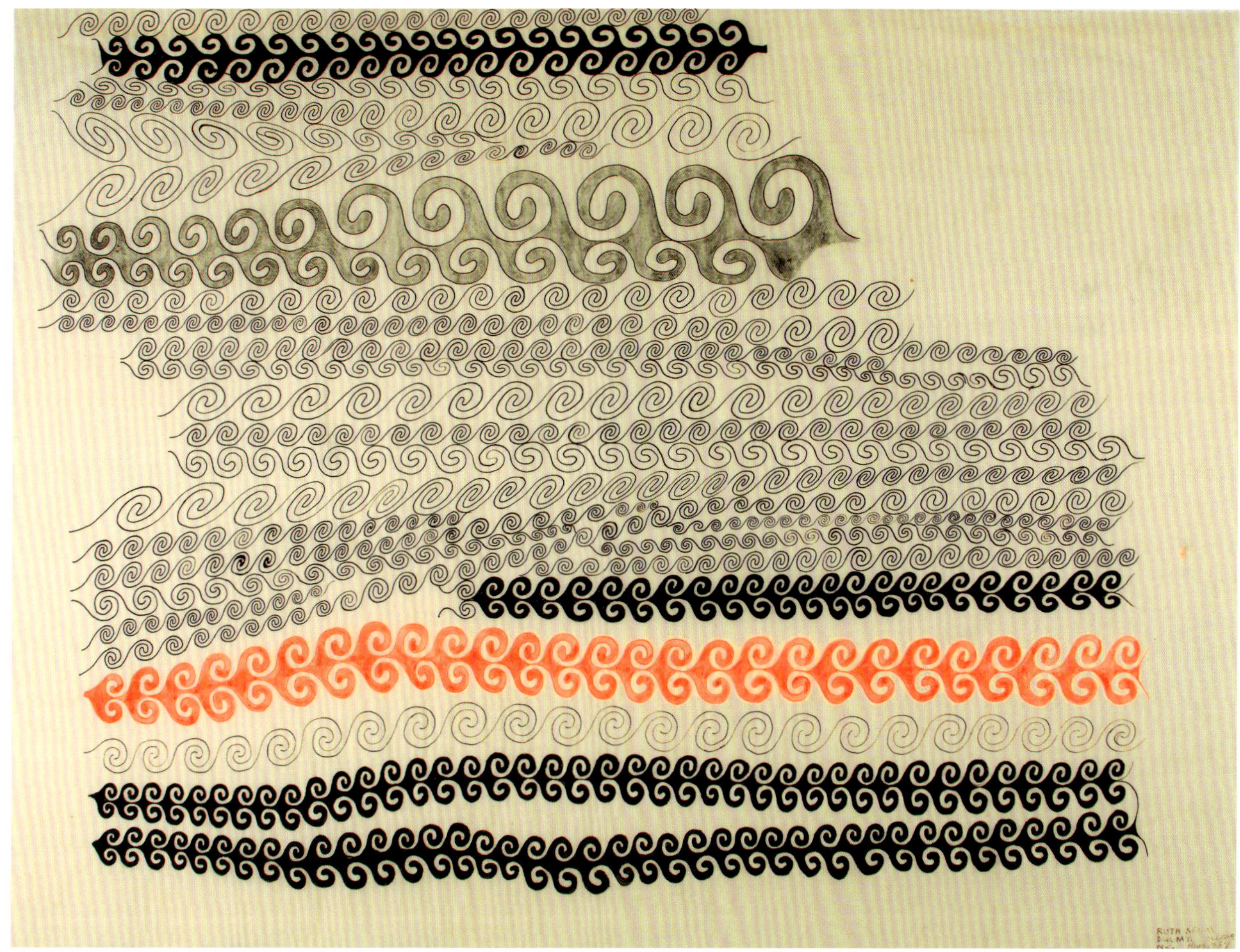

Untitled (BMC.124, Meander Black and Red), ca. 1946–49. Black and red ink with graphite on tracing paper, 17 × 22 inches (43.2 × 55.9 cm)

matière studies that encouraged students to explore properties of humble, everyday materials, such as eggshells and leaves, which they often scrounged and recycled from the school's rural site.

Albers was a formidable teacher whose authoritarian presence was off-putting to many, but not to Asawa, who found his strict and matter-of-fact demeanor stimulating. In a presentation at the San Francisco Museum of Art in 1963 about her former teacher, Asawa remembered that Albers began his class by telling students to "open your eyes and see."[12] His first lesson was to demonstrate the extent of the students' impoverished ways of seeing the world by asking them to draw ubiquitous imagery, such as the Coca-Cola logo, which they often struggled to re-create from memory. Albers would then prompt a series of drawing experiments to deconstruct a familiar motif—such as a student's name. These exercises included drawing and reversing the chosen motif; using both the dominant and nondominant hand to render it; and executing it right side up and upside down. Such simple processes, aimed at sparking the student's powers of observation, rested on practical, hands-on learning. Asawa summarized this key lesson by stating that "with art, your motor sense should be developed at full capacity."[13]

Respect for skills of the hand as a basis for art making was complemented by another of Albers's credos, namely that individual exercises could never be completed—one experiment could only transition into the next. This is particularly evident in a number of works Asawa made as a student based on the aforementioned meander. She pursued this pattern across a number of drawings, paintings, and collages. Executed in freehand, Asawa's meanders visualize her attempts to gain greater control of motor skills, while also demonstrating the ways in which difference could be achieved through repetition. In one untitled drawing, Asawa arranged the meander into rows that stretch, contract, and twist [p. 15]. They unfold in different sizes, directions, colors, and orientations to convey movement and rhythm that is played off the negative space of the page. A commitment to such painstaking exercises may account for the comments Albers wrote on Asawa's report card, describing her as: "Very interested. Developed somewhat toward precision work. Talented and particularly helpful and good as a member of the community."[14]

The curriculum at Black Mountain College underscored to Asawa the value of hands-on efforts, equipping her with a methodology that encouraged her to experiment with form and materials. In 1947, after completing her first year of studies, Asawa traveled to Mexico for the summer, where she learned a technique that translated her investigation of design and line into the third dimension.

Asawa had already visited Mexico before enrolling at Black Mountain College, in the summer of 1945. Her initial trip was stimulating, fortuitously leading to her studies with Clara Porset, a friend of Josef and Anni Albers and a pioneering furniture designer, who spoke highly of the innovative college in North Carolina. But her second sojourn to Mexico in 1947 was more momentous, leading Asawa to discover a technique that she would use to develop her signature work. This time, a setting far removed from the fine arts context triggered her foray into sculpture. While visiting the town of Toluca as a volunteer art teacher for The American Friends Service Committee, Asawa became fascinated with wire baskets designed to hold eggs. With the help of a local craftsman, she learned a looping technique that would become her primary means of expression for decades.[15] The fact that this way of working had taken a strong hold of her imagination can be surmised by the report card she received after returning to Black Mountain for the fall term. Ilya Bolotowsky, a teacher who had previously praised Asawa as "an excellent draftsman," indicated that her interest in drawing had waned, but that she "has done a lot of work with wire construction."[16]

Although working in wire allowed Asawa to leverage her training in painting and drawing, it also inadvertently led her into the third dimension: "I had no intentions of going into sculpture, but found that sculpture was just an extension of drawing. . . . I'm primarily intrigued with, not so much achieving a style, but . . . bringing another personality to wire, which is, I think, an extension of the thinking that Albers tried to teach us."[17] Here again Asawa's imagination was triggered by the exploration of the material: "I'm not so interested in the expression of something. But, I'm more interested in what the material can do. And so that's why I keep exploring."[18]

While the multivalent properties of wire appealed to Asawa, the method she used to explore it prevented her sculptures from being accepted into exhibitions and, more generally, the art world. "It wasn't stone, it wasn't welded steel, it wasn't traditional sculpture. They thought it was craft, or something else, but not art. They couldn't define it in the early fifties when I was starting out. I'd get accepted [into a show] and then I'd get a call that I was disqualified because my work wasn't sculpture. . . . I don't care whether or not someone says that my work is art or is not art. I am interested in finding solutions to problems."[19] These solutions emerged through the rigorous, even arduous manipulation of wire, which formed the basis of Asawa's technique. Far from eschewing associations with labor, her sculpture depended on the skilled work of her hand.

Before she could create a form in space, Asawa had to coil wire around a wooden dowel to produce a series of uniform loops. She then interlocked loops to generate a row. With each new row she could advance the form in one of three ways: keep the same number to maintain the same volume; add an extra loop to a row to expand the form; or overlap two loops in a row to shrink its breadth. Although the technique was based on knitting, Asawa didn't use needles since the "live" loops (e.g., loops that were not yet interlocked with another row) could not unravel because wire holds its shape. Aside from pliers required to coil loose ends and cut the wire, Asawa made everything by hand. She likened the tedium of this process to

> planting five acres of onions during Christmas vacation, or harvesting in July, all of these things. It's very easy in a way for me to do it because it's out of my own past, having worked on a farm and doing many things that were repetitive, like stringing the bean pole for beans to climb up on and picking the beans and sorting the tomatoes, picking tomatoes, sowing and planting onions and gathering them. All of these things make it very logical that I would select a way

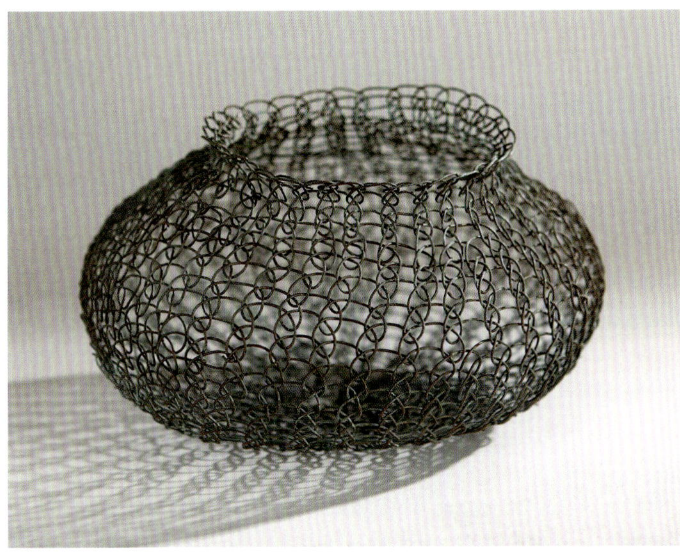

Fig. 5. *Untitled* (S.363, Freestanding Basket) ca. 1948–49. Copper wire, 4½ × 7½ × 7¾ inches (11.4 × 19 × 19.7 cm). Example of an early basket made at Black Mountain College

> of work that would be very similar to that, only done in wire instead of plants.[20]

Seasonal farm work and its cycles were not Asawa's only point of reference: at Black Mountain College students were encouraged to repeat courses without ever earning a formal grade or degree, thus the value of sustained and recurrent work were further reinforced.

It is clear that Asawa saw merit in repeating the same process, loop after loop. Her first works in wire recalled the utilitarian baskets she encountered in Mexico [fig. 5], and a number of undated studies that remain in Asawa's archive point to a host of issues that she may have been working through during her looped-wire experiments. These studies can be categorized into four types. The first consists of flat, saucerlike forms [fig. 6]. Here we witness Asawa examining the properties of wire in different metals—iron, copper, silver, brass, aluminum

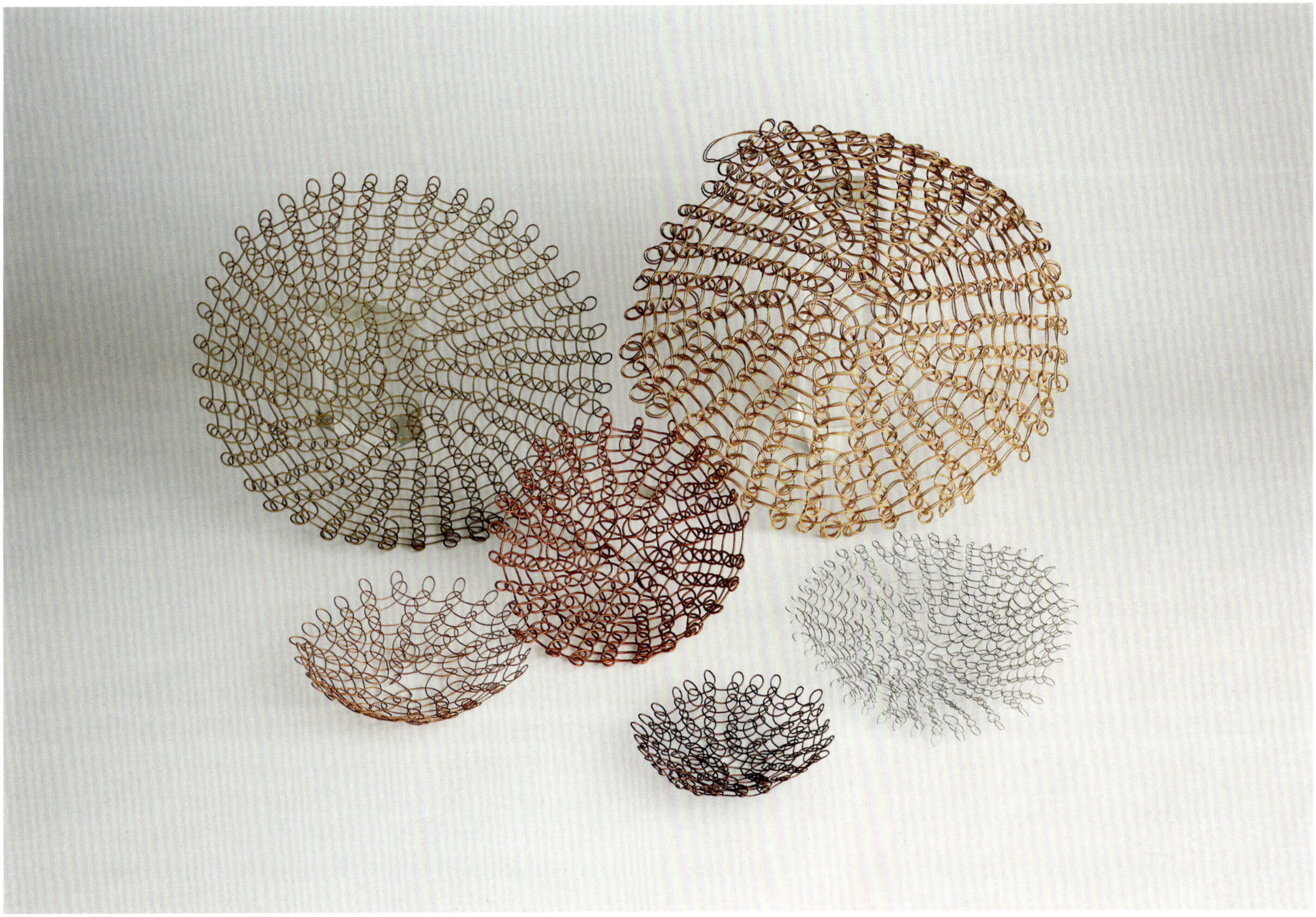

Fig. 6. Studies in different gauges and wires to test appearance, tension, density, and structural properties

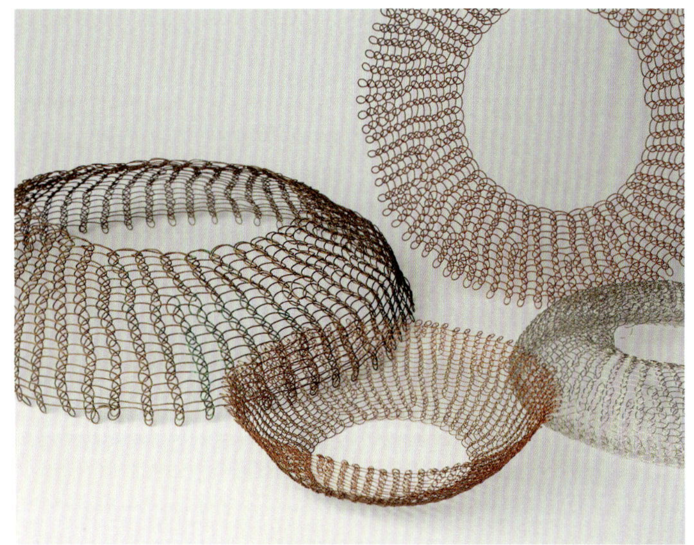

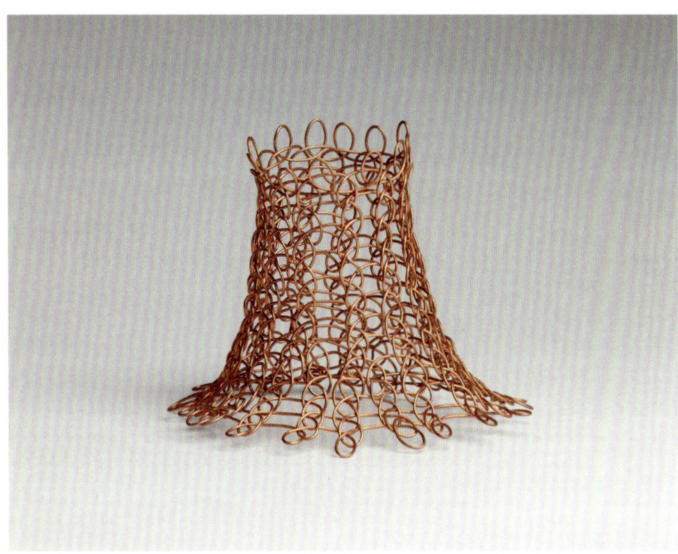

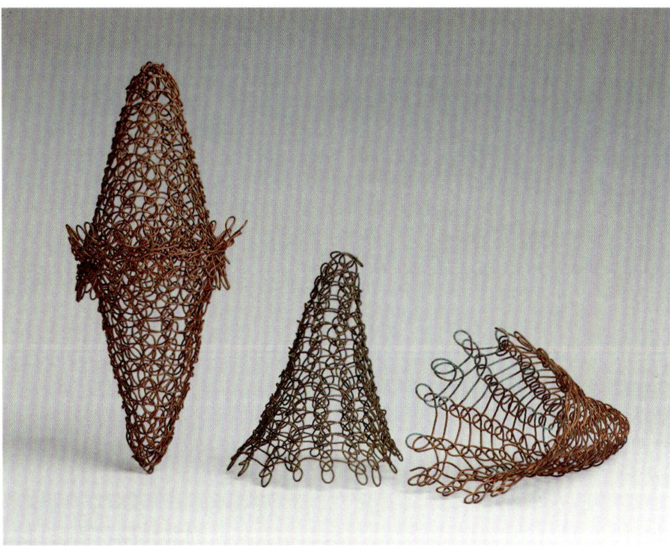

Figs. 7–9. Studies in different gauges and wires to test appearance, tension, density, and structural properties

—while assessing their natural color ranges. She was also experimenting with various formal densities: larger loops result in a more open and permeable surface, while smaller loops yield more tightly knit exteriors. At the same time, Asawa was using different gauges to analyze the linear quality of wire. A wide range of thicknesses enabled her to vacillate between delicate and heavy lines, as she did in her works on paper. The second group of wire studies considers these tests three-dimensionally. These collar-like prototypes are missing a center—a dispensable part of the construction given that the purpose of this experiment was most likely devoted to understanding the tensile quality of wire—and indicate how the material might flex as the construction starts to assume a form in space [fig. 7]. The third group of studies applies these exercises to tubular forms, or necks, that Asawa devised as extensions between lobes [fig. 8]. And finally, the last group reveals Asawa's interest in moving beyond the sphere to study not only conical shapes, but also the ways in which separate forms might intersect and interpenetrate [fig. 9].

Untitled (S.264), a sculpture Asawa made in 1949 (the year that marked her arrival in California from North Carolina), represents one of her major turning points as she moved from open basket forms to hanging looped-wire sculptures [p. 19, left]. Asawa began the sculpture from the lower center with a single strand of wire that she looped into a teardrop shape. She then tapered it into a long and narrow neck and repeated the teardrop form, which terminates in a single loop of wire at the very top that is used to hang the piece. This type of construction meant that the work no longer rested on a flat surface, but could be freely suspended in space. With this work Asawa began a new manner of execution that broke away from prevailing notions of sculpture, in that it defined volume while also being transparent, light, and even permeable. The sculpture could also be read as a two-dimensional line and a three-dimensional object.

Enclosing the surface begged the question of what other types of forms could be articulated and the ways in which those forms could be related to one another. For example, *Untitled* (S.264) is constructed in a single layer from a continuous length of wire. Another method Asawa devised enabled her to join separate and distinct spheres by chain—either by stacking one on top of another, such as in *Untitled* (S.793) [p. 19, right], or by

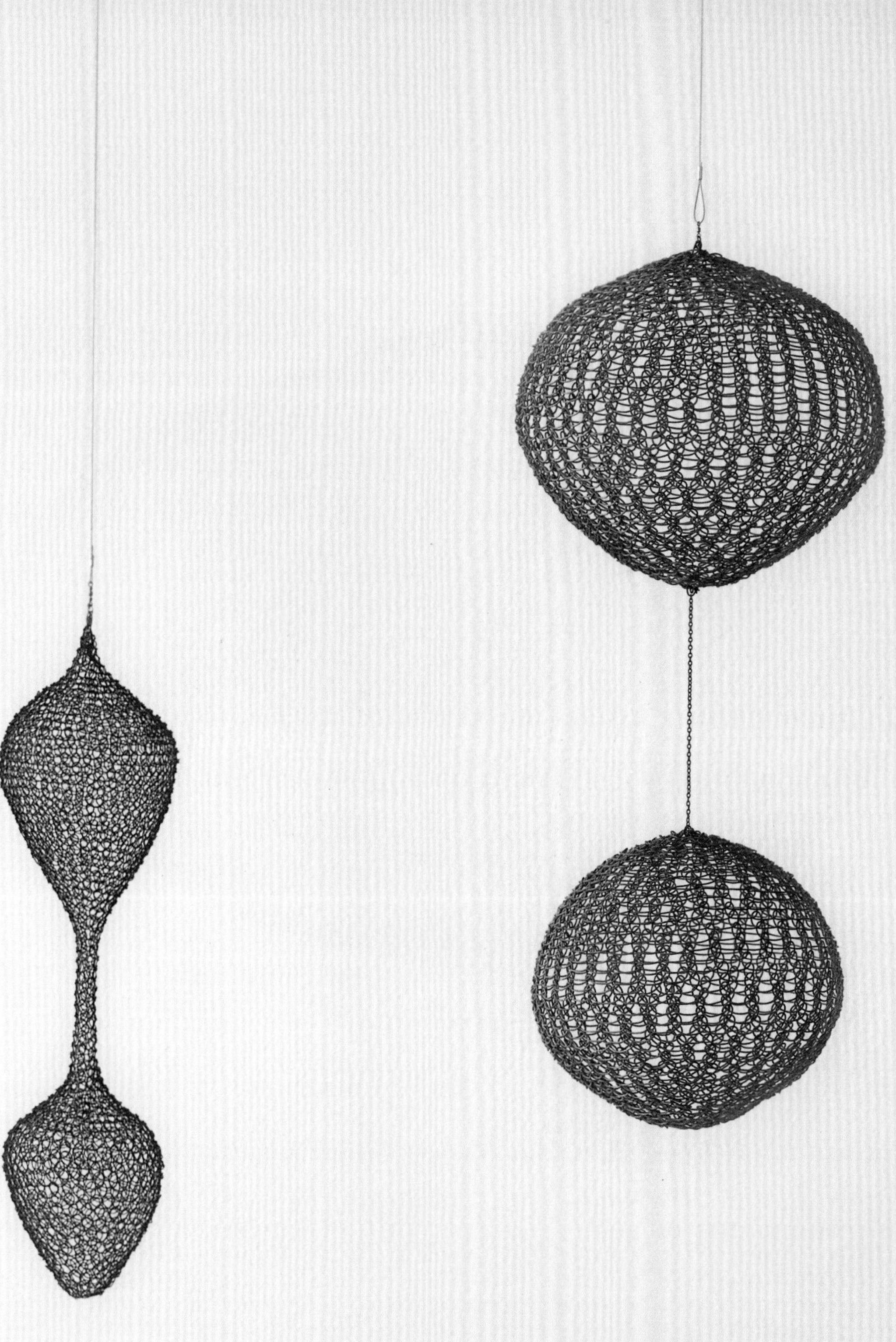

Untitled (S.264, Hanging Two-Lobed Continuous Form), 1949.
Oxidized copper wire, 16 × 4 × 4 inches (40.6 × 10.2 × 10.2 cm)

Untitled (S.793, Hanging Two Spheres Attached with Chain), ca. 1951–52.
Brass wire, brass chain, 18 × 7⅝ × 7⅝ inches (45.7 × 19.4 × 19.4 cm)

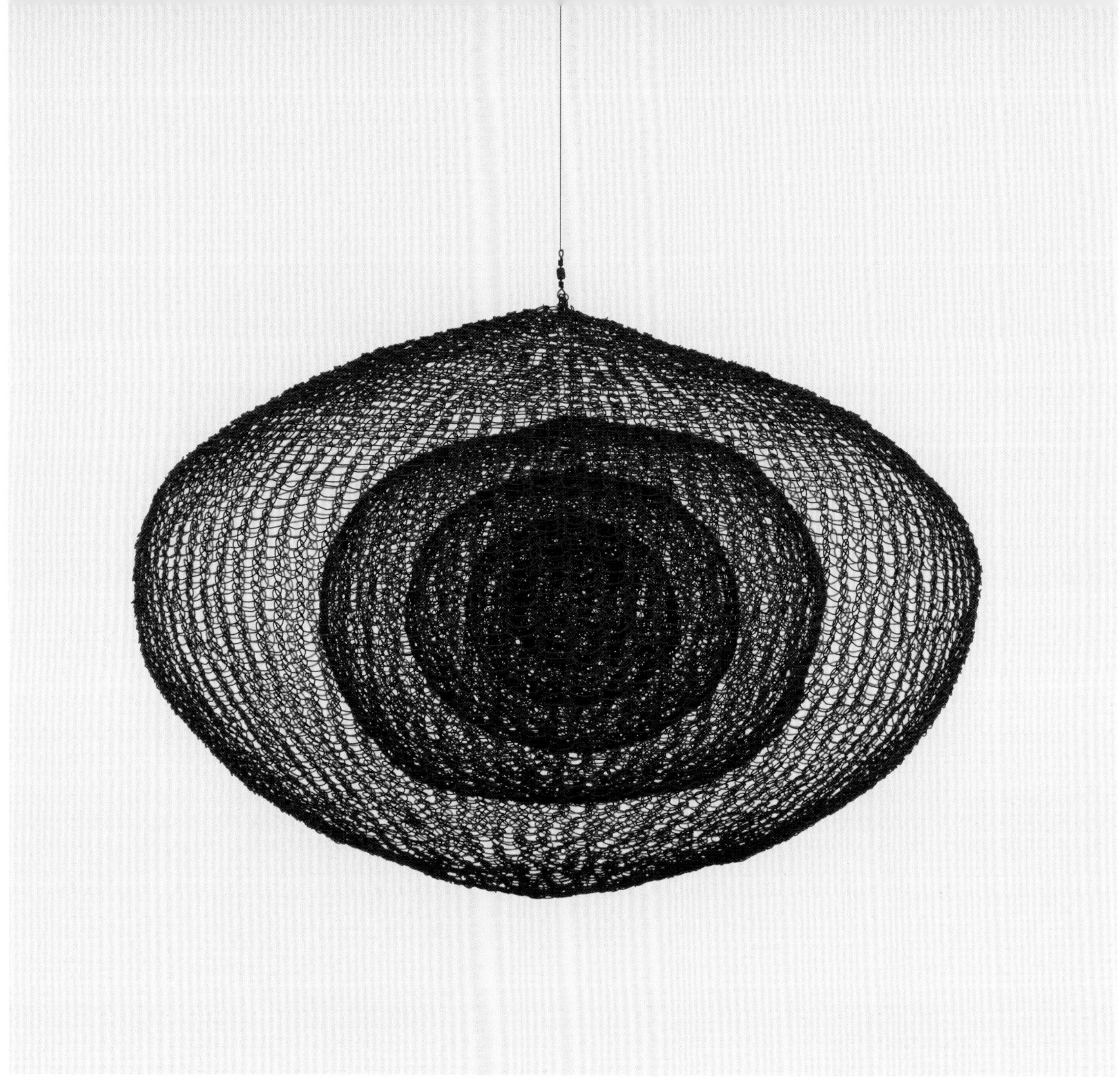

Fig. 10. *Untitled* (S.461, Hanging Single-Lobed, Five Layers of Spheres), ca. 1954.
Iron wire, 15 × 21 × 21 inches (38.1 × 53.3 × 53.3 cm)

nesting them in graduating sizes within one another, as in *Untitled* (S.461) [fig. 10].

By the early to mid-1950s, Asawa's commitment to manual engagement with the material, coupled with her interest in solving an ever-increasing and cumulative set of formal problems posed by her constructions in wire, led her to a series of elaborate permutations. Many of these can be seen in *Untitled* (S.270) [p. 21] and include an increasing number of lobed forms that redirected the sculpture vertically, adding the element of height to the experience of the work. Asawa also started to experiment with different types of wire, which led to often striking variations in color. These complex constructions also started to feature a greater number of interlocking parts that move from the interior out to the exterior of the sculpture (and back again), resulting in intricately overlapping layers that dazzle the eye, but also create a sense of intrigue that invites viewers to examine how the forms intersect.

Opposite: *Untitled* (S.270, Hanging Six-Lobed, Complex Interlocking Continuous Form within a Form with Two Interior Spheres), 1955 (refabricated 1957–58). Brass and steel wire, 63⅞ × 14¹⁵⁄₁₆ × 14¹⁵⁄₁₆ inches (162.2 × 37.9 × 37.9 cm)

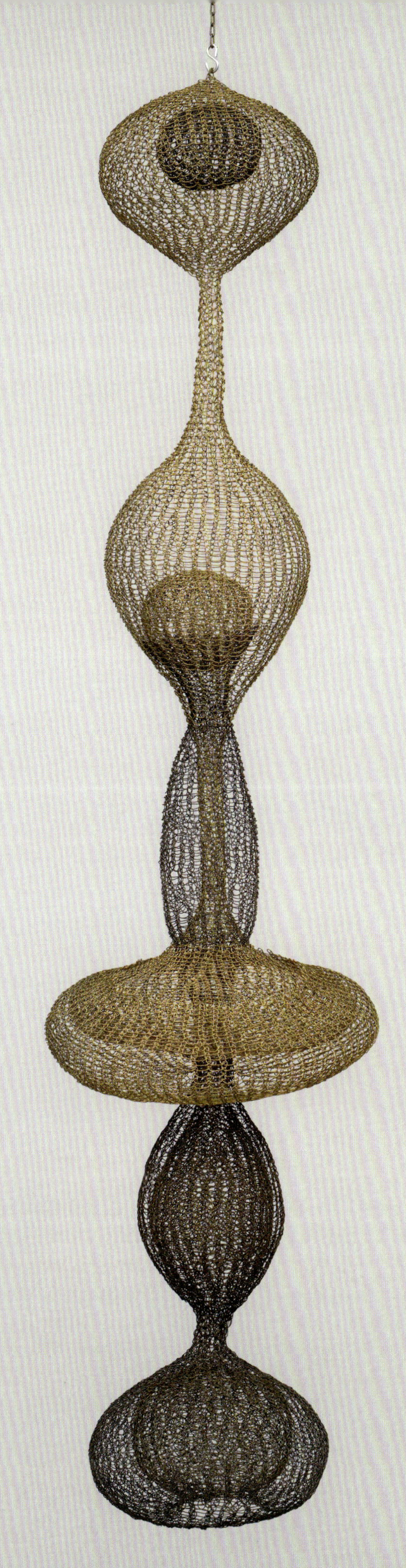

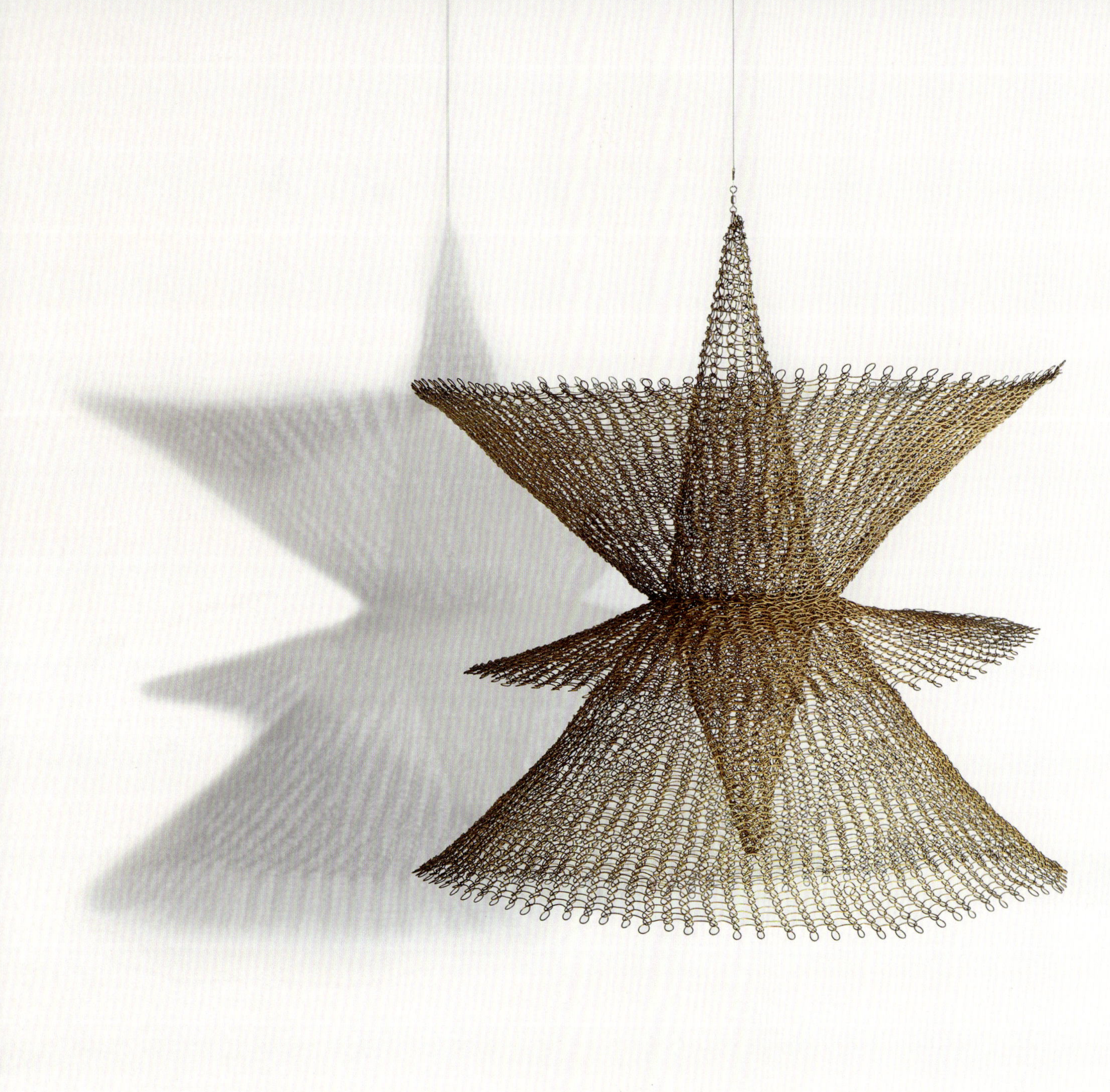

Untitled (S.166, Hanging Two Interlocking Cones with a Center Disc), ca. 1952. Brass wire, 22 × 21 × 21 inches (55.9 × 53.3 × 53.3 cm)

At the same time, Asawa started to open up the surface of her sculptures. Initially she accomplished this by moving beyond the sphere and the lobe to explore conical shapes. *Untitled* (S.166) [above], which eventually interpenetrated and morphed into stacked hyperbolic constructions *Untitled* (S.040) [p. 23, left], are emblematic of this development. Simultaneous to these forms, another type of open construction, as seen in *Untitled* (S.659) [p. 23, right] was arrived at by mistake: in trying to fix a misshapen form, she had to cut the looped surface of one of her sculptures, only to discover that the weight of the work made it twist around its central axis. The incision exaggerated and spread the flared openings she created, which Asawa called "windows," a term she later adopted to describe subsequent sculptural variations of this kind, in which

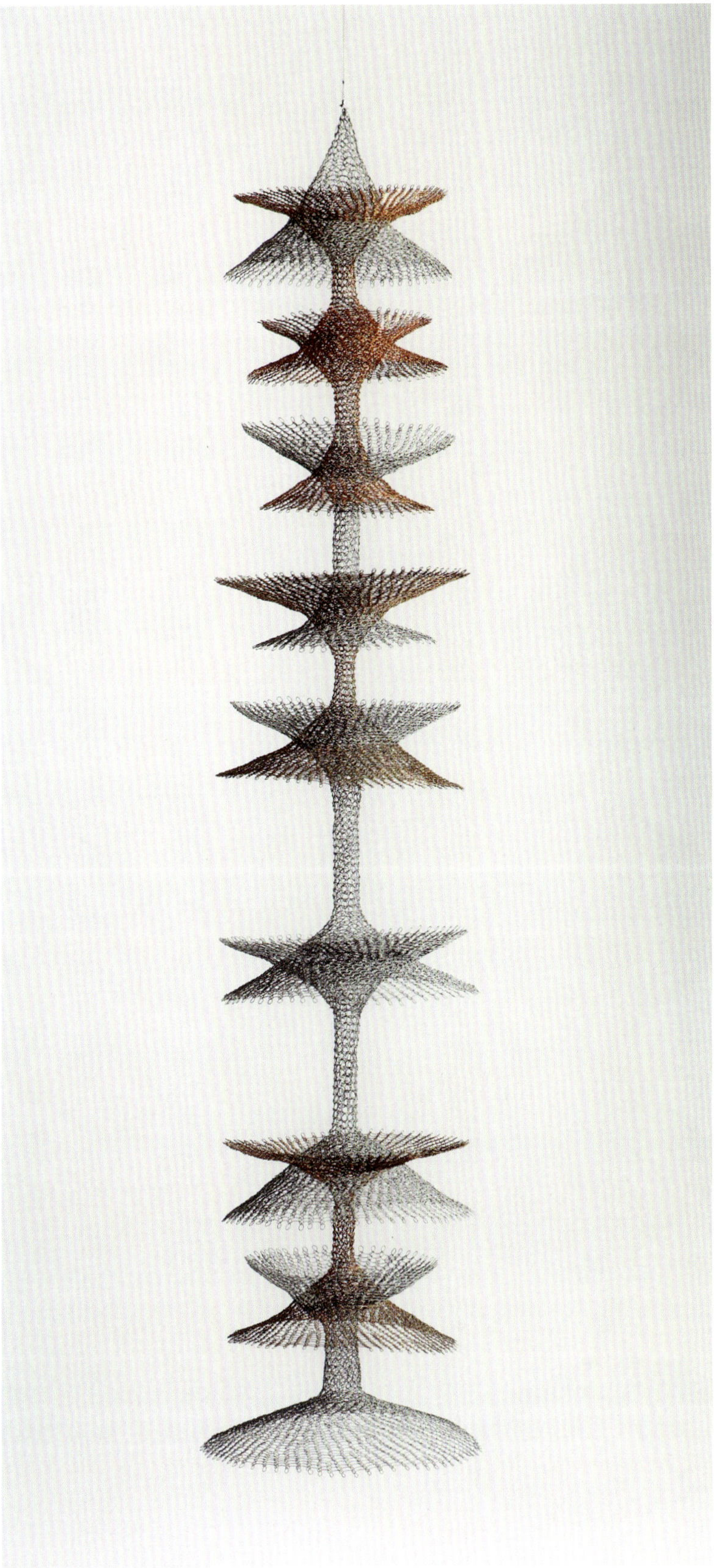

Untitled (S.040, Hanging Eight-and-a-Half Open Hyperbolic Shapes that Penetrate Each Other), ca. 1956. Enameled copper wire and galvanized steel wire, 78 × 16 × 16 inches (198.1 × 40.6 × 40.6 cm)

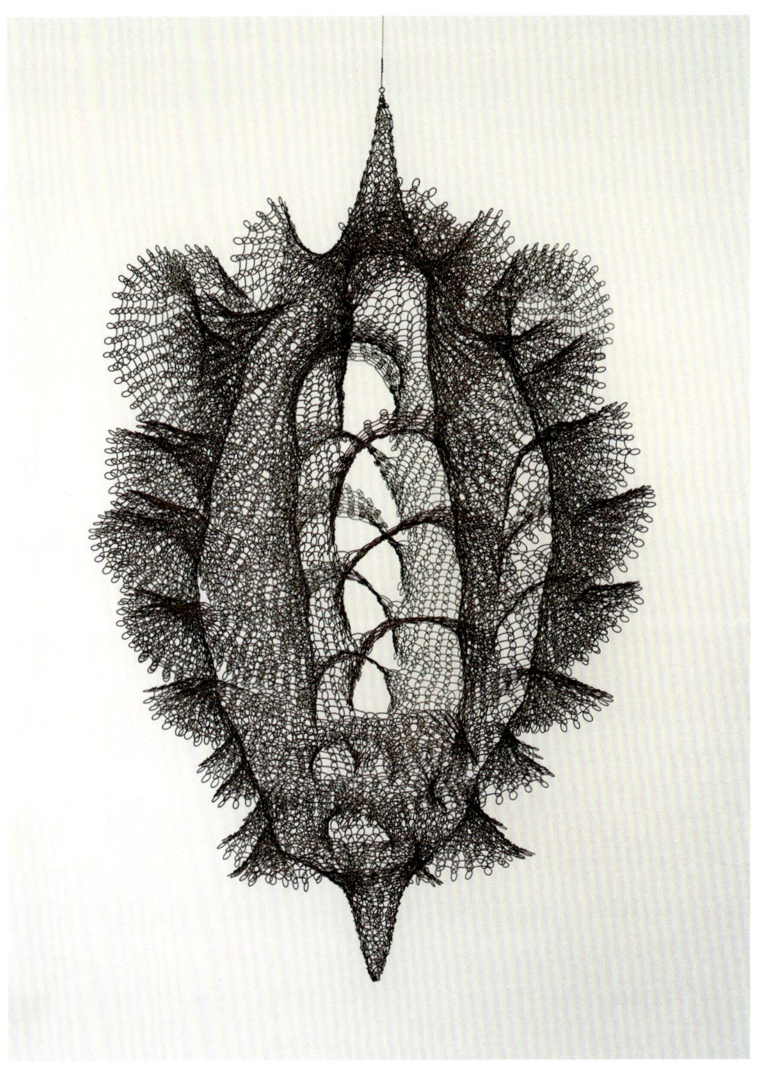

Untitled (S.659, Hanging Single Section, Reversible Open Window Form), ca. 1959. Nickel-plated copper wire, 37½ × 25 × 25 inches (95.3 × 63.5 × 63.5 cm)

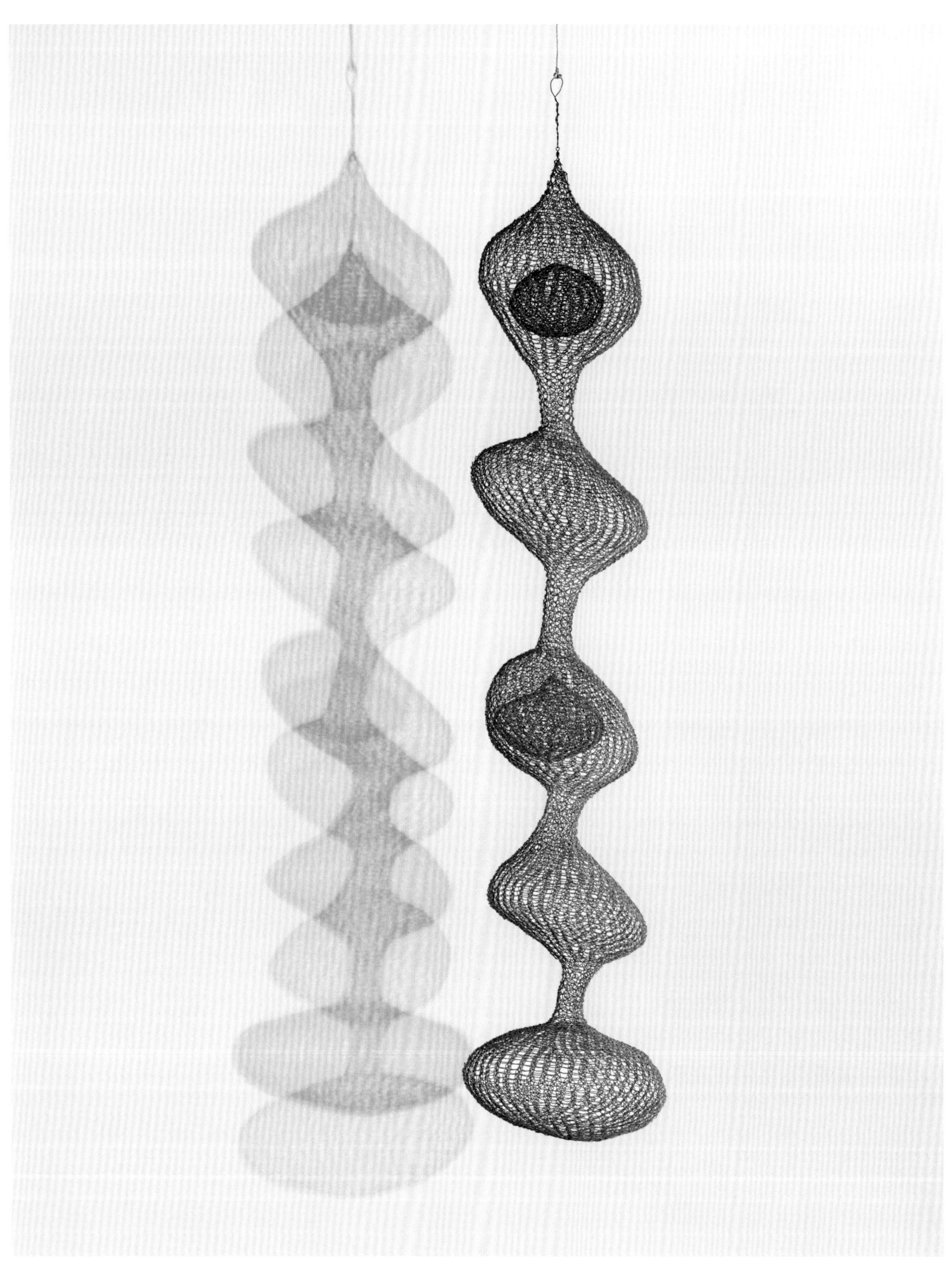

Untitled (S.541, Hanging Five-Lobed Continuous Form, with Spheres in the First and Third Lobes), ca. 1951–54.
Brass wire, 54 × 11 × 11 inches (137.2 × 27.9 × 27.9 cm)

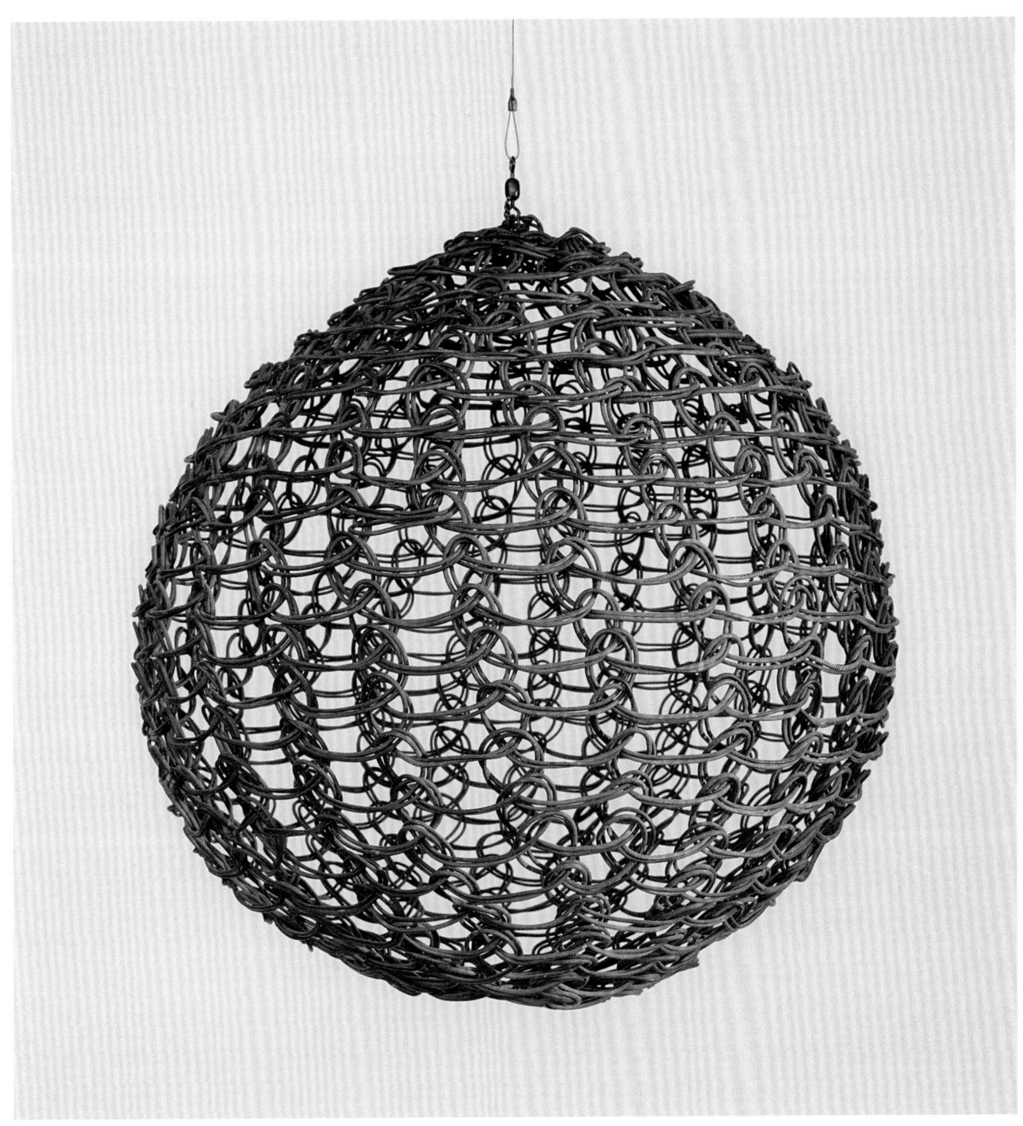

Untitled (S.634, Hanging Sphere), ca. 1968–72. Brass and copper wire, 8½ × 8 × 8 inches (21.6 × 20.3 × 20.3 cm)

the cuts were not literally made but incorporated into the looping process as a further study of open and closed volumes.[21]

Among these experiments, some forms were short-lived. For example, in the early 1950s Asawa developed a method for asymmetrical construction, which resulted in lopsided forms as evident in *Untitled* (S.541) [p. 24] that were quickly abandoned because she deemed the process "too easy."[22] The fact that Asawa found this variation—one that is premised on letting go of order and method—unchallenging is unsurprising given the premium she placed on discipline, effort, and control of the hand. It is therefore perhaps fitting that the period of Asawa's intense and exclusive engagement with the looped-wire technique culminates with a series of sculptures from the late 1960s and early '70s, which show her working with double, and even triple, strands of wire in order to create denser, heavier

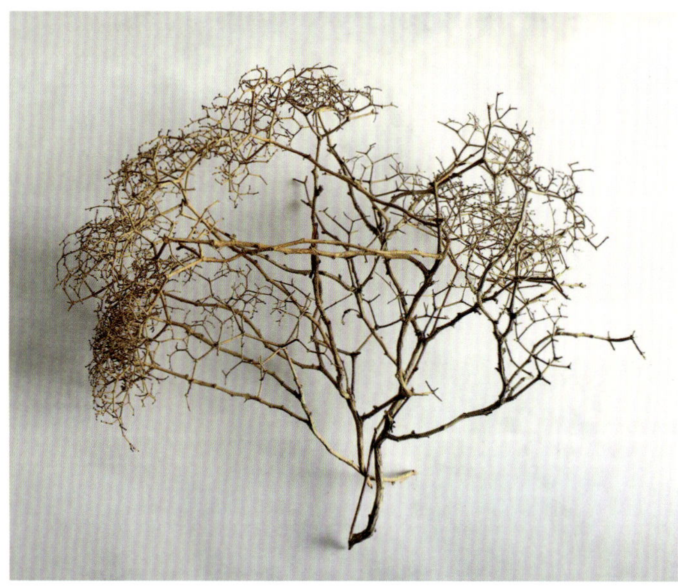

Fig. 11. Desert plant given to Asawa by Paul and Virginia Hassel

surfaces that demanded increased levels of technical proficiency executed through deft maneuvers of the hand, as seen in *Untitled* (S.634) [p. 25].

Taking a cumulative view of Asawa's experiments in looped wire makes the diversity and breadth of this body of work evident. It shows how she translated her approach with a single technique into a set of iterative formal challenges that resulted in a unique sculptural vocabulary. Asawa often related these experiments to phenomena she observed in nature: "If I plant a tomato seed I will get a tomato plant out of it. Then I will get tomatoes from that. . . . I like the steps that one gets from merely planting a seed, or planting a plant. I like what happens, because you know that you get an eggplant every time you plant an eggplant seed. . . . Or what if I've got a cucumber and a mixture, a hybrid. I like that too because I'll get something new. And I like that."[23] As a child growing up on a farm, Asawa would have been deeply familiar with the material transformation she describes in this passage, so it is no surprise that the notion of a seed germinating into a crop would serve as her point of inspiration.

Nature also served as a catalyst for Asawa's next innovation in wire. A desert plant that her friends Paul and Virginia Hassel gave her after their visit to Death Valley in 1962 raised a new set of formal questions that she was eager to address [fig. 11]. She initially drew the tangled plant but after struggling to capture its expanding and twisting form on paper, she shifted to wire, thus beginning a body of work that would become known as the tied-wire sculptures.[24] Instead of looping, Asawa's new method involved bundling, pulling apart, and tying the wire. In a letter to Albers she described her new approach as "very exciting," adding that some works start with as many as "1,000 strands of wire in a bundle; I divide them into 3 bunches of 333 strands. Each bunch is divided again and again until 2 strands are left. I tie each joint with the same wire, so there is no solder used. My tool is a pair of pliers that will cut and twist the wire. The variations are endless."[25]

In addition to providing insight into Asawa's new experiment, this passage is noteworthy as a document of her continued insistence on repetitive hand-making as the basis for her practice. Although she described her working process as monotonous, Asawa never saw this as anathema to innovation.[26] This attitude toward work was in part informed by her studies with Albers, who privileged repetitive, even arduous exercises over self-expression, which he believed would be a natural outcome of the creative, hands-on process. In the 1963 talk Asawa gave at the San Francisco Museum of Art, she summarized Albers's teaching philosophy: "Art is to present vision first, not expression first . . . It's a mistake to let emotion control your pen."[27] A few years later, this sentiment was reiterated to Asawa by her calligraphy teacher, Tobase, who advised her not to "bother with expression. Expression and beauty take care of themselves."[28]

Rewarded by her commitment to the generative qualities of repetition and manual work, Asawa created a great number of tied-wire variations within a year of announcing this new body of work to Albers. The first sculptures, made in 1962, were freestanding, originating from a single stem. Within a year, however, this form expanded into two directions, eventually dispersing into multiple points in space. These types of constructions were initially suspended from the ceiling, but they eventually migrated onto the wall in relieflike permutations of wire, which Asawa diffused into an allover pattern. Whether hanging or wall-mounted, Asawa's tied-wire constructions were always determined by their center, which could be either open or closed. Sculptures with a closed center were defined by an arrangement of overlapping bundles of wire that she divided and tied into dispersing branches [p. 27]. By contrast, sculptures with an open center were

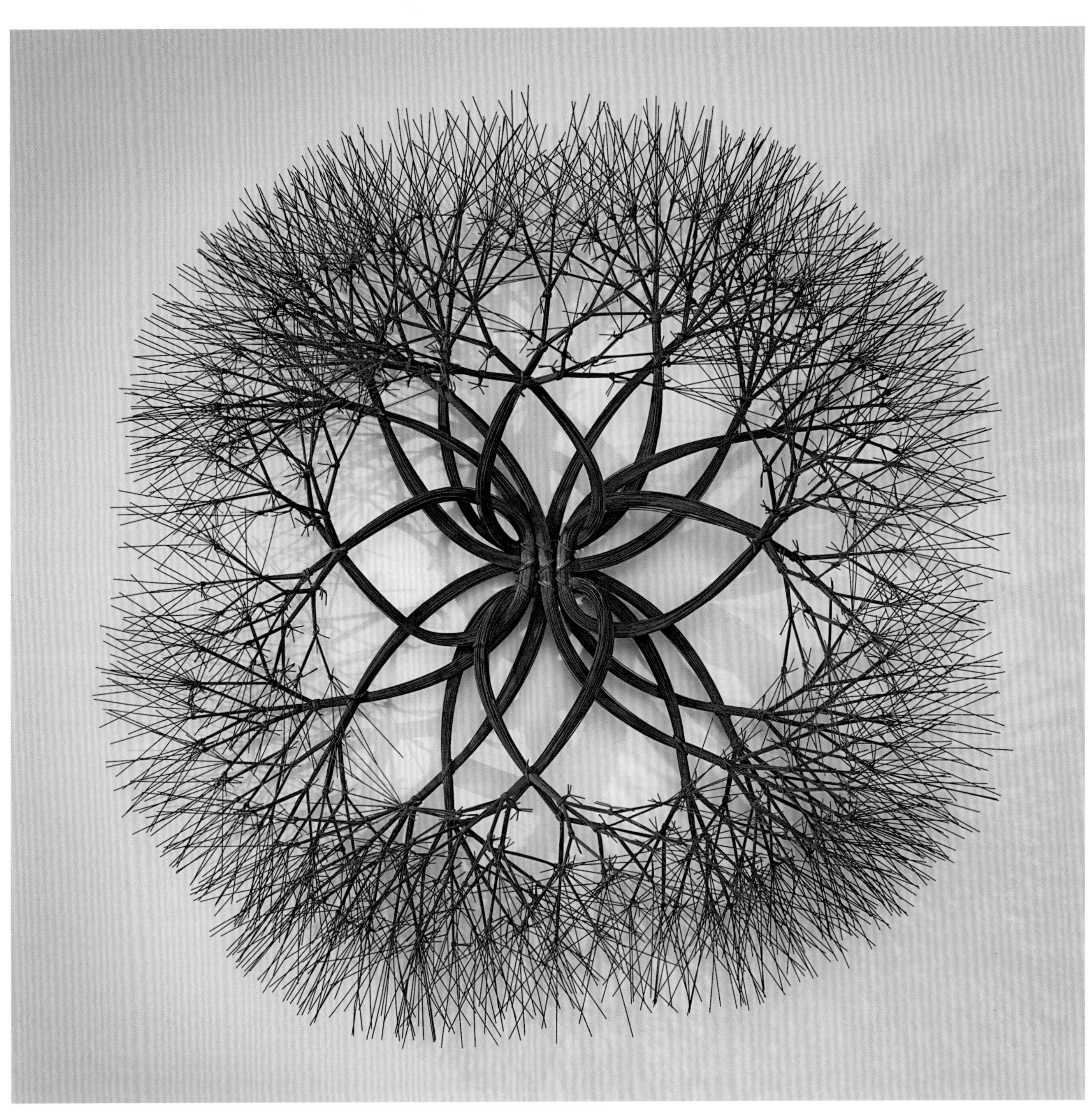

Untitled (S.557, Wall-Mounted Tied-Wire, Closed-Center, Twelve-Petaled Form Based on Nature), ca. 1965–70.
Bronze wire, 38 × 38 × 12 inches (96.5 × 96.5 × 30.5 cm)

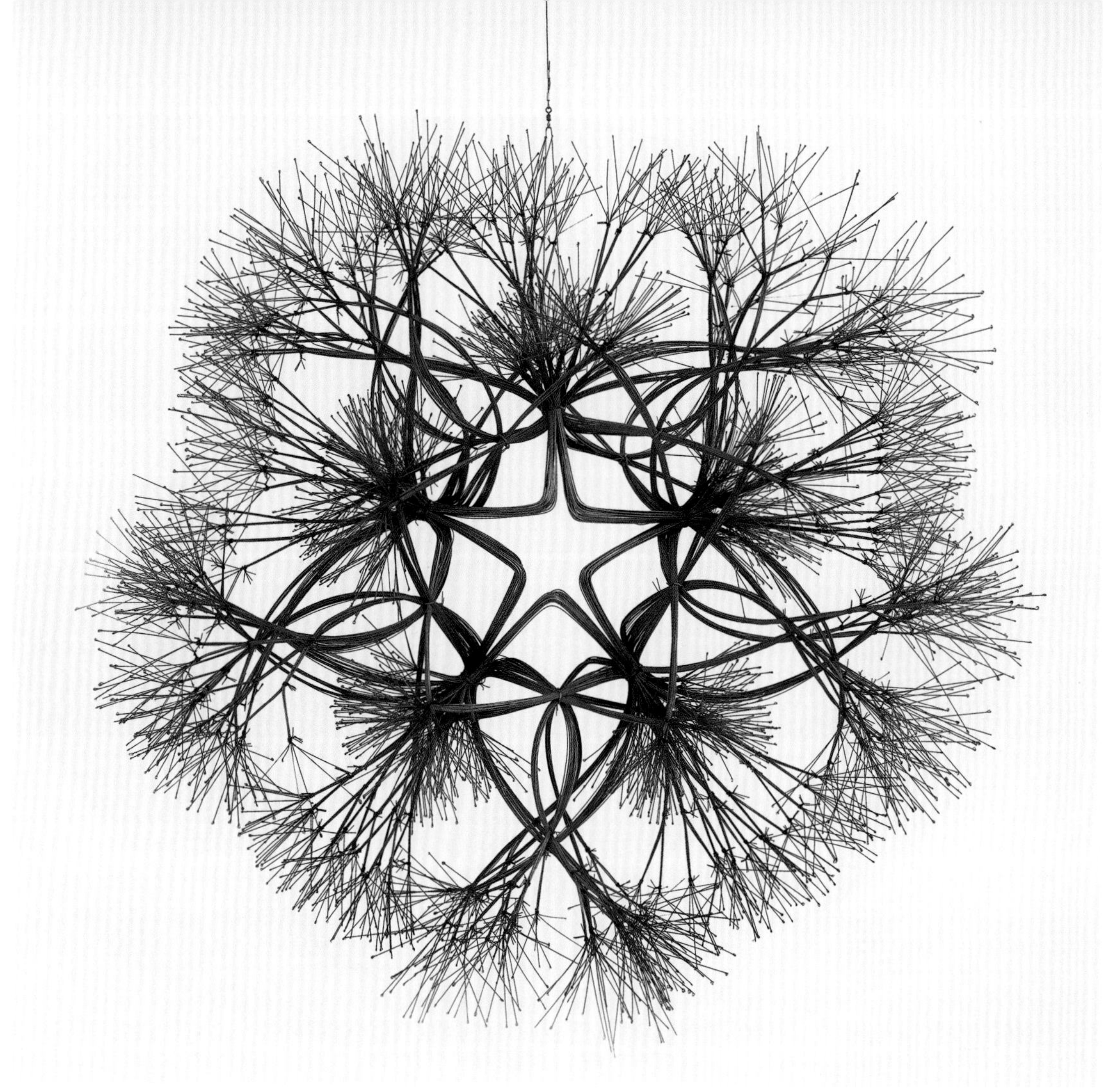

Wintermass (S.187, Hanging Tied-Wire, Double-Sided, Open-Center, Five-Branched Form Based on Nature), ca. 1974. Stainless steel wire tipped with resin, 45 × 46 × 25 inches (114.3 × 116.8 × 63.5 cm)

delineated by radiating strands of wire that articulated a hollow, contoured shape—often a star [above].

Asawa's tied-wire experiments extended beyond the divide-and-tie method. In 1963, a visit to the company that cleaned her sculpture led to the discovery of a chemical process that transformed her tied-wire sculptures into a new, yet related body of work. By 1965 she began to practice this method in her studio by submerging sculptures into an electrically charged sulfuric acid bath, which caused the wire to develop a thick, greenish crust on the metal surface [p. 29].[29] This process was consistent with Asawa's studies at Black Mountain College. The *matière* experiments that Albers championed encouraged students to manipulate the material to uncover new "visual and haptic experiences" without destroying its inherent properties.[30] In the case of electroplating, the acid did not obliterate the wire and its form; rather, it revealed another property of the material. While Asawa embraced the effect and the resulting work, the experiment could not be sustained because the wire eventually "became too brittle at the joints and it cracked off, and it was not technically good."[31] Despite its fragile nature, the electroplating method attests to Asawa's interest in sustaining an iterative practice that continually maps one effort and one set of skills onto the next.[32] These acts of making, however, were not only performed for the sake of art, but they also had a dual purpose within the context of Asawa's family life.

In embracing her role as a parent, Asawa defied the concerns of both Albers and Cunningham, who at different times urged her to moderate her desire to become a mother with her ambition to work as an artist.[33] Between 1950 and 1959 Asawa welcomed six children

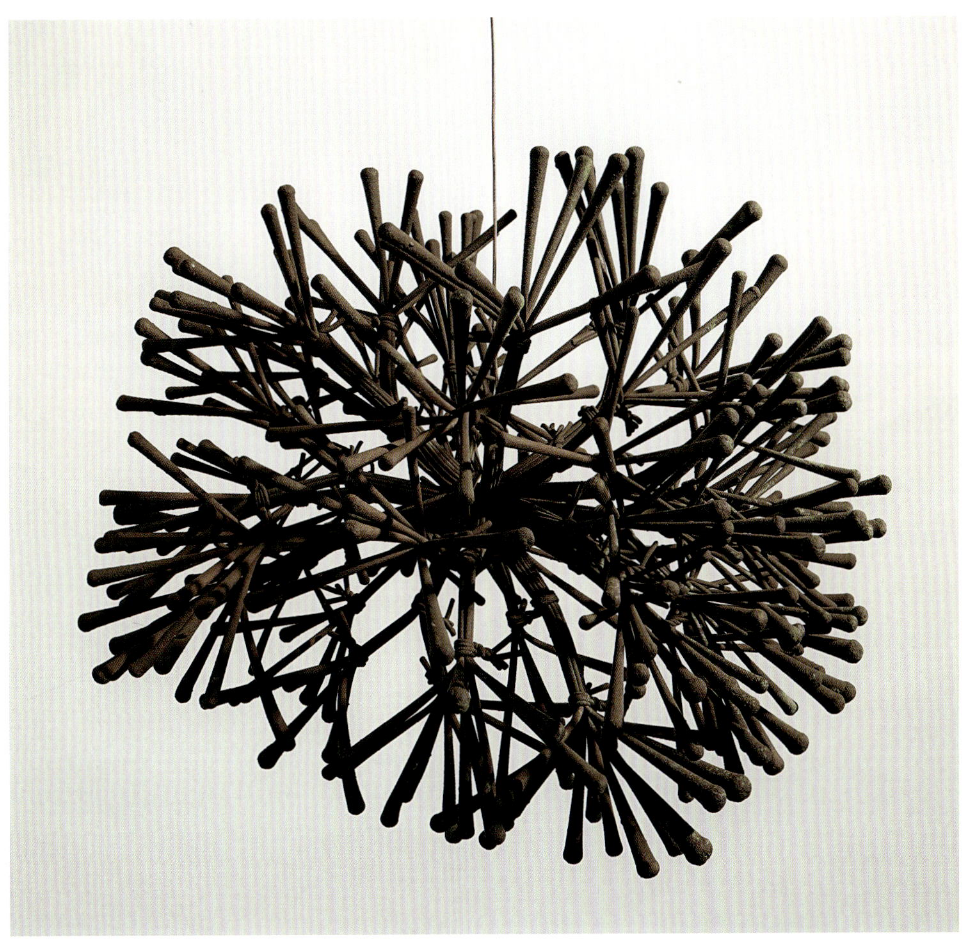

Untitled (S.021, Hanging Electroplated Tied-Wire, Center-Tied, Spherical Multi-Branched Form Based on Nature), ca. 1963. Electroplated copper wire, 10¼ × 10¼ × 11 inches (26 × 26 × 27.9 cm)

while steadily advancing her innovations in wire. Her commitment to maintaining an active practice, however, was not commensurate with the presentation of her sculptures in museums and galleries. While her work reached the public during this decade—including three solo shows at Peridot Gallery, an established New York space for contemporary art, which represented her for a time—Asawa's overall gallery exposure during the 1950s and early '60s was limited. A number of factors have been proffered as explanations: one is financial—Asawa had to bear the responsibility of high shipping costs, and her sculptures would often be returned damaged since institutions didn't know how to properly crate her work. Another oft-cited reason takes into account the reception of her work, particularly the critics' struggle to reconcile the craft method she employed within the context of sculpture.[34] While these explanations hold true, we also cannot discount Asawa's own lack of interest in pursuing opportunities within the museum and gallery setting. Although she and Lanier struggled financially during their child-rearing years, Asawa rejected invitations by commercial firms to design for the mass market (one prospective employer even offered the services of a housekeeper who would tend to her home and children). She was suspicious of these opportunities, deeming them too disruptive, likely to her own practice and her role as a parent.[35]

Asawa's investment in the act of making had a clear purpose. She intentionally worked and displayed her art at home, for her family, instead of a separate and solitary studio environment, in an effort to make her art visible and inspire a strong work ethic in her children. Asawa also engaged them with various tasks. "I think you have to teach kids to work and you can only teach

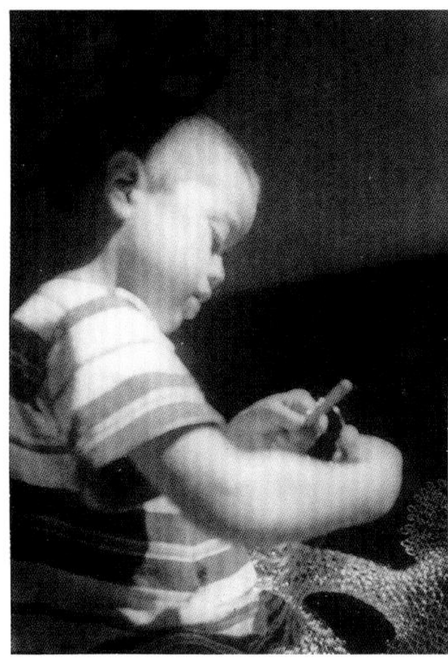
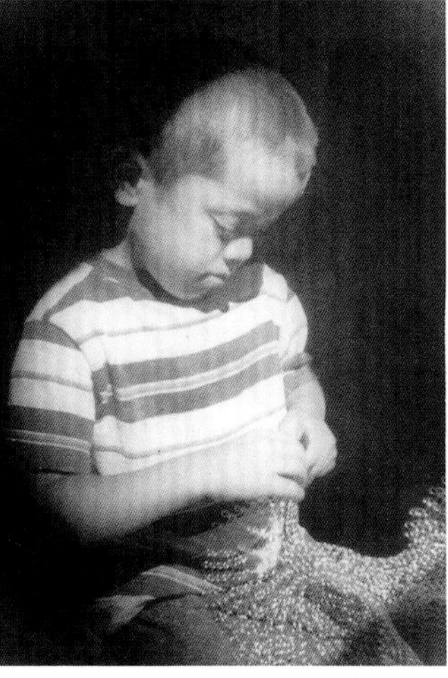

Fig. 12. Asawa's son Hudson coiling wire for his mother, 1956

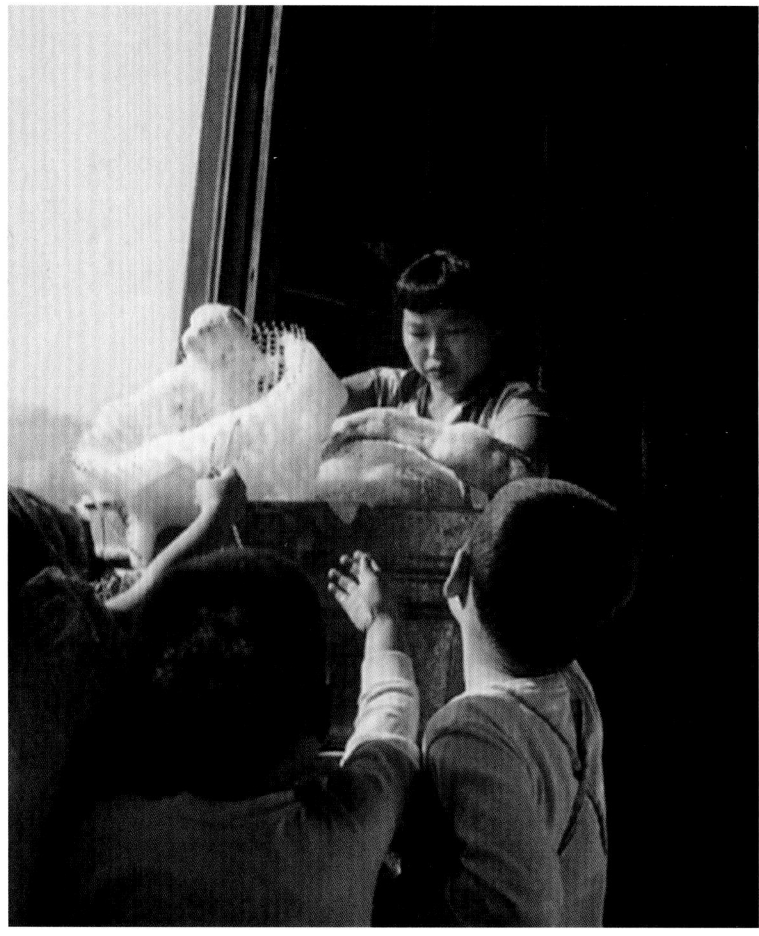

Fig. 13. Asawa washing a sculpture with her children on the back porch of their home on Saturn Street, San Francisco, 1954

them to work if you work. . . . I can't delegate jobs if I'm not doing it. . . . you can't say, 'Go weed the garden,' if you're not doing it yourself."[36] Photographs from the period show one of her sons using a dowel to coil wire [fig. 12], and her children helping to wash her looped-wire sculptures [fig. 13]. These images show how Asawa used art making to set up conditions for learning. For her, work routines took center stage and held transformative potential—not only for shaping her vision, but also for raising her children.

At the same time, Asawa recognized that her efforts were not one sided and that her work as a mother informed her work as an artist. Reflecting later on her larger body of work, which would go on to include several public commissions, including fountains in the Bay Area, Asawa recognized that her many roles were inseparable. "Because I had the children, I chose to have my studio in my home. I wanted them to understand my work and learn how to work. If I hadn't spent all those years staying home with my kids and experimenting with materials that children could use, I would never have done the Ghirardelli and Hyatt fountains."[37] This quote makes clear that through the act of making and displaying her work at home, Asawa directly addressed her children as a key audience for her work. At the same time, the learning environment she put into place was not one directional. The community-centered approach to learning that she inherited from life on the farm and her time at Black Mountain College also inspired Asawa's own practice. Her work at home thus set the stage for her next set of experiments, which she also premised on learning and community building. By the late 1960s, she advanced them into two outward-facing directions.

One began with her volunteering efforts in her children's public schools, which by 1968 had evolved into the co-founding of the Alvarado School Arts Workshop. At its prime the program was active in fifty public schools in San Francisco. Through this initiative, Asawa helped bring working artists into the classroom to teach, but also to bring children out of the classroom and into the garden, so that they could gain hands-on, nature-based experience. Baker's clay—composed of flour, salt, and water, and which she and her children played with—became a mainstay in Asawa's workshops, along with other materials that could be easily found, repurposed, and reimagined (e.g., egg and milk cartons) [fig. 14]. In 1968 Asawa was appointed to the San Francisco Arts Commission to advocate for arts education reform from within the school system and greater public art in San Francisco.

During this period, Asawa also set aside her earlier reluctance to accept commissions. As she transitioned from being a primary caregiver, she began pursuing a number of public commissions, and in 1966 began working on a design for her first fountain, which was cast in bronze. Intended for Ghirardelli Square in San Francisco, the sculpture was envisioned as two nursing mermaids surrounded by frogs and lily pads in response to the site's family-friendly destination in the Fisherman's Wharf area. After the fountain was installed, however, the square's landscape architect circulated a two-page scathing reprimand to newspapers and the art community to inveigh against the sculpture for its "Victorian overtones," petitioning for its removal.[38] Such severe criticism, however, seems to have had little impact on Asawa, who largely continued to eschew abstraction in favor of idyllic iconography for her subsequent public projects.

The outdoor works she created were beloved by the community, earning her the moniker "the fountain lady," which led to, in the words of one art historian, "the wrong kind of renown, at least in the view of contemporary art circles (then, as now)."[39] Asawa's public projects, seemingly at odds with her experiments in wire, have therefore continued to remain on the sidelines of critical considerations of her work. Yet if we consider them in the context of her dedication to learning, making, and iterating, these public works take their rightful place within her practice at large. The bronze casting she began to explore with the Ghirardelli fountain sparked Asawa's imagination and played to her strengths since it entailed a translation of a single form across multiple material permutations. This allowed her to create the fountain's mermaid tails by looping an undulating form in wire, which was then dipped in wax,

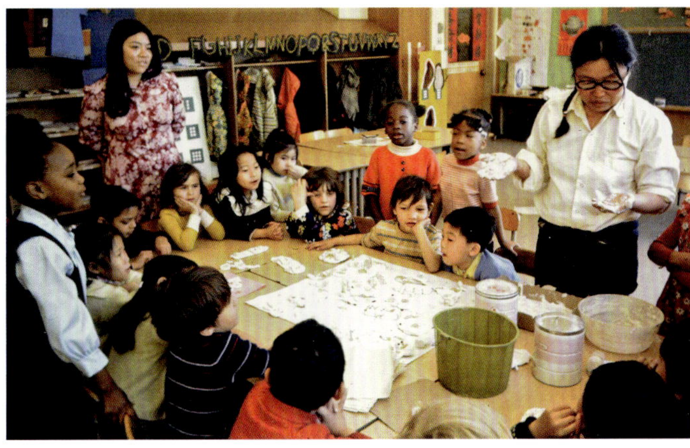

Fig. 14. Asawa demonstrating how to cast small sculptures in plaster at a public elementary school in San Francisco, ca. 1970s

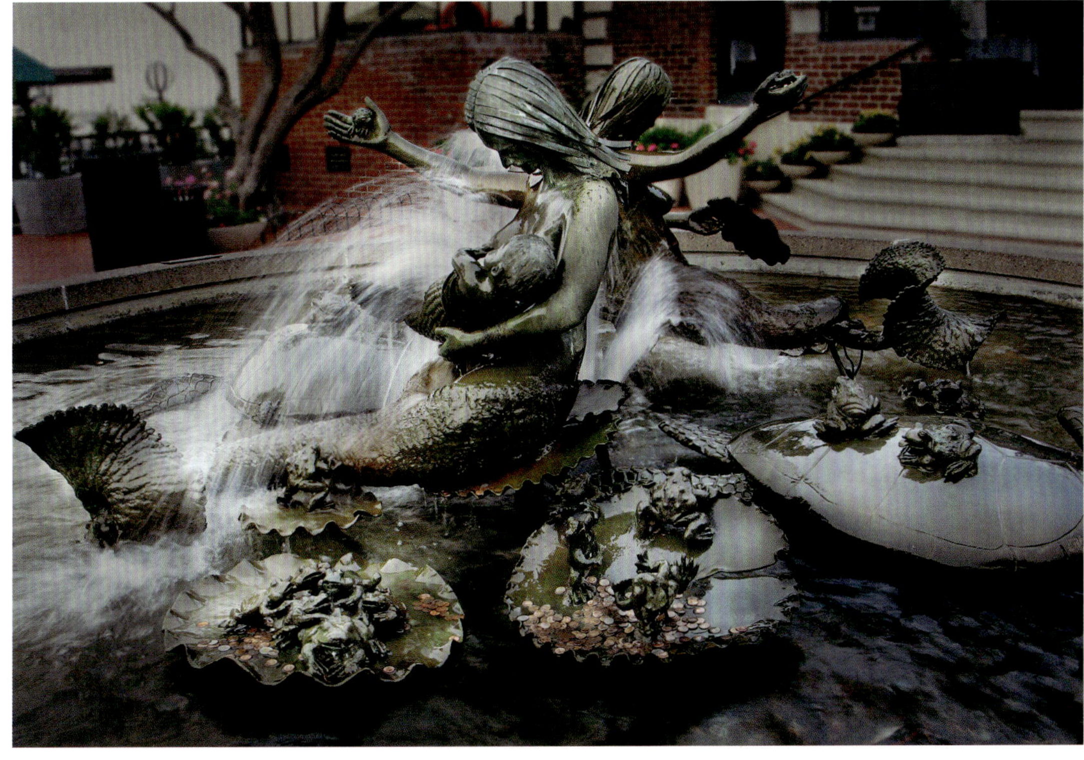

Fig. 15. *Andrea*, Asawa's first public commission, Ghirardelli Square, San Francisco, 1968

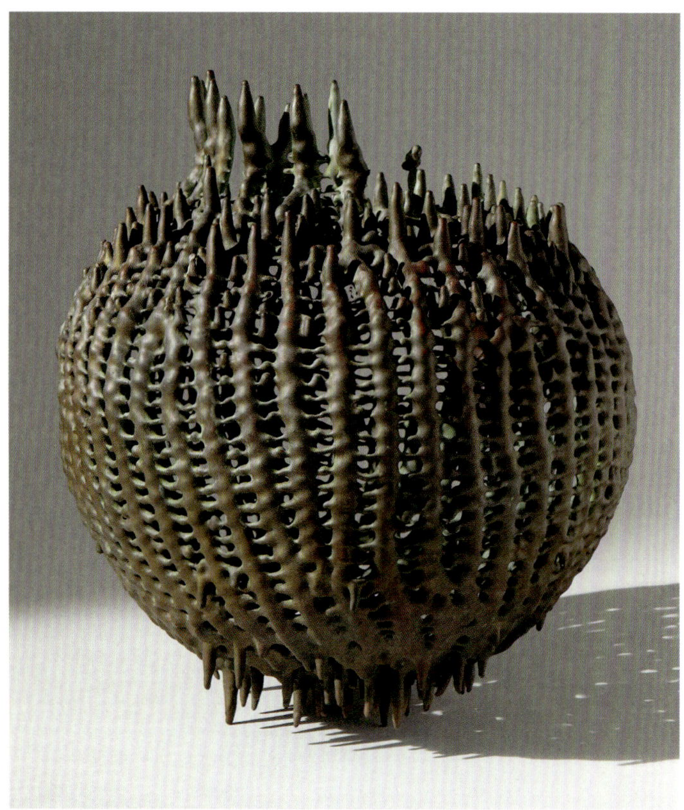

Untitled (S.130, Freestanding Vessel Form), 1996. Bronze, golden green patina, 14 × 13¼ × 13¼ inches (35.6 × 33.7 × 33.7 cm)

invested in plaster, and finally cast into bronze [fig. 15].[40] Soon she refined this processes into a new direction with her looped-wire sculpture. Works such as *Untitled* (S.130) [above], exemplify this new hybrid undertaking. Despite the multiple processes involved, the sculpture retains a sense of formal clarity: the gridded construction in looped wire, present in each finished one-of-a-kind work, remains visible, as does the process of casting, which is evident in the sculptures' final form. Asawa extended these experiments from the late 1960s and 1970s into the 1990s by casting nontraditional materials, such as folded paper (pp. 118–19) and baker's clay, that came directly out of her work with children.

Much like her earlier explorations in looped wire, in her later works Asawa maintained a straightforward approach to both material and execution. By sustaining an extended commitment to a single medium and investigating the full range of its inherent properties, Asawa demonstrated the potential of simple means to profound ends.

•

Asawa's aesthetic philosophy reflects a synthesis of her personal and professional histories, which, like the meander design, were in many ways intertwined. In an undated artist statement, she makes rare mention of her family's secular relationship to Zen Buddhism while also addressing the intersection of Taoist philosophy and Josef Albers's teachings at Black Mountain College. Aside from demonstrating the expansive range of philosophical touchstones Asawa encountered over the years, the statement provides a revealing window into her approach to life and work:

> I am a double Zen Buddhist. Both father and mother were, without dogma, plain dirt farmers. I am an ox in the Chinese zodiac. "Chop wood, carry water." Albers introduced his students to Laotse, Ying/Yang, positive/negative, in/out, hard/soft. I have used his poetry style to convey what I have been trying to do for the past 59 years of my life.
>
> Work days days work
> Draw life life draws
> Love family family loves[41]

The full proverb Asawa cites above reads: "Before enlightenment, chop wood, carry water. After enlightenment, chop wood, carry water." Asawa's statement makes clear that daily hard work is not a burden; rather, it is necessary for leading a deeply rewarding and productive life, including—and especially—her life as an artist. Asawa's early training on her parents' farm and at Black Mountain College taught her that studying, carrying out chores, and making art worked on a continuum. She would live this approach throughout her entire career, including during those summers spent in Guerneville, where she carved the meander on redwood doors with her children, for their home.

Ruth Asawa drew the spiral line of her life's work, her family, the objects she brought into the world, and the community she contributed to through her generous and influential activities. The line didn't follow any precisely charted course, but it moved steadily across time and space; it was neither directed toward any specific destination, nor was it aimless. It was successively iterating, always searching for itself, following the thread, all along the line she was creating.

Notes

1. Ruth Asawa's application materials for a 1952 Guggenheim Fellowship, Ruth Asawa Papers (M1585), Department of Special Collections and University Archives, Stanford University Libraries, Stanford, California.
2. Conversation between the author and Asawa's children, Aiko Cuneo and Hudson Lanier.
3. Asawa, quoted in an oral history interview with Albert Lanier, conducted by Paul Karlstrom and Mark Johnson of the Archives of American Art, Smithsonian Institution, San Francisco, June 21 and July 5, 2002, unpaginated.
4. See Tiffany Bell, "Ruth Asawa: Working from Nothing," in *Ruth Asawa* (New York: David Zwirner Books, 2018), 11–27; Mary Emma Harris, "Black Mountain College," and Jacqueline Hoefer, "Ruth Asawa: A Working Life," in *The Sculpture of Ruth Asawa: Contours in the Air*, ed. Daniell Cornell (San Francisco: Fine Arts Museums of San Francisco; and Berkeley: University of California Press, 2006), 42–66 and 10–29.
5. See Emily K. Doman Jennings, "Critiquing the Critique: Ruth Asawa's Early Reception," in *The Sculpture of Ruth Asawa*, 128–37; and Robert Storr, "Ruth Asawa: Sketches of the Cosmos," in *Ruth Asawa: Line by Line* (New York: Christie's, 2015), 19–37.
6. See Sarah Archer, "Maker to Market: Ruth Asawa Reappraised," *Journal of Modern Craft* 8, no. 2 (July 2015): 141.
7. Ibid., 141–54.
8. Asawa, "Artist's Statement," in *Ruth Asawa: Completing the Circle* (Fresno, CA: Fresno Art Museum, 2001), n.p.
9. Asawa in Katie Simon, "A Conversation with Ruth Asawa, Artist," *Artweek* 26, no. 8 (August 1995): 18.
10. Undated statement on early life and work, Ruth Asawa Papers.
11. Ibid., unpaginated.
12. Draft for a 1963 talk on Josef Albers at the San Francisco Museum of Art, Ruth Asawa Papers.
13. Harris, "Black Mountain College," 56.
14. Black Mountain College report card, summer term 1946, Ruth Asawa Papers.
15. In many interviews Asawa mistakenly described her work as "crocheting." In fact, her technique is more closely aligned with knitting; however, this term is also limiting, given that Asawa worked with her hands and did not use needles. Looping is perhaps the most accurate term to describe how Asawa built her forms.
16. Black Mountain College report card, first term 1947/1948, Ruth Asawa Papers.
17. Asawa, quoted in an interview by Mary E. Harris, San Francisco, December 19, 1971, 9.
18. Asawa, quoted in an interview with Joanne Iritani of the Florin Japanese American Citizens League Oral History Project, San Francisco, April 7, 2001, 51–52.
19. Asawa in Simon, "A Conversation with Ruth Asawa, Artist," 18.
20. Asawa, quoted in an oral history interview with Harriet Nathan, "Art, Competence, and Citywide Cooperation for San Francisco," San Francisco, February 15, 1974; March 15, 1974; June 28, 1974; October 25, 1974; and January 16, 1976, 35.
21. Asawa, Harris interview, 9–10.
22. Conversation between the author and Asawa's daughters, Addie Lanier and Aiko Cuneo.
23. Asawa, Karlstrom and Johnson interview.
24. Hoefer, "A Working Life," 21–22.
25. Asawa, letter to Josef Albers, April 26, 1963, Ruth Asawa Papers.
26. Asawa, Nathan interview, 35.
27. Draft for a 1963 talk on Josef Albers at the San Francisco Museum of Art, Ruth Asawa Papers.
28. Ibid.
29. Asawa, letter to Josef and Anni Albers, February 2, 1965, Ruth Asawa Papers.
30. Michael Beggs, "Josef Albers: Photographs of Matières," in *Leap Before You Look: Black Mountain College, 1933–1957*, eds. Helen Molesworth and Ruth Erickson (Boston: Institute of Contemporary Art; and New Haven: Yale University Press, 2015), 86.
31. Asawa, unpublished interview with Aiko Cuneo, September 24, 2003.
32. See Evolution of Form section on pages 130–44.
33. Hoefer, "A Working Life," 21–22, and Asawa, Karlstrom and Johnson interview.
34. Bell, "Working from Nothing," 22.
35. Asawa, Nathan interview, 37–38, 129.
36. Ibid., 36.
37. Asawa, "Interview with Sculptor Ruth Asawa: Artist Remembers Painful Days of Internment During World War II," *Noe Valley Voice* 13, no. 10 (December 1989/January 1990): 20.
38. George Draper, "Scorn for a New Sculpture: Ghirardelli Square Controversy," *San Francisco Chronicle*, March 26, 1968.
39. Archer, "Ruth Asawa Reappraised," 143.
40. The San Francisco Art Foundry, headed by Onno de Ruijter, cast the sculpture.
41. Asawa, undated statement on early life and work, Ruth Asawa Papers.

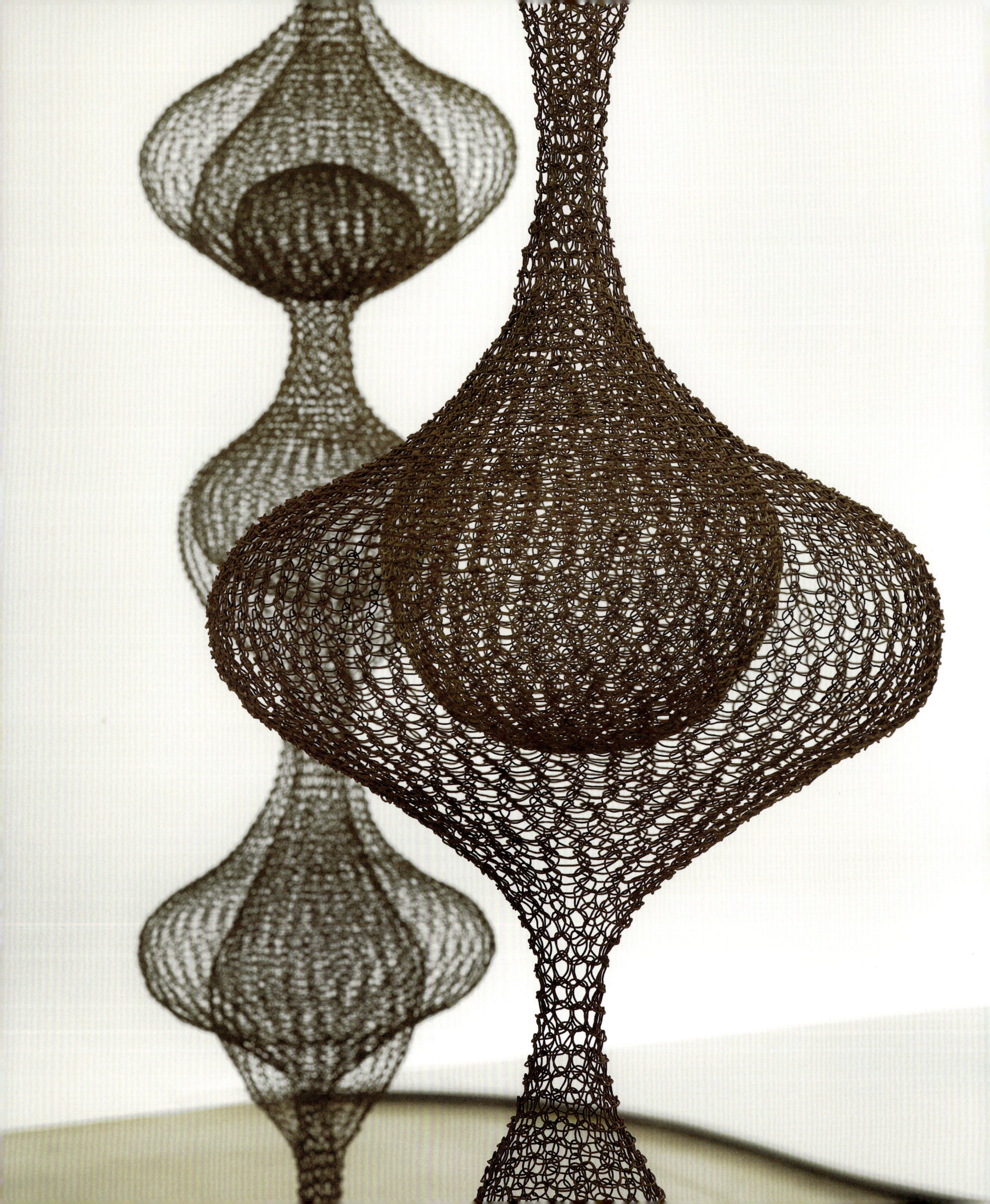

"San Francisco Housewife and Mother"

Helen Molesworth

Doing is living. That is all that matters.

—Ruth Asawa

For quite some time the story of art in the post–World War II period has been told beginning with either Arnold Newman's or Hans Namuth's iconic photographs of Jackson Pollock [figs. 1 & 2]. These images, meant to herald a new era in the history of art, proclaimed the self-evident truths that Pollock, particularly his swaggering masculine identity, connoted American art's radical break with European easel painting, and art as it was understood up until the war. And yet for a while now feminists—myself included—have been telling other stories, with other beginnings. Indeed, it seems that one of feminism's hallmarks as a hermeneutic is its endless propositional mode, one in which the writer or the artist basically says: "I wonder what happens if we start this another way?" This is one of those stories.

Several years after Newman's photos of Pollock appeared in *Life* magazine, the photographer Imogen Cunningham made a photograph known as Ruth Asawa and her children at home on Saturn Street, San Francisco (1957), a ravishing, complicated, and subtly indelible black-and-white image depicting exactly what is described [fig. 3]. In the background, we see the picture's ostensible subject, Asawa, working on the floor, bent over an in-progress sculpture, both hands tending to the wire that was her most essential material. Her face is doubly occluded; for not only does she look down at her hands and her work, but we see her through the semi-transparent looped wire mesh that forms the bottom edge of the lower section of one of her large hanging sculptures. We are afforded a partial view of two sculptures as well as four of Asawa's children, each of whom is as absorbed in their own activities as their mother is in hers. One child squats and looks intently at images on a table; another gazes off as if in a daydream; her eldest daughter is caught mid-motion, waving a long wooden dowel—the tool Asawa used to loop her wire—and, like a conductor's baton, the stick is blurred at its tip. All the while her baby sits naked on the floor jauntily sucking down the contents of his bottle. In addition to the suspended sculptures and drawings laid out on the table, we see a toy banjo; dead center on the floor, a spool of wire.

Cunningham regularly photographed Asawa in her home, and the strong friendship they enjoyed transcended their age difference (Cunningham was forty-three years older than Asawa), their ethnicity (Asawa was Japanese American and Cunningham was what we still call white), and their vastly different circumstances: Asawa had a husband and six young children, and Cunningham, after her divorce and raising three children of her own, lived a fiercely solitary life. However, both were artists and mothers, and their shared attributes enabled an intimacy to which Cunningham's photographs of Asawa clearly attest.

To hold Cunningham's image of Asawa in relation to Namuth's and Newman's equally engaging images of Pollock is almost laughable in its simplistic reliance on art history's favorite method of analysis, "compare and contrast," though in this case, it bears consideration: Pollock, newly branded as the "action painter," stands, stalks, and moves energetically, Asawa is seated and focused; Pollock is alone, Asawa is surrounded by her children; Pollock is portrayed as a master, mid-masterpiece, Asawa is engrossed in making what, at the time, was routinely perceived to be a craft object or an objet d'art; and finally, Pollock is male and Asawa female, which means that all of the other antinomies at play here end up being ruthlessly marshalled along the binary axis of gender.

And yet, perhaps feminism's rhetorical alignment of differences along gender lines, while meant to elucidate how the structural dimension of patriarchy functions to exclude women artists from the canon, also tends toward a reinscription of those gendered divisions—of labor, ideas, and methods. One of the effects of this is that any recovery of the attributes which are gendered female typically means a rewriting of those modalities as possessing the same value as things gendered male, hence leaving in place the structures of value that have historically precluded women and artists of color from the annals of Western art history in the first place. Not surprisingly, part of the reception of Cunningham's photo has been to see it as confirming Asawa's status as a "San Francisco housewife," a phrase used by a contemporaneous critic's assessment of her work. Decades later, writer and curator Sarah Archer neatly summed up Asawa's early reception:

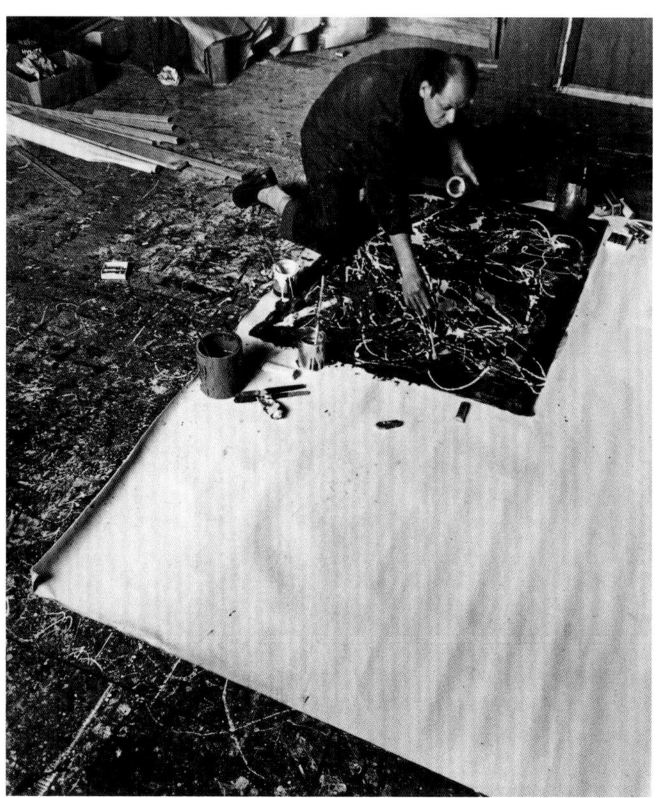

Fig. 1. Arnold Newman, Abstract Expressionist painter Jackson Pollock at work in his Long Island studio January 3, 1949, in East Hampton, New York

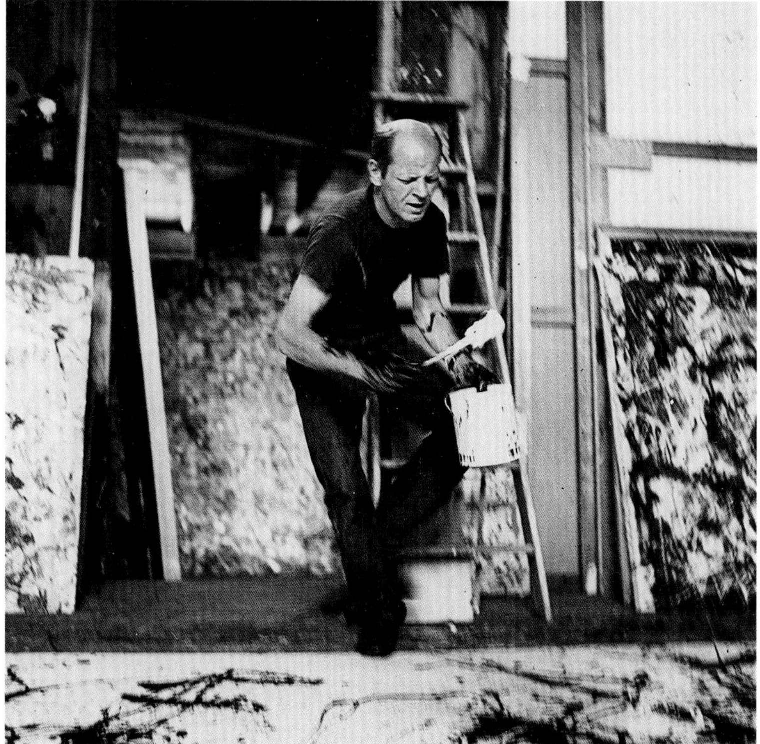

Fig. 2. Hans Namuth, *The Artist in 1950*, research photograph associated with the exhibition *Jackson Pollock*, December 19, 1956–February 3, 1957, at the Museum of Modern Art, New York. Gelatin-silver print, 8 × 8 inches (20.3 × 20.3 cm)

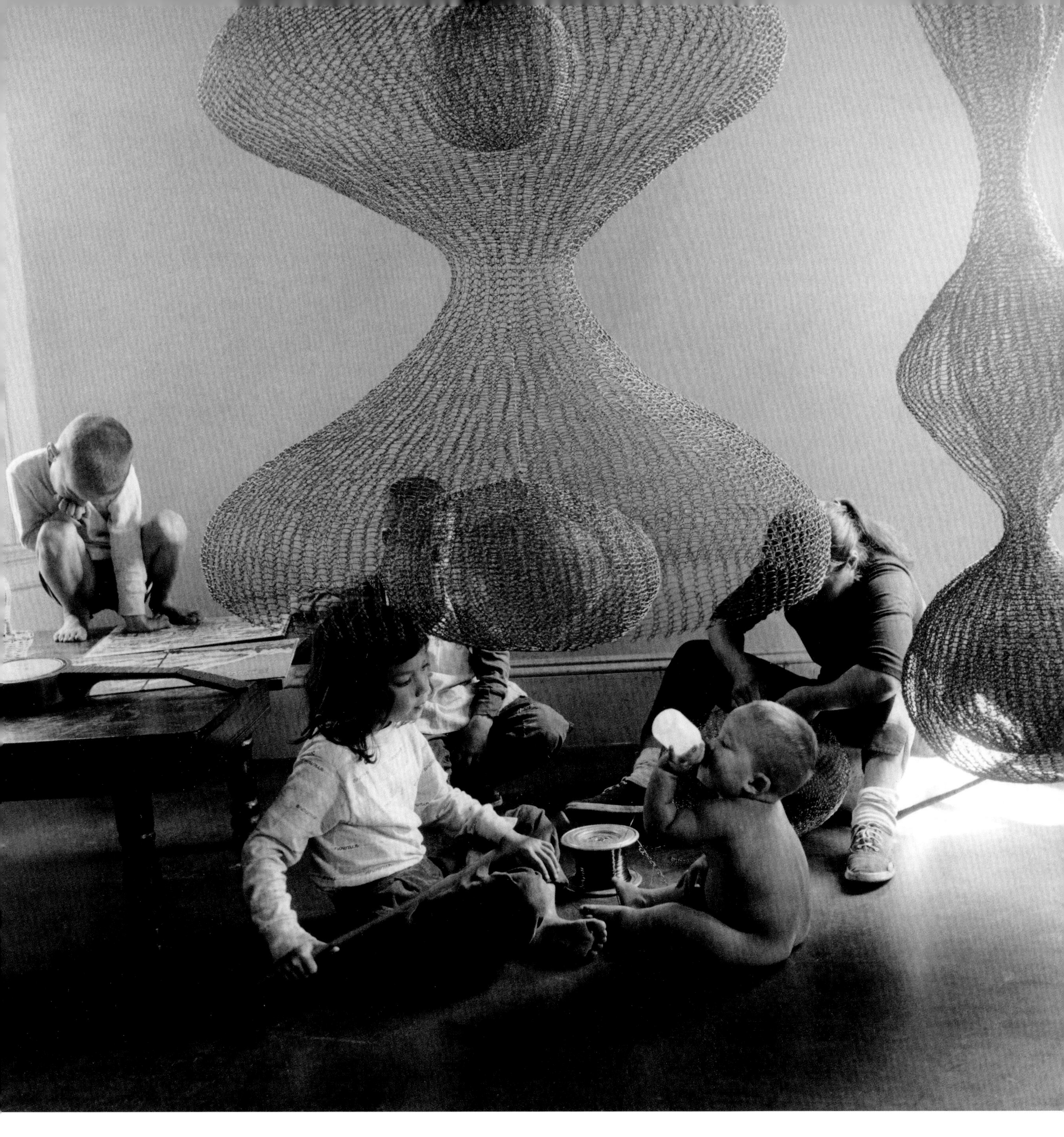

Fig. 3. Ruth Asawa and her children at home on Saturn Street, San Francisco, 1957. Photo by Imogen Cunningham

> The reviews of Asawa's 1956 solo exhibition at the Peridot Gallery were generally complimentary of her skill and aesthetic sense, but dismissive of her work with regard to the larger context of contemporary art practice. The review in *ArtNews* left little room for interpretation: "These are 'domestic' sculptures in a feminine handiwork mode." The *New York Times* review described her work as "beautiful, if primarily only decorative objects in space."[1]

The reasonable desire to "combat" the images of Asawa as a wife and mother of Japanese origin first, and as a mere craft hobbyist second, has tended toward readings of her work that assert the formal attributes of her work as divorced from any of her identities. This has produced critical assessments such as, "nor does her work directly correspond to her Japanese heritage or her role as a mother and wife."[2] I certainly don't want to see those identities as overriding any and all of her innovative formal concerns with the putative subject matter that emanates from such categories, but I don't entirely want to take "wife," "mother," and "Japanese" off the table either. My hope is that feminist art history can begin to work toward a more sensitive hermeneutic, one striated with degrees of complexity about these matters. I crave a discipline capable of negotiating the formal and the biographical, one skillful at navigating systems of value that are cognizant of their sexist formation but not beholden to reiterating that sexism at every turn. My proposition is as follows: if we compare these images of Pollock and Asawa at work, can we see Asawa's resolve in having fully embraced being a mother (hardly a detriment, or something that needs to be negated) so that that she might fully possess the identity *artist*? Might Cunningham's image potentially offer an altogether different model of who and what an artist is?[3]

For instance, Cunningham's photograph of Ruth Asawa and her children depicts art making as an inherently social activity rather than a solitary one. And within this space of sociality, society, and family, we see that the field of play in which Asawa operates is filled with—and energized by—other forms of creativity. Not only is Asawa one person among others, but her creative work is but one example of art in the picture. I view the drawings on the table and the musical instrument laid next to them as harkening back to European allegorical paintings depicting the creative arts, even the gently gathered arrangement of the figures in the picture seems to ride slipstream on the history of such pictorial compositions. In Cunningham's picture, however, the central female figure is neither allegorical, nor is she a "typical" mother. She is neither exclusively concerned with her children, nor is her identity as an artist in any way at risk. Rather, what the picture makes abundantly clear is that Asawa fully inhabits the role of artist and mother with seeming ease, without sacrificing one modality to the other. This interests me deeply, for it seems to offer a way out of the impasse of thinking that motherhood (and by extension other forms of labor historically gendered female) is either antithetical to being an artist, or is not a form of labor equal to the labor of being an artist.[4] What can such a reframing of Asawa's practice—and art making in general—afford us? While my focus here is primarily on Asawa's early sculptures, my hope is that some of the interpretive strategies I'm thinking about might be equally applicable to her later tied and bundled wire sculptures, her lifelong practice of making casts of the faces of her friends and family, and her extraordinary drawings.

Cunningham's photograph shows Asawa at work on the type of artworks she would ultimately become best known for—albeit belatedly. Ranging in size from handheld to over twenty-one feet long, these airy sculptures hang suspended from the ceiling, literally upending the problem of the base or pedestal that has plagued sculpture from its inception. If the twentieth century's radical answer to the problem of the base was to place the work directly on the floor (e.g. Constantin Brancusi), Asawa took the less traveled path of suspension (established by Alexander Calder) and studied the forces of gravity through an exploration of weightlessness. The lightness came from her extraordinary technique of looping thin pliable wire into basketlike forms that are both nested within one another as well as extending vertically to achieve the length and the effect of the human form.

The genesis of this shape was a set of drawings, made while Asawa was a student at Black Mountain College, where she and her peers danced under the tutelage of Merce Cunningham. In these student drawings, beautifully colored blue, green, and purplish, biomorphic shapes and double-lobed forms float on a series of grounds [p. 39]. Their motif repeats both on the page itself and across many drawings, lending the works a provisional attitude somewhere between doodling and practicing. That she would have seen some bodies as awkward and others as graceful, though all

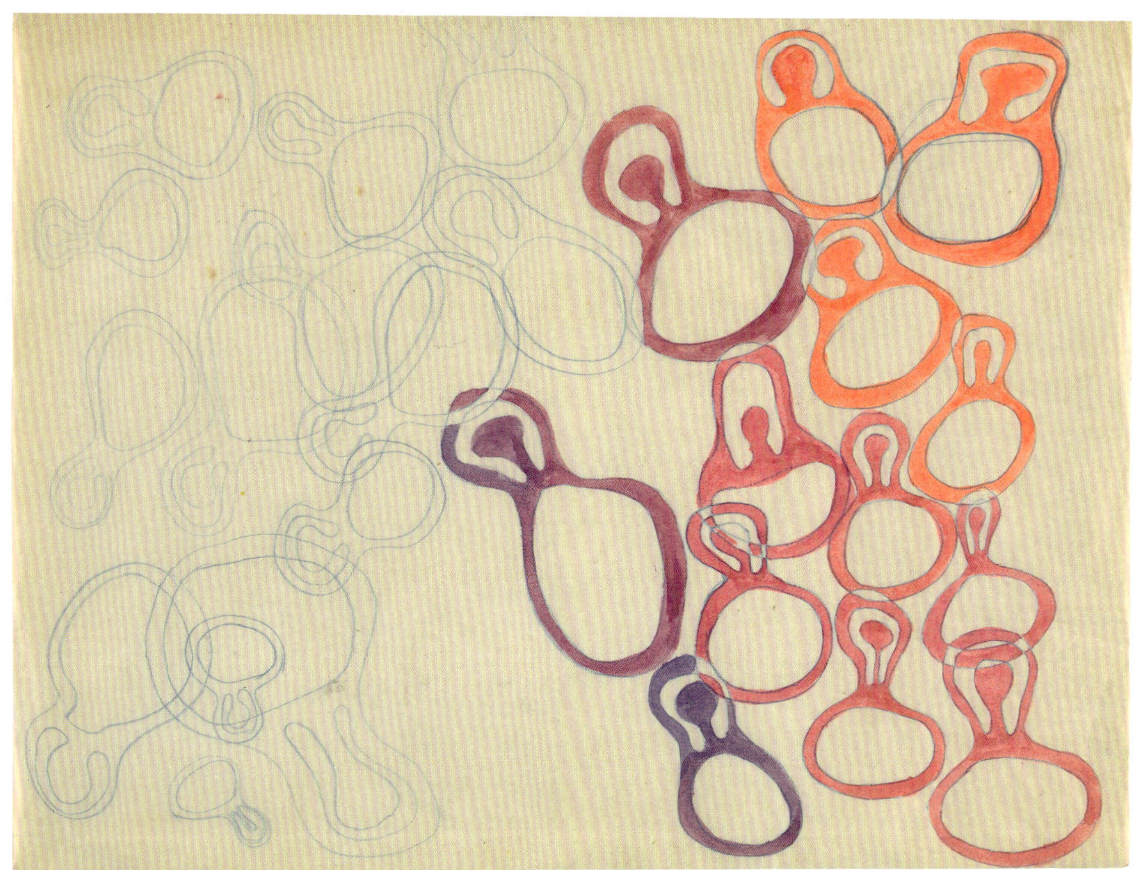

Untitled (BMC.144, Dancers), ca. 1948–49. Blue colored pencil and watercolor on tracing paper, 8 × 10½ inches (20.3 × 26.7 cm)

engaged in acts of repetition in space, seems to me germane to how we might begin to talk about the sculptures as well.

Many of Asawa's sculptures are permanently on view at the de Young museum in San Francisco, in an installation that the artist participated in, and one that mirrors the arrangements in the family home she shared with her husband, the architect Albert Lanier (whom she met when they were both students at Black Mountain College). Photographs of the sculptures in the Asawa-Lanier home reveal dynamic groupings, in which heights of the artworks vary, sunlight streams through and around them, and their repetitive internal forms are amplified by the repetition of the forms as a whole [fig. 5]. This installation set the template for how these works would be displayed moving forward. (Recent exhibitions of Asawa's work at Hauser & Wirth gallery in Los Angeles and at David Zwirner gallery in New York signal the persistence of her vision.)

More than merely looking stylish in the aggregate, which they undeniably do, when installed in groupings such as these the sculptures double down on the work's formal attributes. As already noted, Asawa's use of wire displays a play and tension with weight: the sculptures simultaneously deny and acknowledge gravity. This doubleness is further compounded by her extraordinary facility with positive and negative space. The exploitation of negative space comes through several avenues: each of her works plays with one of sculpture's primary binary oppositions—solid and void—recasting it as a meditation on empty and full, in which "empty" reads as negative space, and the very distinction between empty

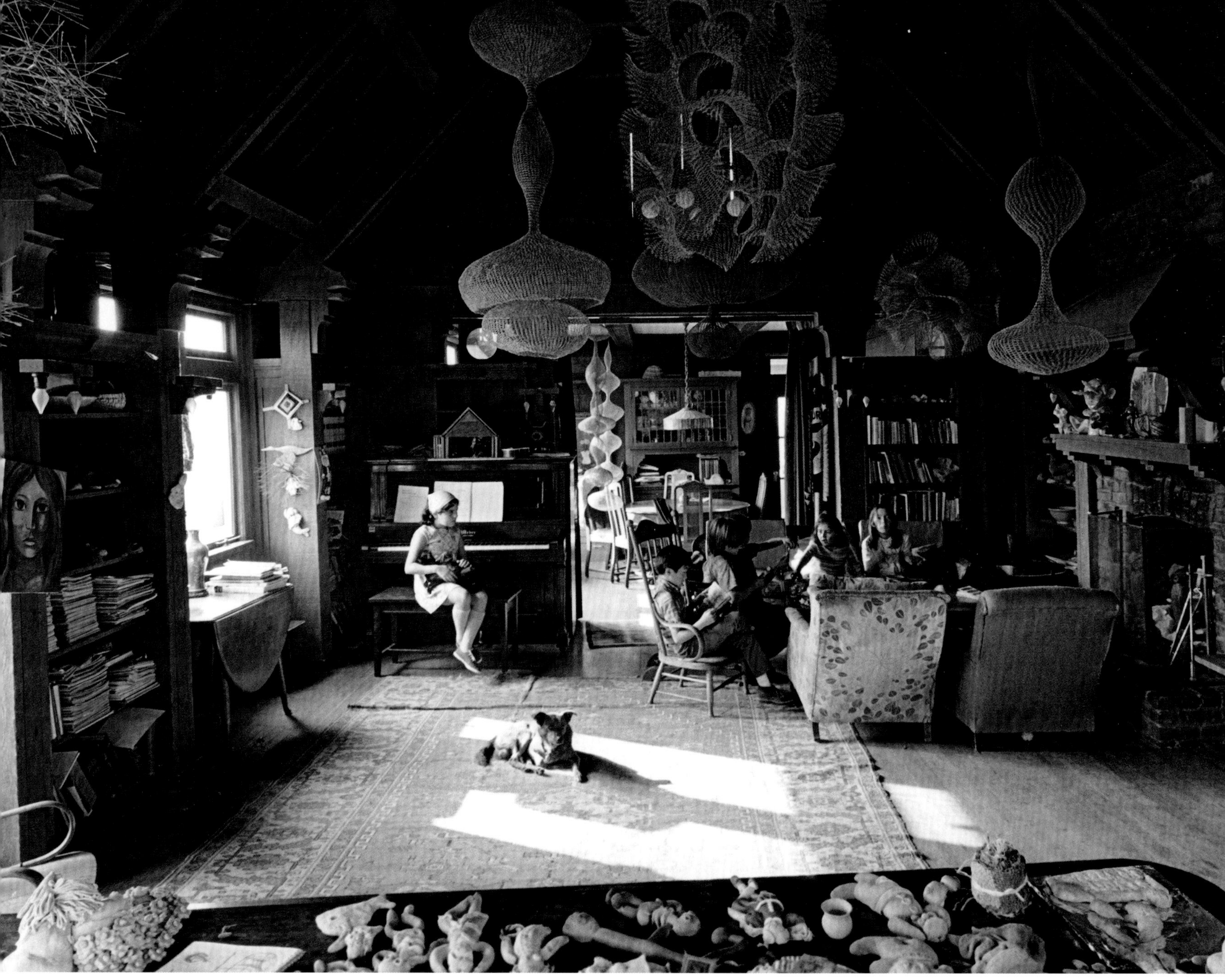

Fig. 5. Ruth Asawa's Living Room, San Francisco, 1969. Photo by Rondal Partridge

and full is attenuated by the continuous inside/outside movement of the looped wire. When the works are suspended in close proximity to one another, the undulating negative spaces in between the individual sculptures are almost as dynamic as the actual objects, and viewers can simultaneously take in the negative spaces internal to each object along with the sculptures themselves. Finally, the works' transparency creates beautiful shadows that feel so intentional as to be part of the work itself, and this shadow play both alludes to and functions as a kind of meta-commentary on negative space as one of sculpture's formal attributes.

While Asawa is undoubtedly mining the formal properties of sculpture, she is doing so by linking sculpture back to the medium of drawing. Not a purist when it comes to matters of medium, Asawa's use of wire allows a visual morphology to occur between the looping wire of her sculptures and the undulating line of her drawings. A heterogenous modernist, we find her everywhere paying attention to the specific formal concerns of a given medium while at the same time allowing subtle overlaps and contingencies to develop between them.

Asawa's preferred method of installing her sculptures demonstrates her engagement with that most enduring of modernist tropes—repetition and difference. She aligns repetition and difference alongside negative and positive space, allowing us to see these binaries in parallel relation, which in turn presents the interpretive possibility that Asawa's sculptures might be proposing a structural framework that governs relations between things. For instance, Asawa's manipulation of negative and positive space makes clear her sculptures complete and utter inextricability as a dialectical image. Cunningham's photographs of the individual artworks readily convey that within each object there is no hierarchical distinction between the empty and full forms, that distinction is suggested through the linguistic apparatus that cleaves these two types of space in half, designating one as "positive" and the other as "negative." At times even making both positive and negative prints of her photographs, Cunningham interprets the "problem" of negative and positive in sculptural space as being analogous to the specific visual operations inherent to photography [fig. 6].

What might it mean to think about these formal attributes—all of which are performed with an undeniably sophisticated sense of aesthetics—through the lens of motherhood? Might we begin to consider allusions to cells, embryos, fetuses, and whole human bodies in these forms? And can we see these things without overstating them? I don't mean to say that Asawa's work is "about" the generative power of the female body, but I do want to talk about how her particular set of formal problems is not exclusively formal, for Cunningham's image and the narrative of Asawa's life seem to suggest something other. This might be one way of looking at the Cunningham image, in which Asawa is working on a sculpture while appearing to be inside of it; it's a kind of uncanny conflation of maternal and fetal development with artistic production. And might Cunningham herself have been interested in extending this quality of Asawa's works when she printed them as negative images, in which they appear downright cellular in structure? I am intrigued by how these plays with inside and outside, empty and full, negative and positive, and their possible allusions to biology might be part of the wordless dialogue transpiring between Asawa and Cunningham in their dual roles as artists and mothers.

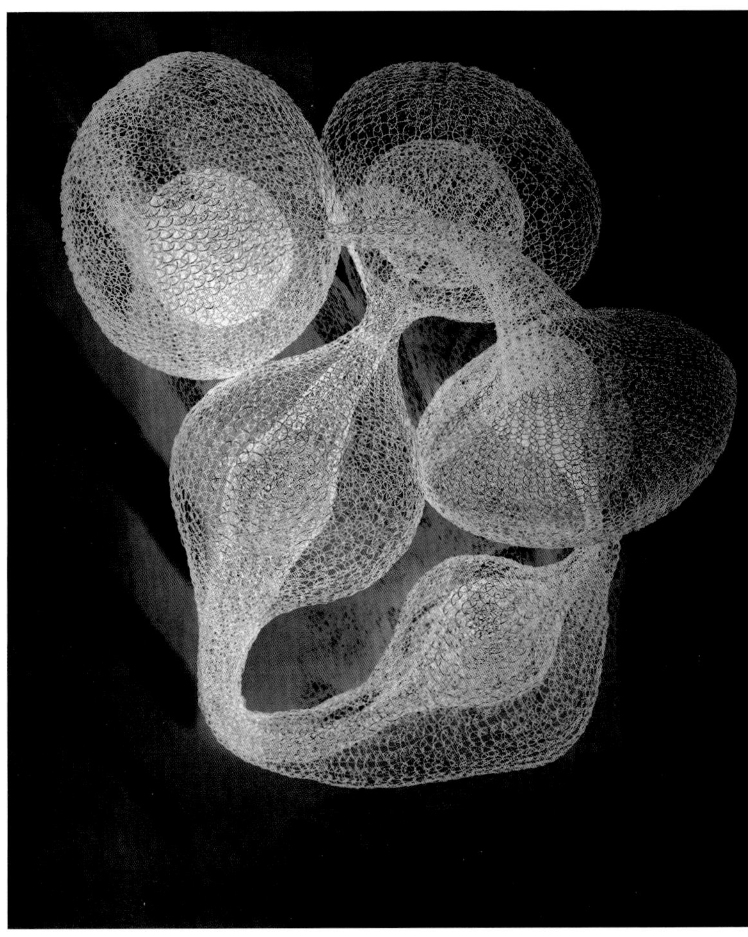

Fig. 6. Ruth Asawa's Hanging Sculpture 2, *Untitled* (S.535), 1951 (negative). Photo by Imogen Cunningham

Similarly, if we think about Asawa's early sculptures in concert with her history of making casts of her friends' and family's faces and we combine that with her work to bring artists into the San Francisco public schools, can we connect the dots of her concerns as being deeply immersed in the idea that art and life are deeply intertwined, which would in turn allow us to see her as interested in repetition and difference both as a modernist trope *and* as a structuring feature of being the mother of six children, who by their very existence and actuality are a living embodiment of the repetition and difference enabled by DNA?[5] In this regard might we read her castings project as a literalization of the formal attributes of her abstract sculptures (especially as casting is one of the most indelible modes of playing with negative and positive space, solid and void, repetition and difference)? Can we see in Asawa's intensely social activities—her belief in public education and art in public spaces—a commitment to art not as a solitary endeavor but as part of a profoundly social network? And might these questions help us to see the later tied-wire sculptures, whose tree- and branch-like forms are bound together with a repetitive coiling of wire, as a kind of bundling, a keeping together of disparate energies that branch out into the world even as they remain connected to others? And given how the previous description of the work could also be read as a depiction of family life in general, could we then jump to a discussion of how all of the sculptures might articulate something of the great mystery of siblings? For what are siblings if not the elucidation of parity and difference, interrelatedness and autonomy, being bound together by a common thread, and so on?[6]

Given that Asawa's time at Black Mountain College was so crucial to the development of her personal artistic idiom, I think a brief exegesis on her influential teacher Josef Albers's attitudes toward form makes sense. For Albers, form was not separate from the problem of content. Rather, his writing, teaching, and art practice all seem to indicate that in his mind, there was no content without form. Albers taught that form was a "never-ending performance," as his longest project, Homage to the Square, clearly demonstrates. Albers's decades-long formal play with color relations was a continual testing of perception in the name of ethics.[7] For it was through his explorations of one individual color's relationship to another color that he could articulate that there was indeed no qualitative difference between colors. What a viewer felt about color was different from how they perceived it, and the task of both the artist and the viewer is to negotiate that gap between perception and feeling with critical awareness. These were the rich and clearly rewarding lessons on tap for Asawa and her peers at Black Mountain College.

I think Asawa's work in general, and her suspended sculptures in particular, are deeply indebted to this "Albersian" idea about what an artwork does. If one of the tasks of the artist is to work on problems of form through acts of repetition, in a manner that permits an actual and theoretical engagement with the issues of making and perception, such that those activities can be used to help gain a greater understanding of the world we inhabit and create, then can we think of Asawa as doing this work from the ethical position of the mother within the framework of the family? And since Asawa did not produce sentimental images that extolled the nuclear family above all other social formations, and instead sought to engage deeply with her community, through her children, and even more specifically through the apparatus that creates society—the public school[8]—can we open up a discursive field around her work that links her interests in wire and sculpture, in negative and positive space, in repetition and difference, in the social, to her dynamic position as an artist and a mother, as a Japanese American, as a product of progressive education, and as a believer in arts education? To put this another way, were Ruth Asawa's family, their home, and these activities her art world [fig. 7]?

These questions and the field of inquiry they map out suggest to me that the proper name Ruth Asawa, and the remarkable oeuvre attached to that name, can now open the story another way and stand in for the mid-twentieth century's early efforts at rethinking the definition of artist. So I'd like to end with a bit of a provocation: it seems difficult—but readily available—to recoup the maternal or the position of the mother in relation to the identity "artist." Less so is any possibility of rethinking "housewife." One effect of art history's reclamation of female artists has been to argue that critics have historically missed the formal integrity and sophistication of women's work because the overriding framework of identity was allowed to obliterate the "true" or "real" concerns and/or intentions of the artist. But what if the denigrated terms hold knowledge that we need? What if instead of insisting that women artists be judged by the same formal parameters as their male counterparts we instead ask what the terms "mother"—or even the more scandalous, and typically pejorative "housewife"—might have to teach us about being an artist? What does a housewife-artist look like? Late in life Asawa offered a small clue in an interview contained in a volume titled *On Women Turning 70*: "Something very important I want to tell women is that it's never too late but don't wait until it's too late, because you won't have the energy. You should do a little bit at a time. It's important to learn how to use your small bits of time. All those begin to count up. It's not the long amounts of time you have that are important. You should learn how to use your snatches of time when they are given to you."[9]

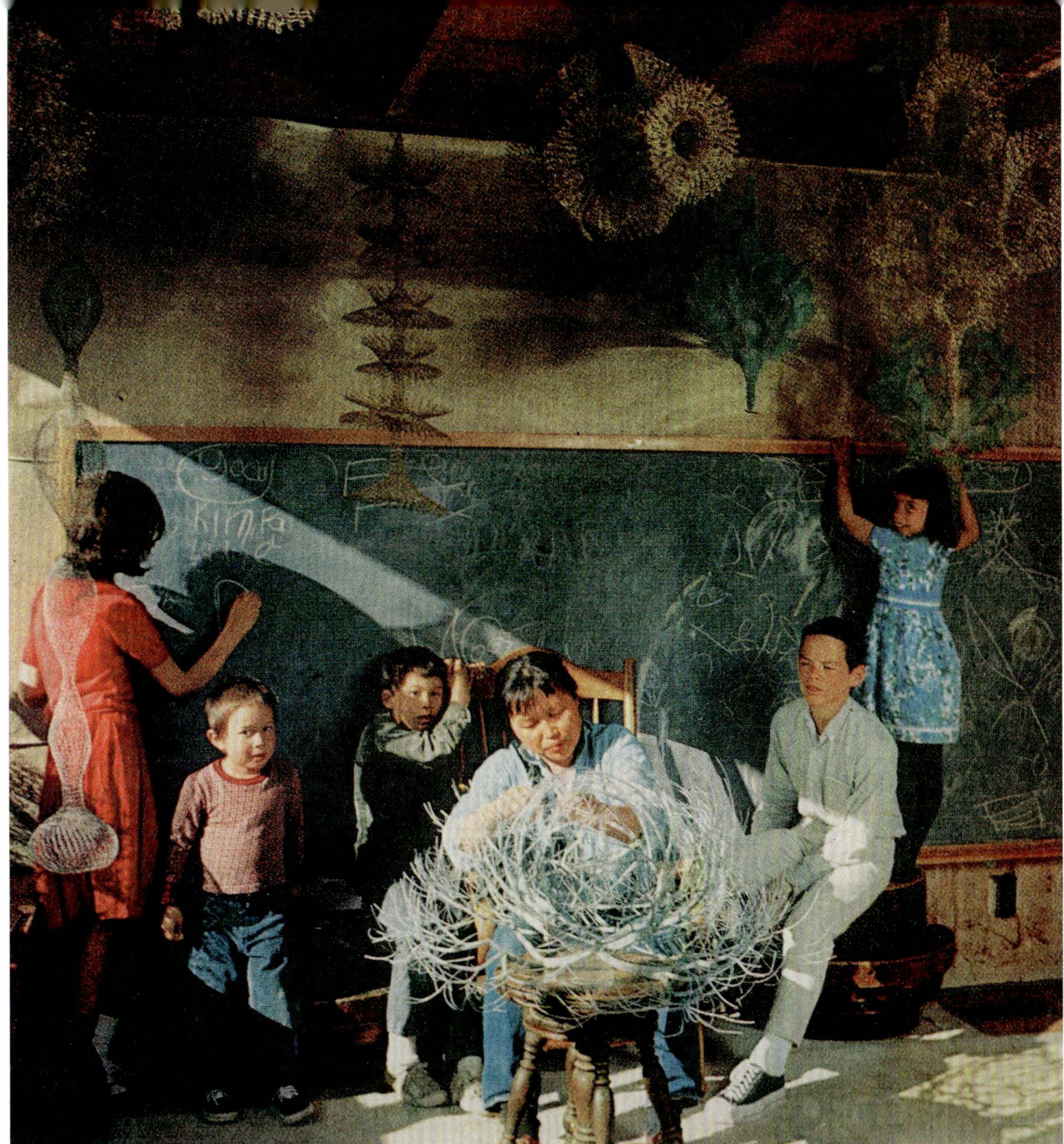

Fig. 7. Asawa with five of her six children in the sunroom of her Noe Valley home in San Francisco, 1964

Notes

1. Sarah Archer, "Maker to Market: Ruth Asawa Reappraised," *Journal of Modern Craft* 8, no. 2 (July 2015): 146.

2. Emily K. Doman Jennings, "Critiquing the Critique," in *The Sculpture of Ruth Asawa: Contours in the Air*, ed. Daniell Cornell (San Francisco: Fine Arts Museums of San Francisco; and Berkeley: University of California Press, 2006), 137.

3. In this essay I focus almost exclusively on the role of mother due to an interest in the ways in which being a mother and being an artist are typically offered as an antinomy. This isn't to deny the intersectionality that structures Asawa's person and her work, but rather to continue an avenue of inquiry that began with the figure of the "artist mother" in my essay on the work of Anna Maria Maiolino, "Mother Knowledge." See *Anna Maria Maiolino* (Los Angeles: The Museum of Contemporary Art; and New York: DelMonico Books/Prestel, 2017), 164–71.

4. The single most sustained effort to think through the problem of the Mother-Artist dyad comes in Moyra Davey's edited volume *Mother Reader: Essential Writings on Motherhood* (New York: Seven Stories Press, 2001). See in particular Susan Rubin Suleiman's "Writing and Motherhood" and Nancy Houston's "Novels and Navels."

5. Much of my thinking about the logic of sameness and difference and its relation to siblings comes from Juliet Mitchell's *Siblings: Sex and Violence* (Cambridge, UK: Polity Press, 2003).

6. In his essay on Asawa, John Yau writes that "Robert Smithson's description of Hesse's work as 'psychic models of a very interior person' seems equally applicable to Asawa's wire constructions." I think my questions here are in this spirit: to see in the formal the structure of subjectivity and its intelligences rather than a one-to-one correspondence between identity and subject matter. In *Ruth Asawa: Objects and Apparitions* (New York: Christie's, 2013), 20.

7. For more on Albers and form, see my essay "Imaginary Landscape," in *Leap Before You Look: Black Mountain College, 1933–1957* (Boston: Institute of Contemporary Art; and New Haven: Yale University Press, 2015), 25–73.

8. For more on Asawa's work in San Francisco public schools, see "The Alvarado Art Workshop, 1968–1973" by Sally B. Woodbridge in *Contours in the Air*, 222–26.

9. Cathleen Rountree, ed., *On Women Turning 70: Honoring the Voices of Wisdom* (San Francisco: Jossey-Bass, 1999), 83.

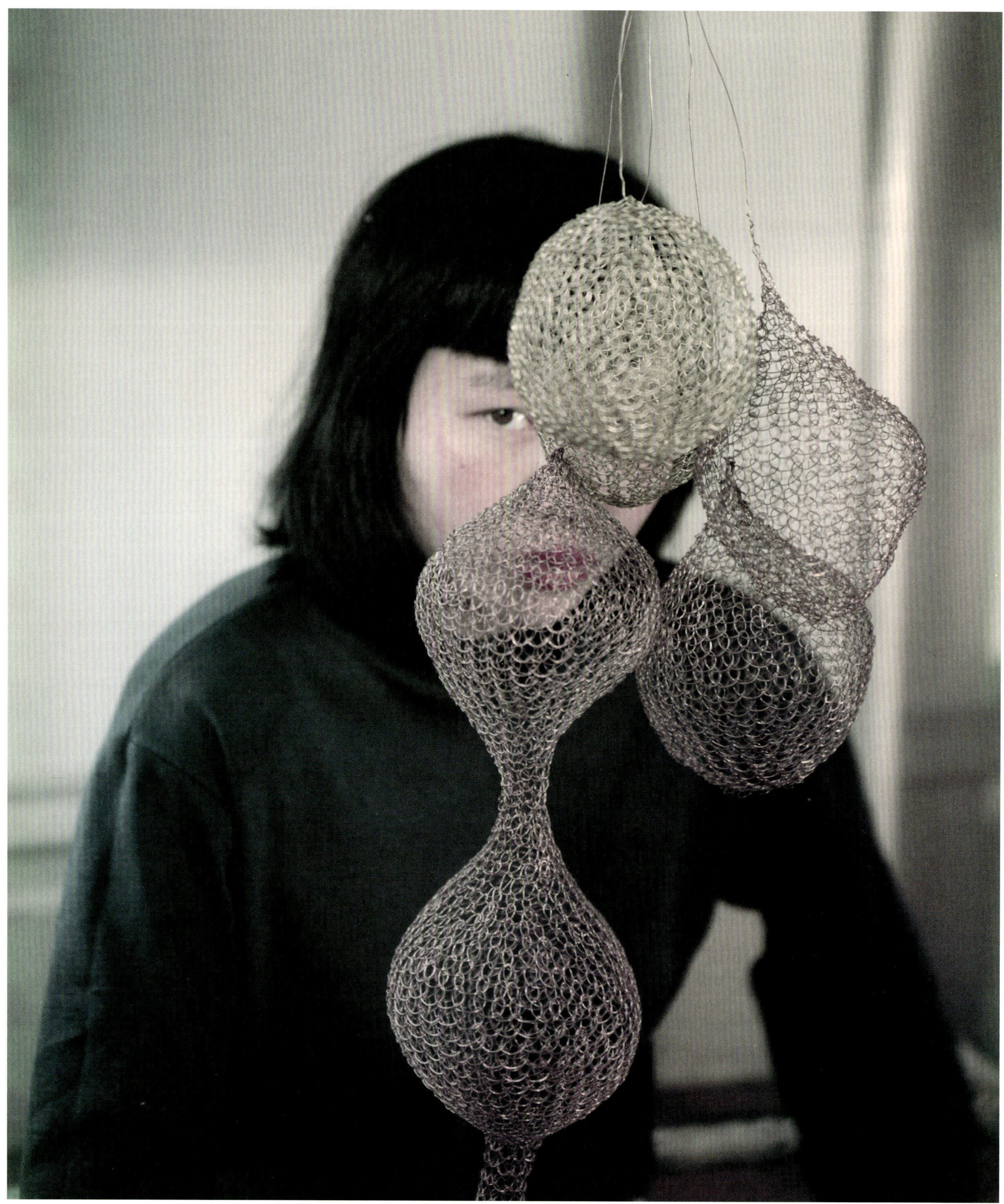

Fig. 1. Ruth Asawa, 1951. Photo by Imogen Cunningham

Transparency and its Other

Aruna D'Souza

It was in college that I experienced for the first time the feeling of being an individual, a minority of one.

—Ruth Asawa

This statement by Ruth Asawa about her experience at Black Mountain College in the 1940s fascinates me. In its brevity, it encapsulates Asawa's life as a Japanese American woman negotiating American culture—enduring the injustices of being interned during World War II, and the irony of finding herself at a progressive college in the segregated South because anti-Asian racism had prevented her from completing her education degree up north. "I experienced for the first time": It is an expression of relief at finally being able to put aside the labels that had dogged her for most of her life, the labels that had marked her as not simply different but also, in the wake of Pearl Harbor, a "traitor." "[T]he feeling of being an individual": It is a statement about the expansion into the self, freedom from the ways she had been raced and othered until this point, an extension into space, an ascension into subjectivity after being so long a faceless threat.

And then: "A minority of one."

This last phrase, "a minority of one," sounds like a sharp intake of the breath that inflated and buoyed the earlier part of the sentence, contracting the individual to a solitary—to my ear infinitesimal—singularity. To be an individual means to stand out from the undifferentiated crowd. Being a minority of one, on the other hand, means barely counting.

She reiterated this idea, poignantly, when she wrote to her future husband Albert Lanier, whom she met at Black Mountain College, about the difficulties they would face as a mixed-race couple. She begins with reference to her family's imprisonment in an internment camp, and goes on to contrast the trauma of being marked as other in public space with the solace of imagining herself as a "citizen of the universe":

> [W]e have all suffered intolerance innocently. I no longer want to nurse such wounds; I now want to wrap fingers cut by aluminum shavings, and hands scratched by wire. Only these things produce tolerable pains. You will have to look at me on a streetcar or bus when you hear someone shout, "dirty Jap." I hope we never have to experience it, but expect it, but do not fear it. I've overcome most of the fear. I've reached a point where I can no longer nurse such stupidity. *This attitude has forced me to become a citizen of the universe, by which I grow infinitely smaller than if I belonged to a family or a province or a race. Then I can allow myself to pass and not be hurt as mortally by ugly remarks.*[1]

There are contradictory impulses, then, in both of these short articulations of Asawa's understanding of selfhood. An almost endless expansion outward—into full subjectivity, into citizenship—and a simultaneous contraction to infinite smallness. The optical correlates of these are visibility and invisibility—or, we might say, transparency and its other.

•

When we speak of Asawa's looped-wire sculptures, we often speak of transparency, and rightly so. It is one of the qualities the artist sought when she took a single wire and repeated the e-shaped loop that she had learned from Mexican basket weavers on her trips to villages there in the summer of 1947. This simple method, in her hands, resulted in an almost infinite variety of lobed, single and nested biomorphic and cosmic forms over the course of her career. Frequently suspended from the ceiling in clusters, they evoke amoebas, seaweed, coral, the moment a new star is born in the ether or an egg begins to break free from an ovary, bodies, wombs, and so on and so forth—a universe of associations, often overlapping and multiplying. But the simple looped stitch itself, formed around a dowel, never changed:

> It's an amazing technique. All my [looped] wire sculptures are made from the same loop. And there's only one way to do it. The idea is to do it simply, and you end up with a shape. That shape comes out working with the wire. You don't think ahead of time, *this is what I want*. You work on it as you go along. You make a line, a two-dimensional line, then you go into space, and you have a three-dimensional piece. It's like drawing in space.[2]

Asawa once said that she borrowed the notion of transparency from Josef Albers, her teacher at Black Mountain College: "I liked the idea," she said, "and it turns out my sculpture is like that. You can see through it. The piece does not hide anything. You can show inside and outside, and inside and outside are connected. Everything is connected, continuous."[3] This continuity was dependent on the unbroken line—the single wire that weaves the form without interruption; even the forms within forms are made from this one single filament.

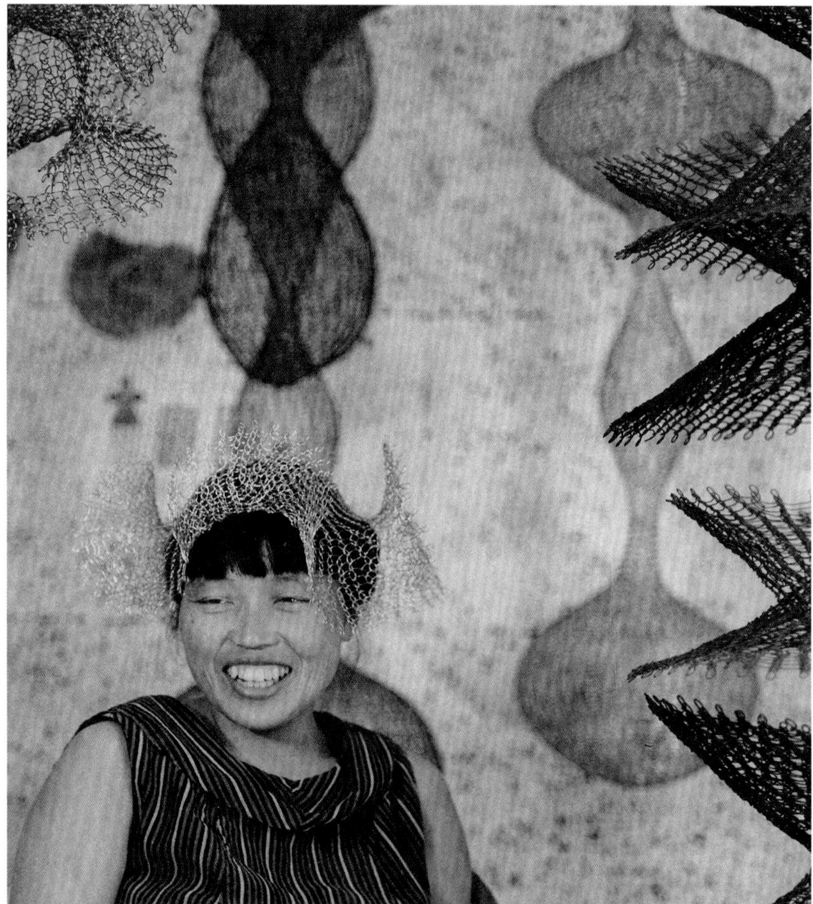

Fig. 2. Ruth Asawa wearing *Untitled* (S.762), 1958. Photo by Paul Hassel

> I was interested in . . . the economy of a line, making something in space, enclosing it without blocking it out. It's still transparent. I realized that if I was going to make these forms, which interlock and interweave, it can only be done with a line because a line can go anywhere.[4]

The mobility of line—its ability to go anywhere—is a kind of invisibility, like a person so inconsequential she can enter any space unnoticed. And this transparency, formed by the line's ability to slip through space and still function as a boundary, was imagined by Asawa to model an almost human form of coexistence, one in which space (or even that which fills the space, namely air) is not consumed or occupied but simply borrowed momentarily: "I am able to take a wire and go into the air and define the air without stealing it from anyone. A line can enclose and define space while letting the air remain air. You can see right through most of my sculpture."[5]

•

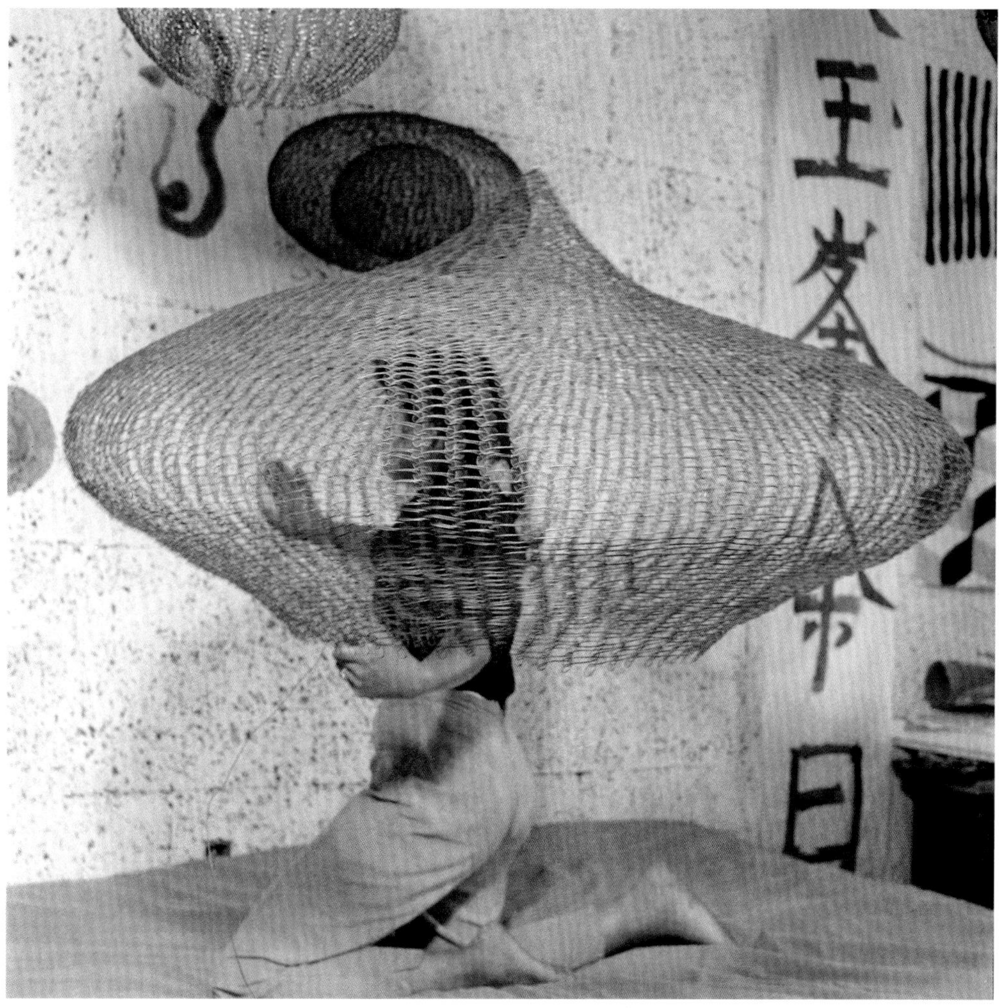

Fig. 3. Ruth Asawa, 1957. Photo by Imogen Cunningham

This is true, to a point. The open mesh of Asawa's forms, determined by the size of the dowel around which she looped her iron, galvanized steel, copper, or brass wire, allow us to see through them, sometimes revealing another lobe, or several, contained within. But a circa 1951 photograph by Asawa's friend Imogen Cunningham of the artist peering out from behind a cluster of simple wire droplets reveals how complicated this transparency, this continuity, this connection of inside and outside, actually is [fig. 1]. We can see Asawa's pink lips through one of the orbs on the left, the line of her jaw, and her green shirt behind. But near the top, where two of these "transparent" forms overlap, the doubling and thickening render her left eye invisible, even while her right peers out at us warily. One form overlaps her shoulder on the right of the image, softening the black of her shirt to a gainy grey; just above, two wire forms sit cheek-and-jowl with the other, creating a darkened curved shape that mirrors, if imperfectly, the contour of Asawa's body.

Others were seemingly fascinated by photographing Asawa inside her sculptures, or sometimes wearing them [fig. 2]. In part, this was an effective way of showing how the artist made her deceptively simple forms—working both inside them and out, building the inner globules as she worked the enclosing orbs—from something as simple as wire. In 1957 Cunningham made a series of pictures of Asawa sitting on her bed constructing a large pendulum [fig. 3]. She appears underneath it in some of the images, examining it closely; in others, her upper body is fully contained by it, as her fingers work expertly. It is as if we are seeing her

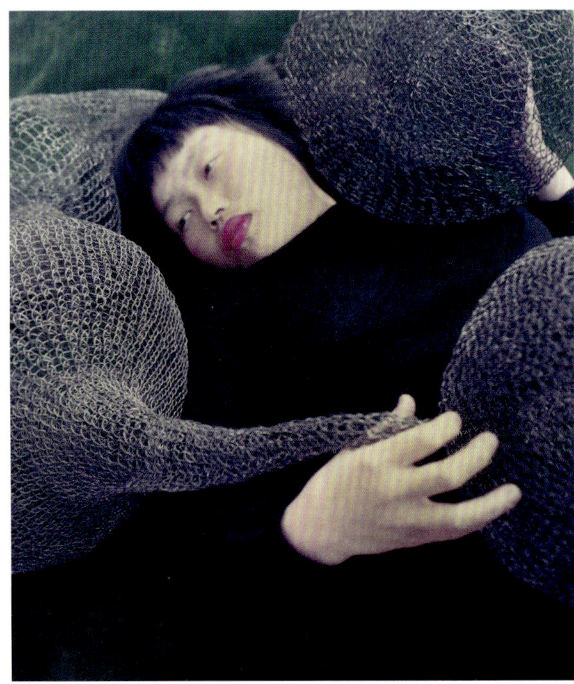

Fig. 4. Ruth Asawa, 1951. Photo by Imogen Cunningham

in a fishbowl; the screen of looped wire distorts her figure, bends it optically. We see her as a function of transparency, but not fully, not truly. We can only see through.

An earlier Cunningham photograph shows the artist with one of her pieces, a column that swells out and contracts in, creating an undulating series of bulges, wrapped around her; she lies back, nestled into it, gazing away from the camera, hands gently caressing the wire form [fig. 4]. The effect is almost startlingly sensual, erotic even. While Asawa would later in her career go on to create origami-like objects meant to be worn by, draped over, or tunneled through by dancers at the San Francisco School of the Arts, Cunningham's photograph of the artist entwined in her sculpture is marked by its stillness. In another image from the same year, she sits upright, the sculpture held in both hands. Again Asawa looks away from the camera, out of the frame. In this case, the mood is not so much sensual as uneasy; the wire piece becomes a form of protection, a barrier, a cage. It was the poet John Yau who pointed out that

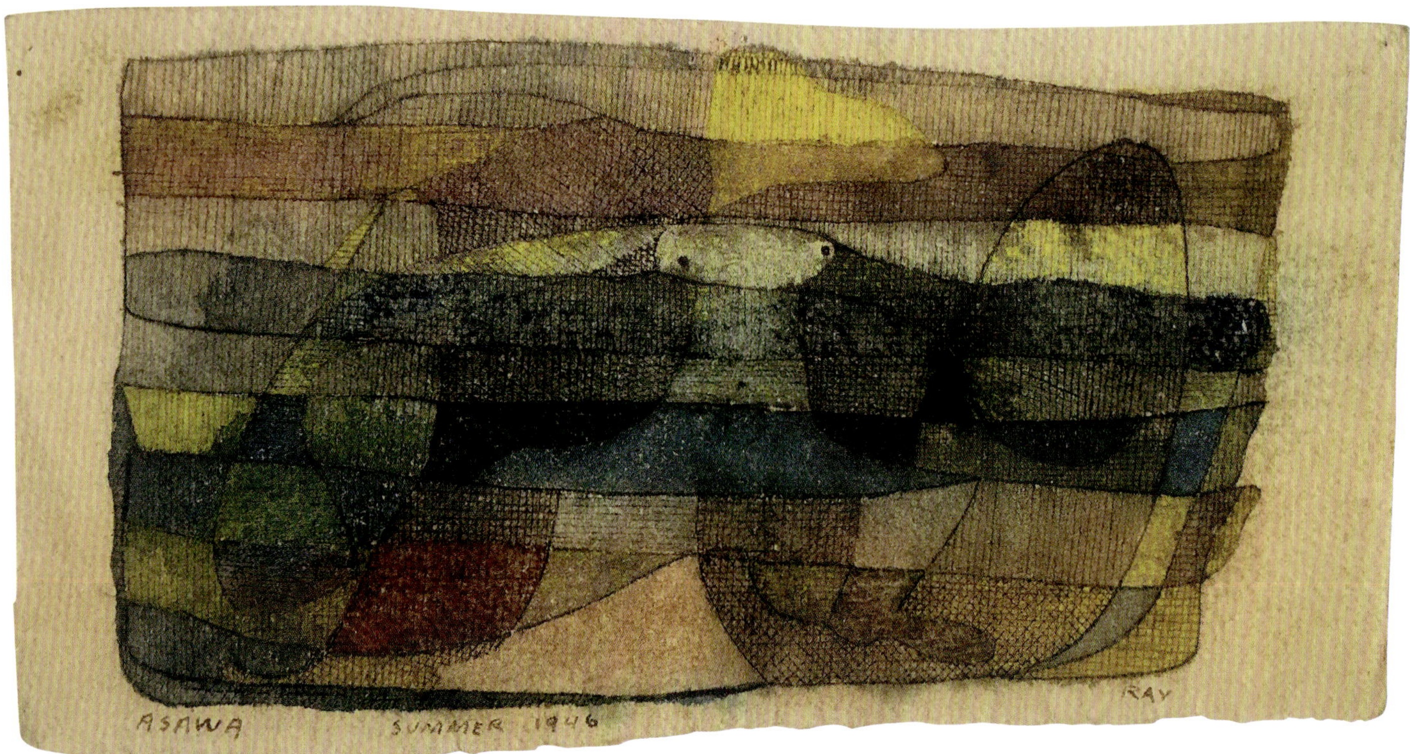

Fig. 5. Ray Johnson, *Asawa Summer 1946*, 1946. Ink and watercolor on paper, 3⅜ × 6 inches (8.5 × 15.2 cm). Private collection

Asawa's looped stitch produced chain mail as easily as it did organic abstractions in her hands.[6]

Like Cunningham, Asawa's Black Mountain College classmate Ray Johnson must have also recognized in his friend this play between openness and distance, between transparency and its other. In *Asawa Summer 1946*, he pictured her veiled behind a transparent scrim of delicate lines, her body an abstracted biomorph, almost like a sea creature [fig. 5]. She is barely discernible behind the screen of hatch marks except for two nipples that point in slightly different directions, like the eyes of a myopic squid. She is faceless. Her body does not disappear behind this web of markings so much as fuse with them; she is neither projected onto this screen nor hidden by it, but woven into it. She is a function of, even a component of, her work.

•

But we should not imagine that this play of visibility and invisibility, of the simultaneous presence and effacement of the self, is merely a facet of the artist's personality, of her particular way of being in the world. On the contrary, it is also an essential part of the viewer's experience of the work. Grouped in installations, as Asawa tended to favor from the earliest moments of her career, the sculptures separate and overlap to create complex shadows, shifting the transparency and opacity of each individual piece, as the viewer moves around the room. She was preternaturally skilled at imagining her sculpture not in terms of solidity, but as a feature of negative space. But negative space is not simply an abstraction: it frames a view. Our bodies, the bodies of those looking at her work, are seen in and through those interstices.

However, this is hardly a formalist's game of hide and seek: not simply an optical experience, but a politics. The phenomenology of Asawa's practice is, at its root, a vision of how viewers can and should interact in communal space. By becoming almost invisible—becoming a minority of one, contracting into the infinitely small—we become citizens of the universe. In the same way that the sculptures sometimes occlude and sometimes frame (heighten the visibility of) their neighbors, so too do people coming into momentary contact bring out the humanity of those to whom they are proximate. How does one make sculpture that does not steal any air? This formal and material question was very much framed by Asawa in human terms: how does one exist in communal space without diminishing the next person? How does one live in the world without stealing a neighbor's humanity?:

> Each material has a nature of its own, and by combining it and by putting it next to another material, you can change or give another personality to it without destroying either one. So that when you separate them again, they return back . . . to [their] familiar qualities. . . . It's the same thing that you don't change a person's personality, but when you combine them with other people, other personalities, they take on another quality. But the intent is not to change them, but to bring out another part of them.[7]

The idea that one must remain true to the nature of their materials—whether paper, paint, or metal wire—in pursuit of formal innovation was a foundational tenet and a principle of art making for Albers, who certainly imparted this to his students. In the hands of young Ruth Asawa, this aesthetic became an ethic. This is the paradox of Asawa's play with transparency and its other, with the presence and occlusion of the human body that her sculpture offers up in turn: via our willingness to be *seen through*, we become part of something much larger—a community.

Notes

1. Asawa, letter to Albert Lanier, December 29, 1948, in *Ruth Asawa* (New York: David Zwirner Books, 2018), 7. Emphasis mine.
2. Jacqueline Hoefer, "Ruth Asawa: A Working Life," in Daniell Cornell, ed., *The Sculpture of Ruth Asawa: Contours in the Air* (San Francisco: Fine Arts Museums of San Francisco; and Berkeley: University of California Press, 2006), 16.
3. Ibid.
4. Cornell, "The Art of Space: Ruth Asawa's Sculptural Installations," in *Contours in the Air*, 138.
5. Ibid., 143.
6. John Yau, "Ruth Asawa: Shifting the Terms of Sculpture," in *Ruth Asawa: Objects and Apparitions* (New York: Christie's, 2013), 19: "Paradoxically, the structure is a kind of armor, at once protective, as well as a vulnerable form in which inside and outside are visible at the same time."
7. Karin Higa, "Inside and Outside at the Same Time," in *Contours in the Air*, 41.

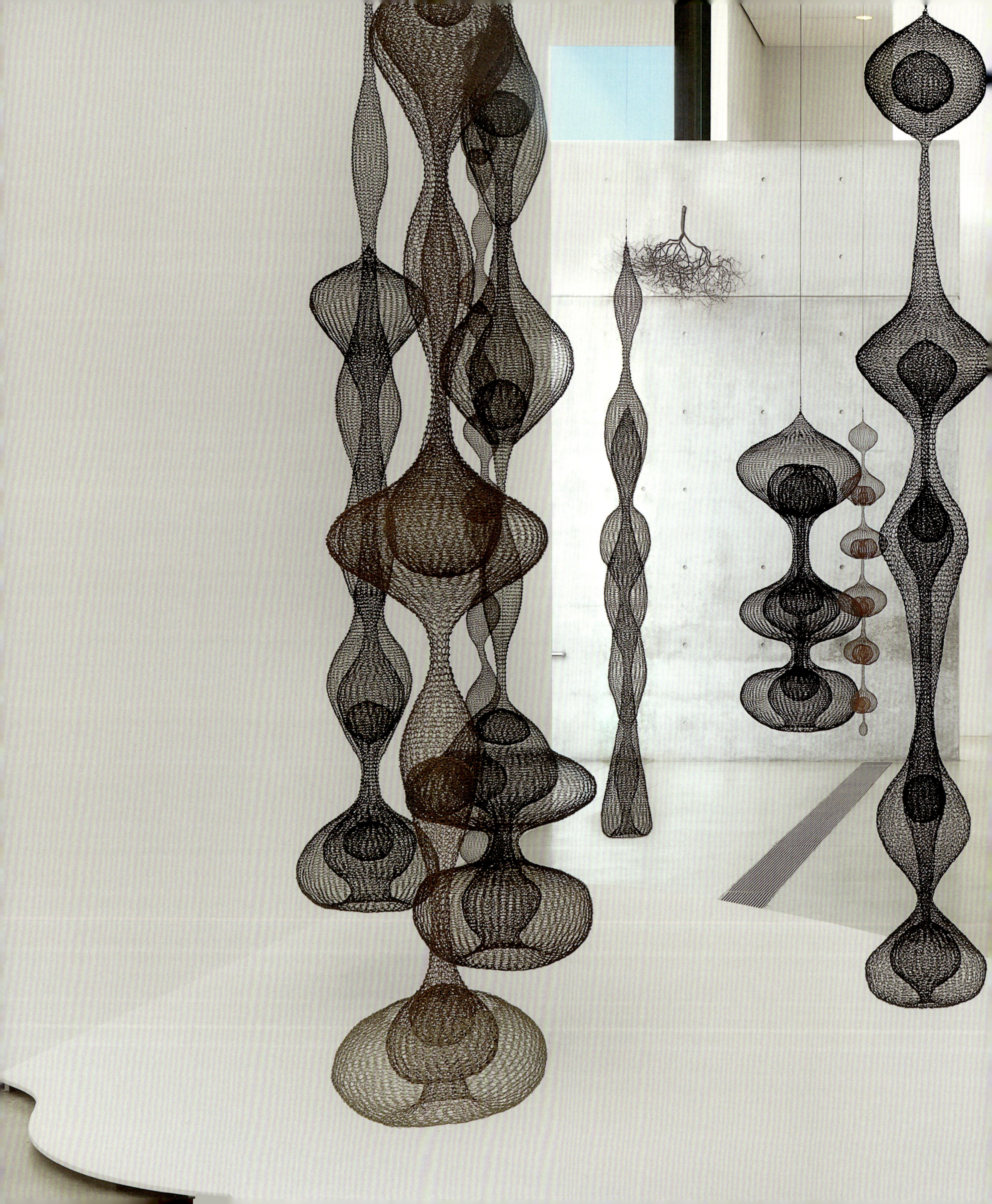

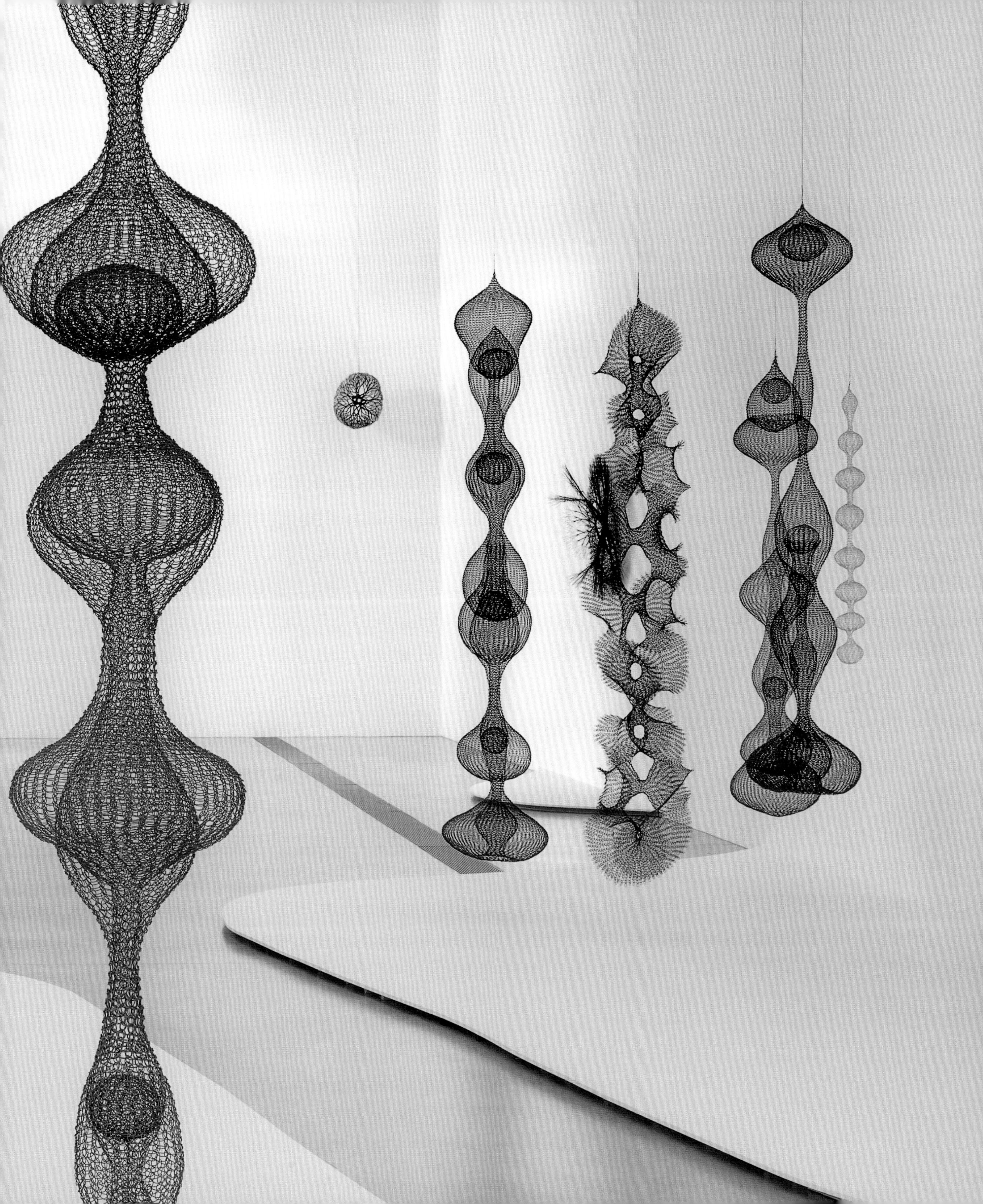

Artworks

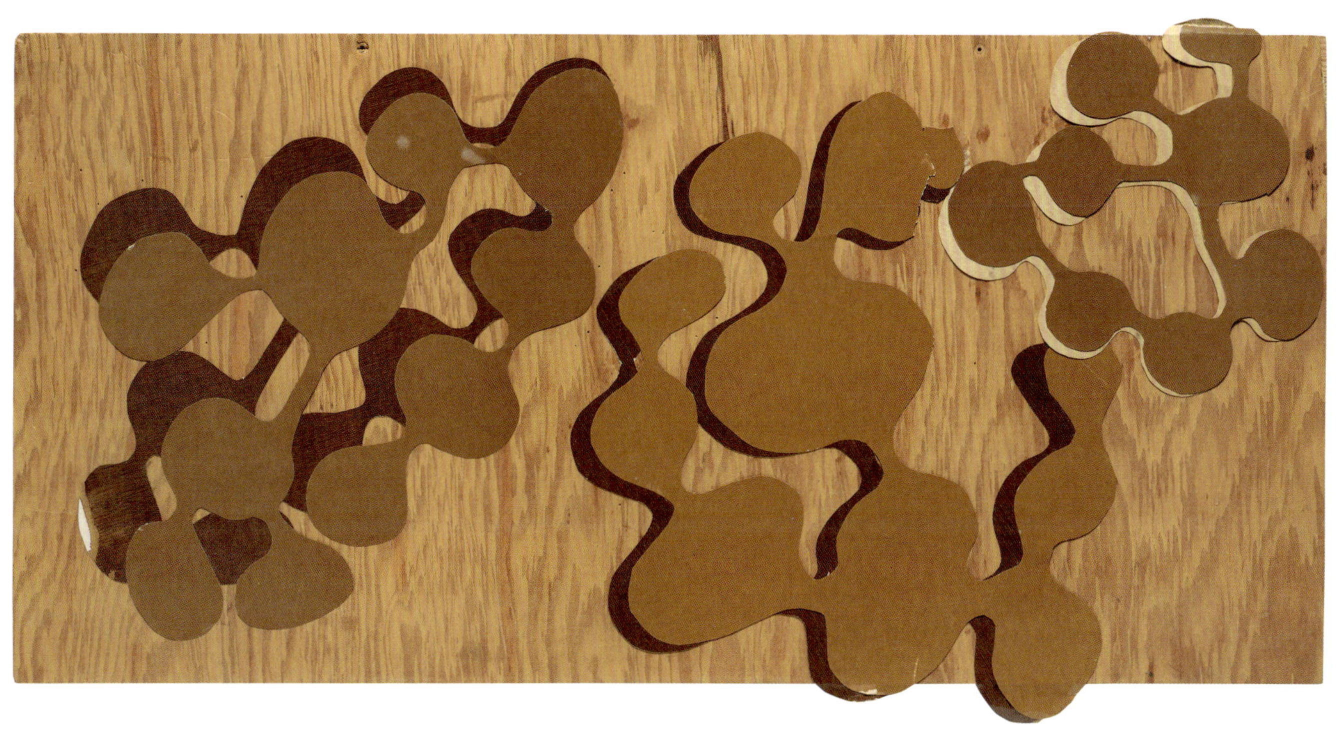

Untitled (BMC.119, Early Organic Biomorphic Forms), ca. 1946–49.
Cut coated papers in brown and white on plywood, 14 15/16 × 27 15/16 inches (38 × 71 cm)

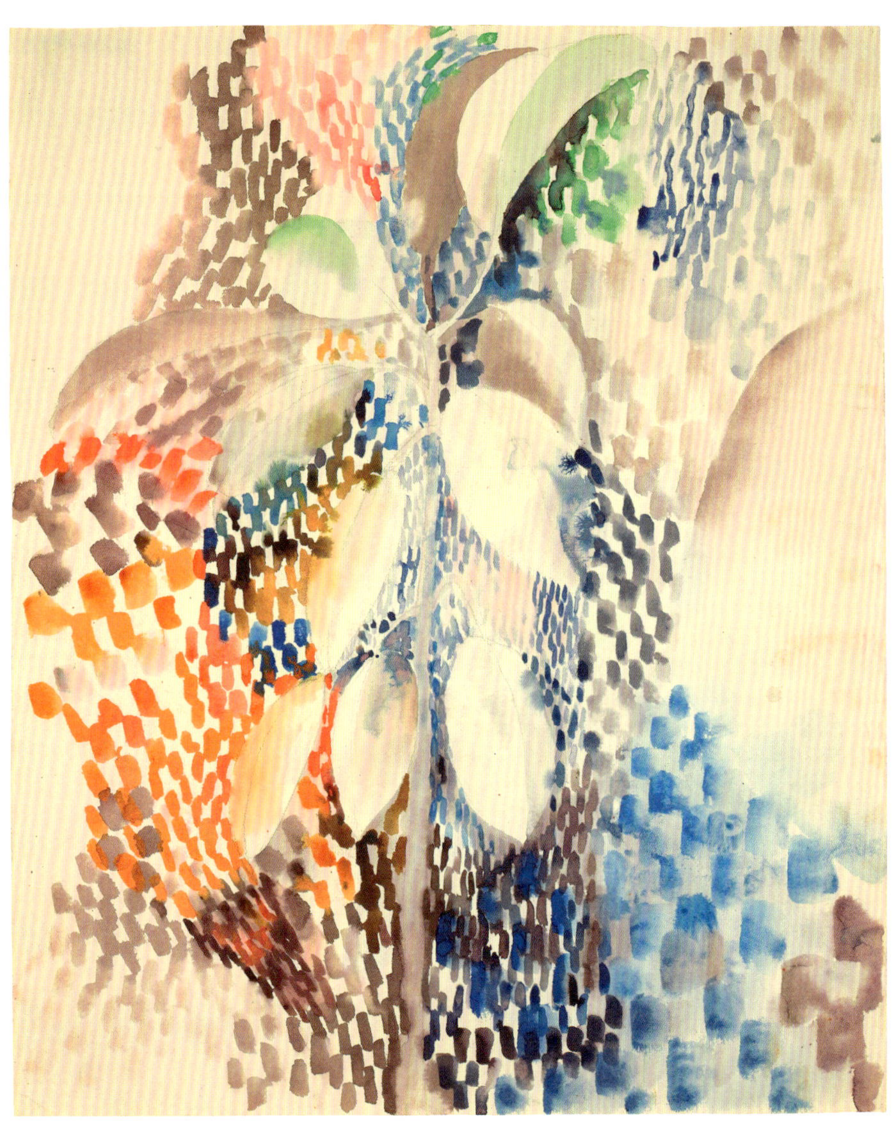

Untitled (BMC.66, Stem with Leaves: "Background" Painting), ca. 1948–49.
Watercolor over graphite on paper, 19¾ × 16 inches (50.2 × 40.6 cm)

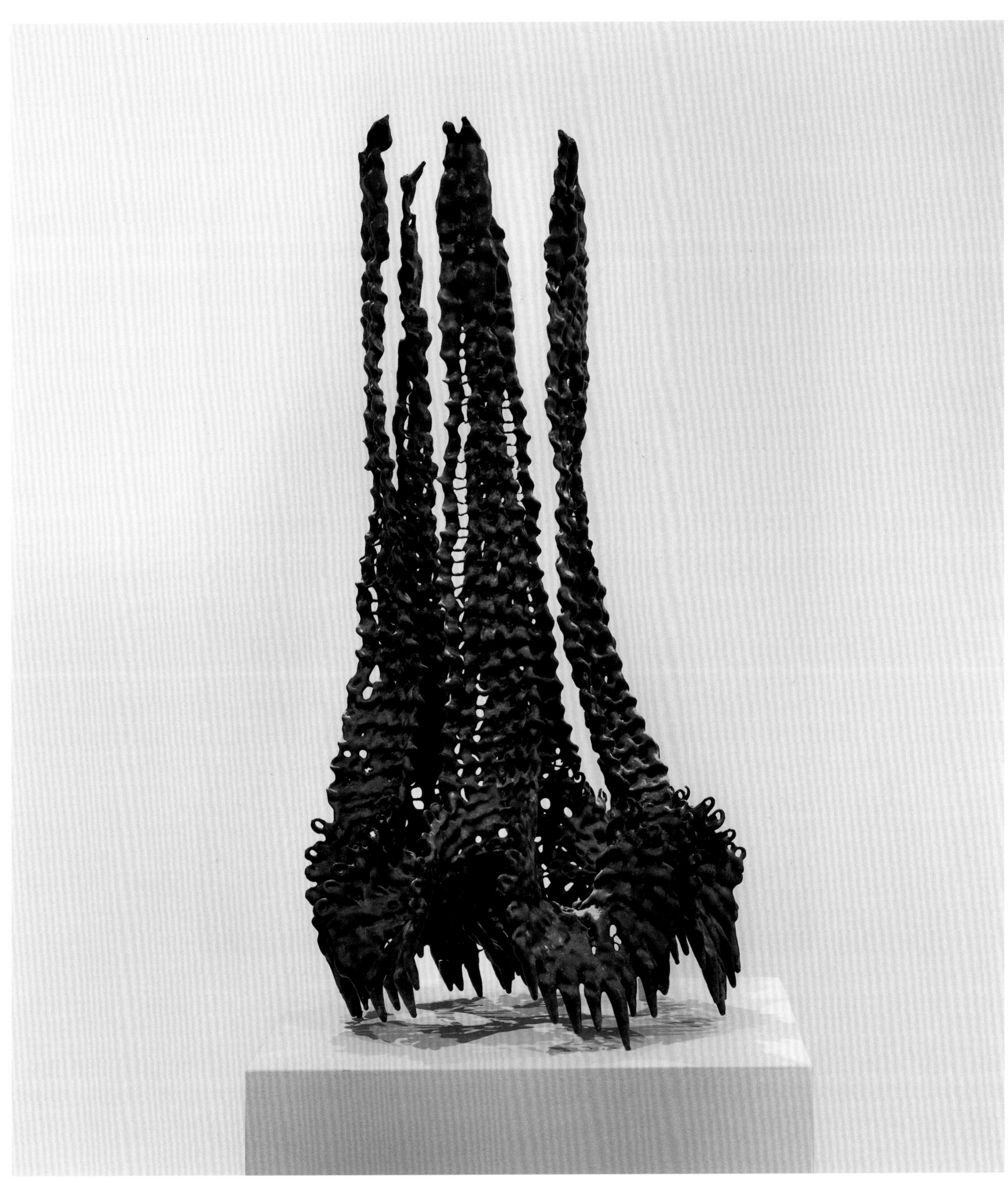

Untitled (S.004, Freestanding Stalagmite Form), 1997.
Bronze, golden brown patina, 23 × 11 × 11 inches (58.4 × 27.9 × 27.9 cm)

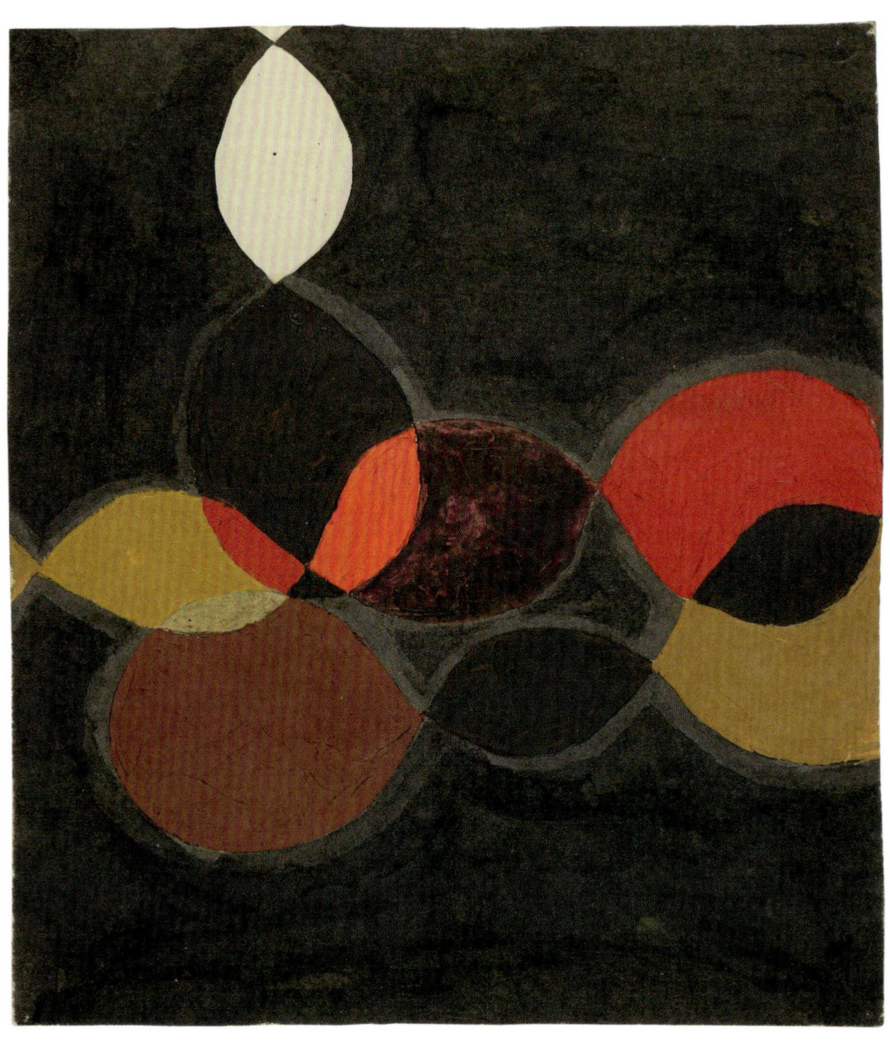

Untitled (BMC.83, Dogwood Leaves), ca. 1948–49.
Oil and watercolor on paper, 9½ × 8¼ inches (24.1 × 21 cm)

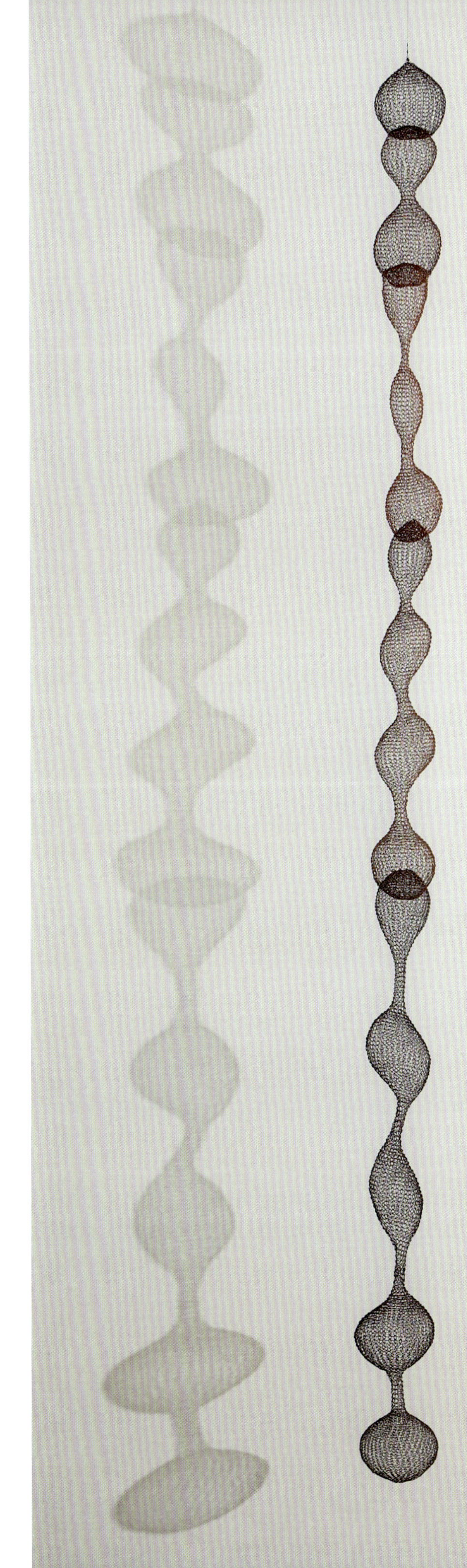

Untitled (S.334, Hanging Fifteen-Lobed [Seven Open and Eight Interlocking] Continuous Form), ca. 1953–55. Enameled copper wire, 134 × 8 × 8 inches (340.4 × 20.3 × 20.3 cm)

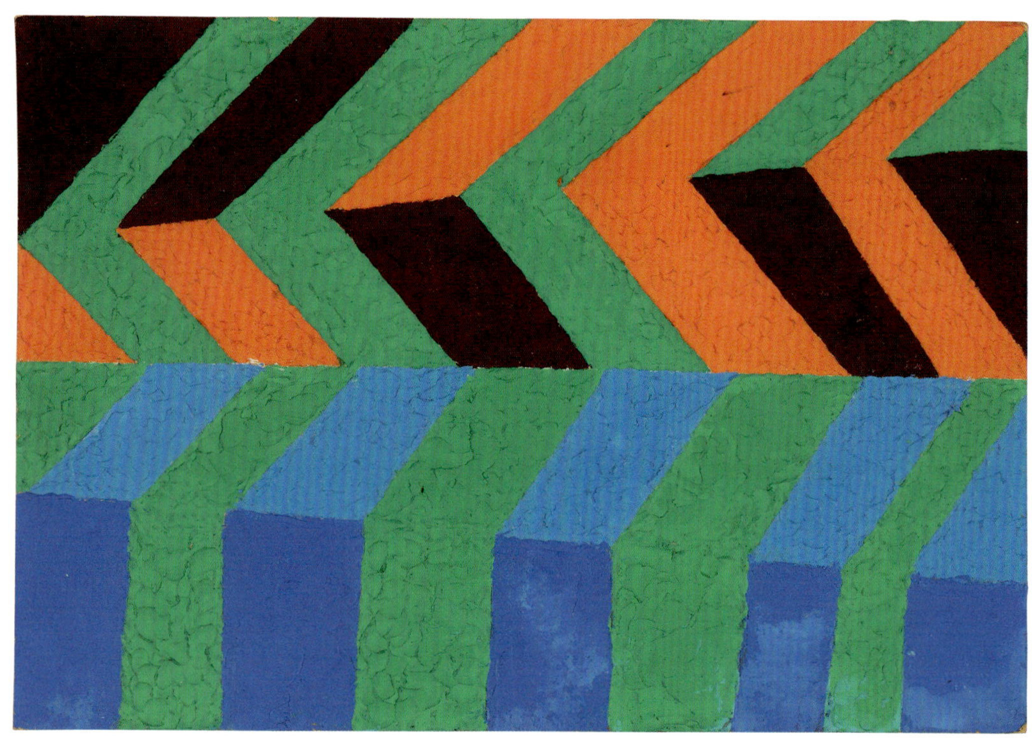

Untitled (BMC.96, In and Out), ca. 1948–49.
Oil paint on paper, 6½ × 9¼ inches (16.5 × 23.5 cm)

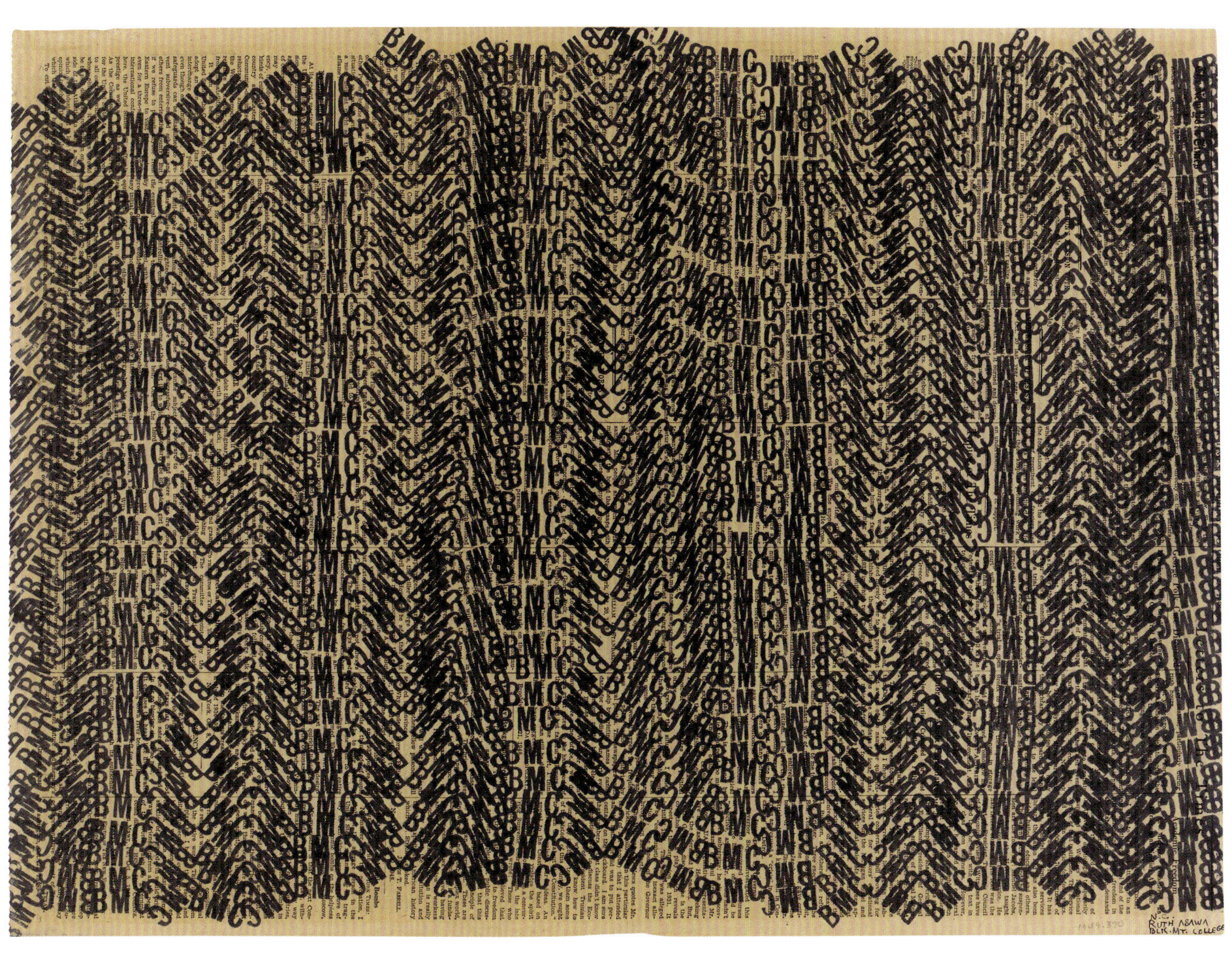

Untitled (BMC.117, BMC Laundry Stamp on Newsprint), ca. 1948–49.
Stamped black ink on newsprint, 16½ × 22 inches (41.9 × 55.9 cm)

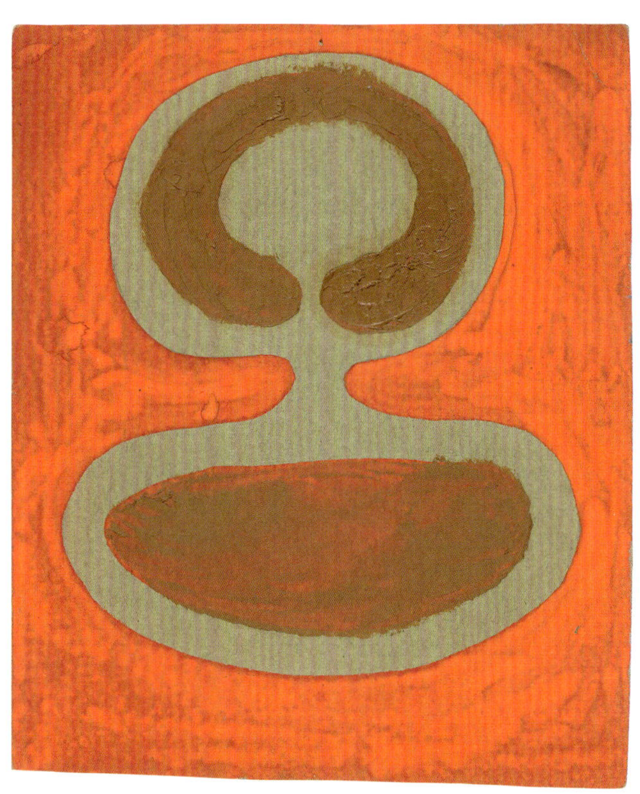

Above: *Untitled* (BMC.143, Dancer), ca. 1948–49. Oil paint on paper, 6¾ × 5½ inches (17.2 × 14 cm)

Opposite: *Untitled* (S.535, Hanging Five-Lobed Continuous Form within a Form with Two Interior Spheres and One Teardrop Form), 1951. Iron and brass wire, 87 × 12½ × 12½ inches (221 × 31.8 × 31.8 cm)

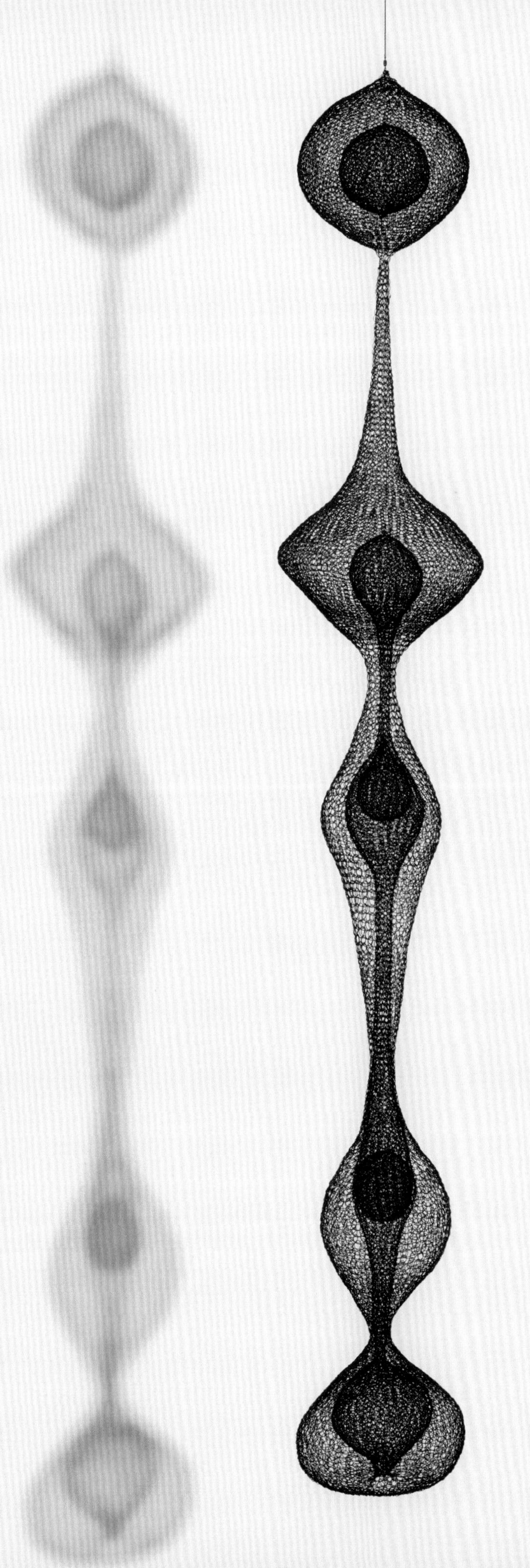

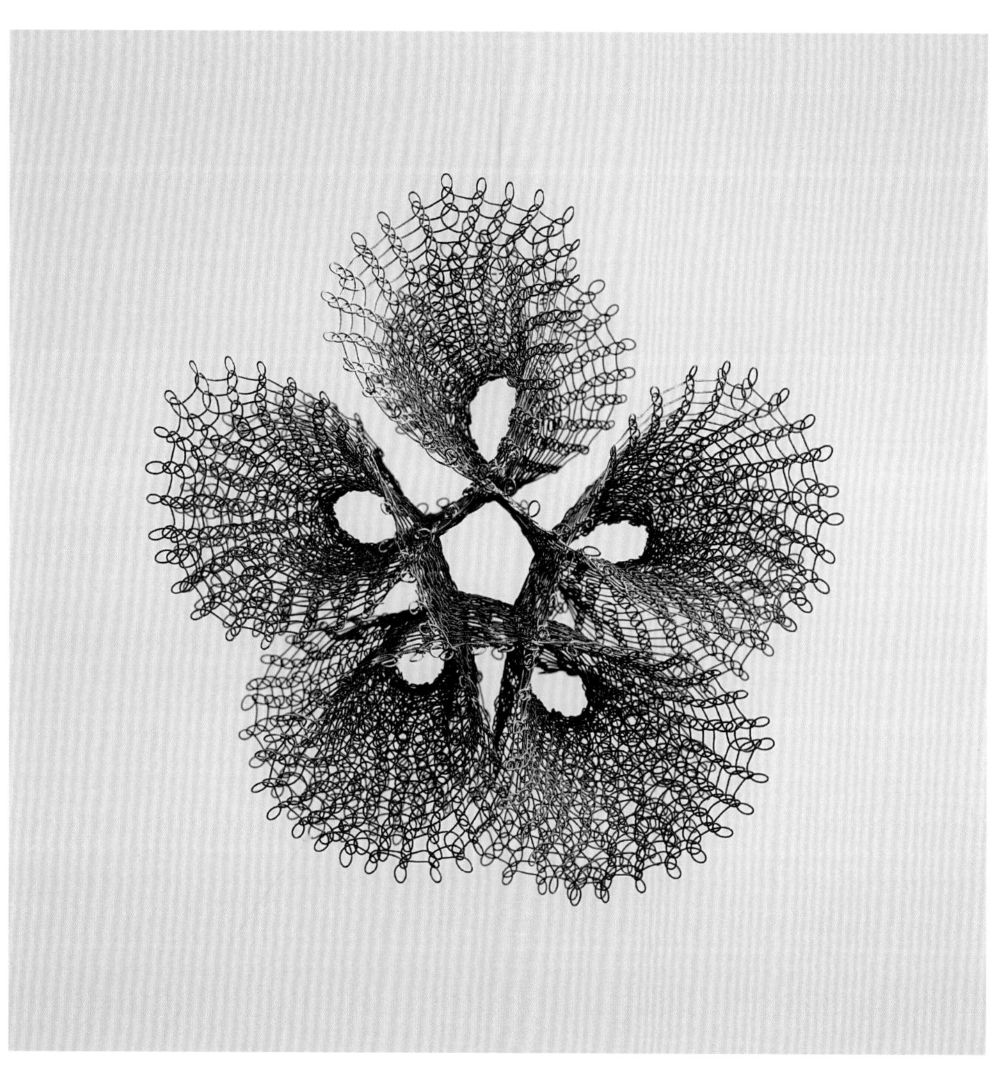

Untitled (S.306, Hanging Miniature Five Interlocking Double Trumpets), ca. 1978.
Copper wire, 5½ × 5½ × 4 inches (14 × 14 × 10.2 cm)

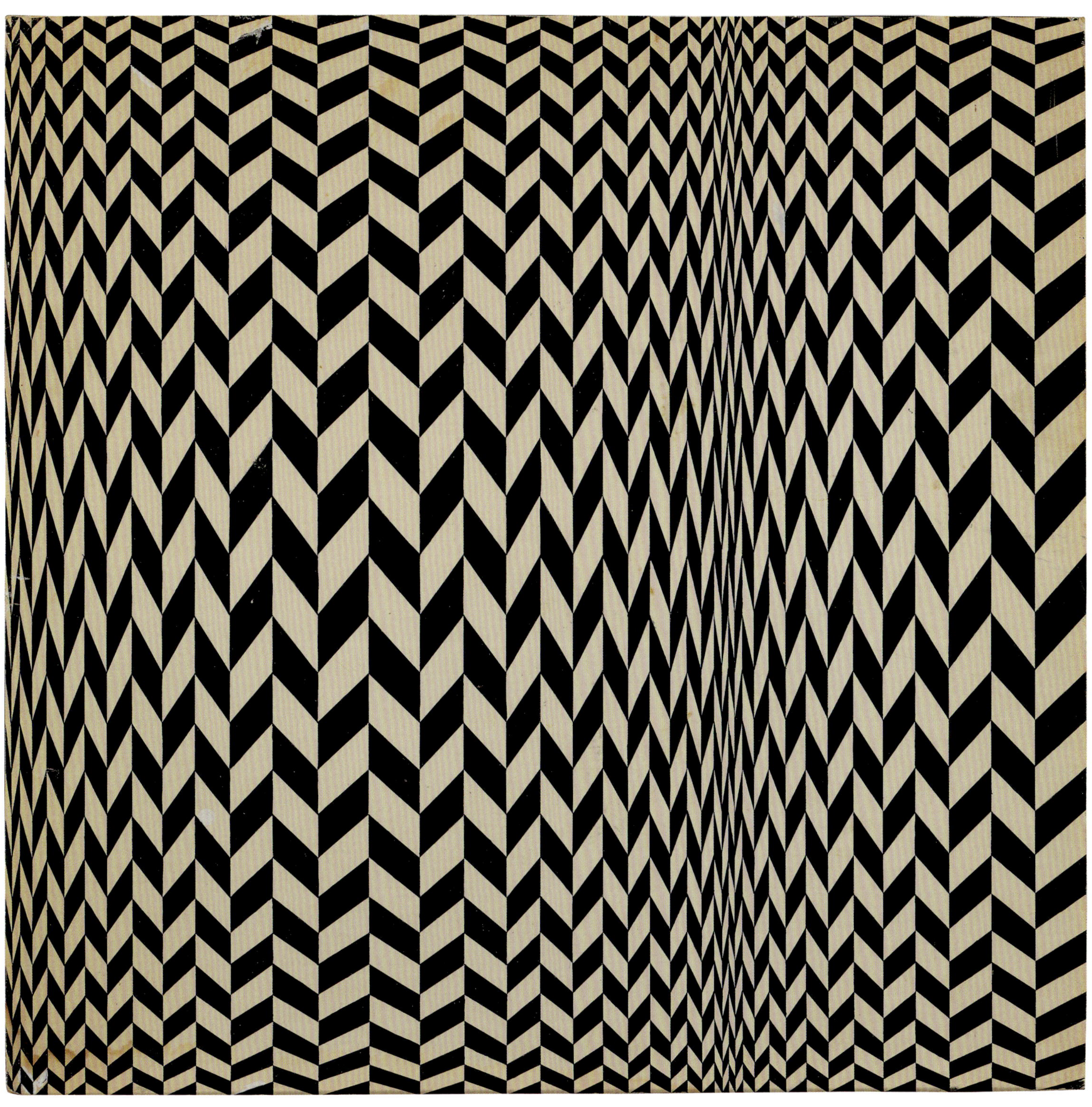

Untitled (SF.003, Undulating Parallelograms), ca. 1951–52.
Pen and brush and black ink on gouache on board, 27 × 27 inches (68.6 × 68.6 cm)

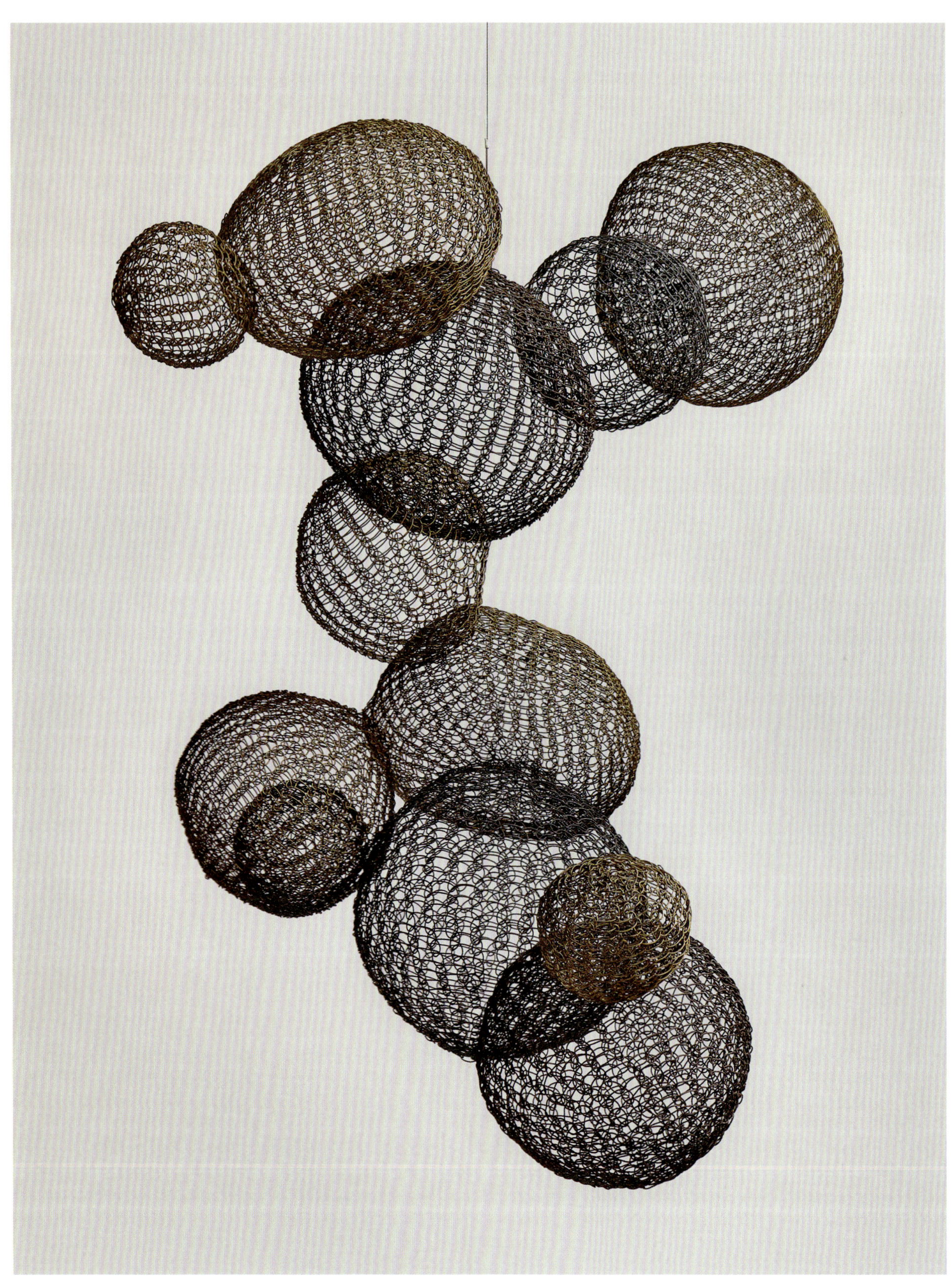

Untitled (S.089, Hanging Asymmetrical Twelve Interlocking Bubbles), ca. 1957.
Galvanized steel, brass, and iron wire, 26 × 22 × 17 inches (66 × 55.9 × 43.2 cm)

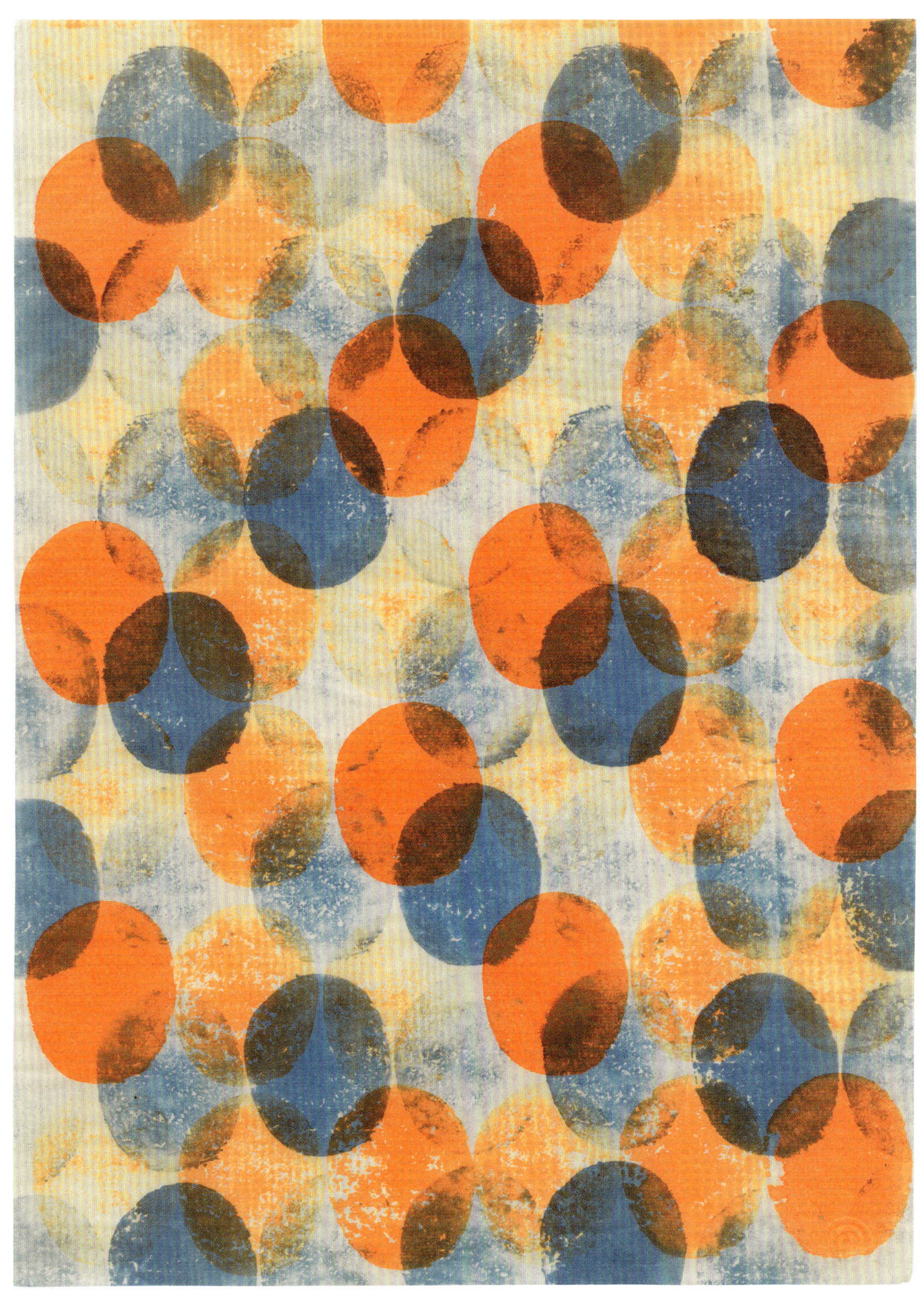

Untitled (SF.046b, Potato Print, Blue/Orange), 1951–52.
Blue and orange ink on paper, 14 × 10 inches (35.6 × 25.4 cm)

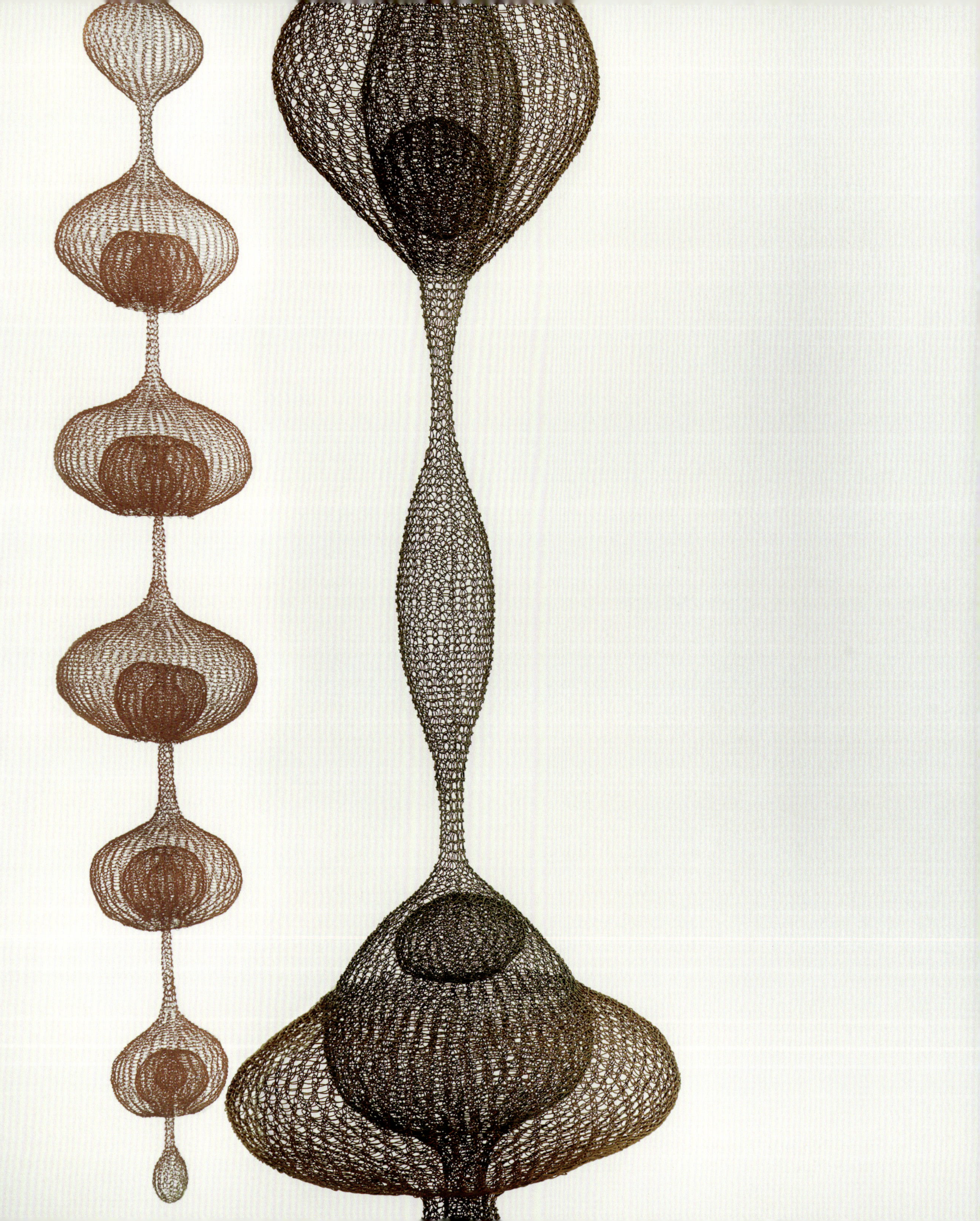

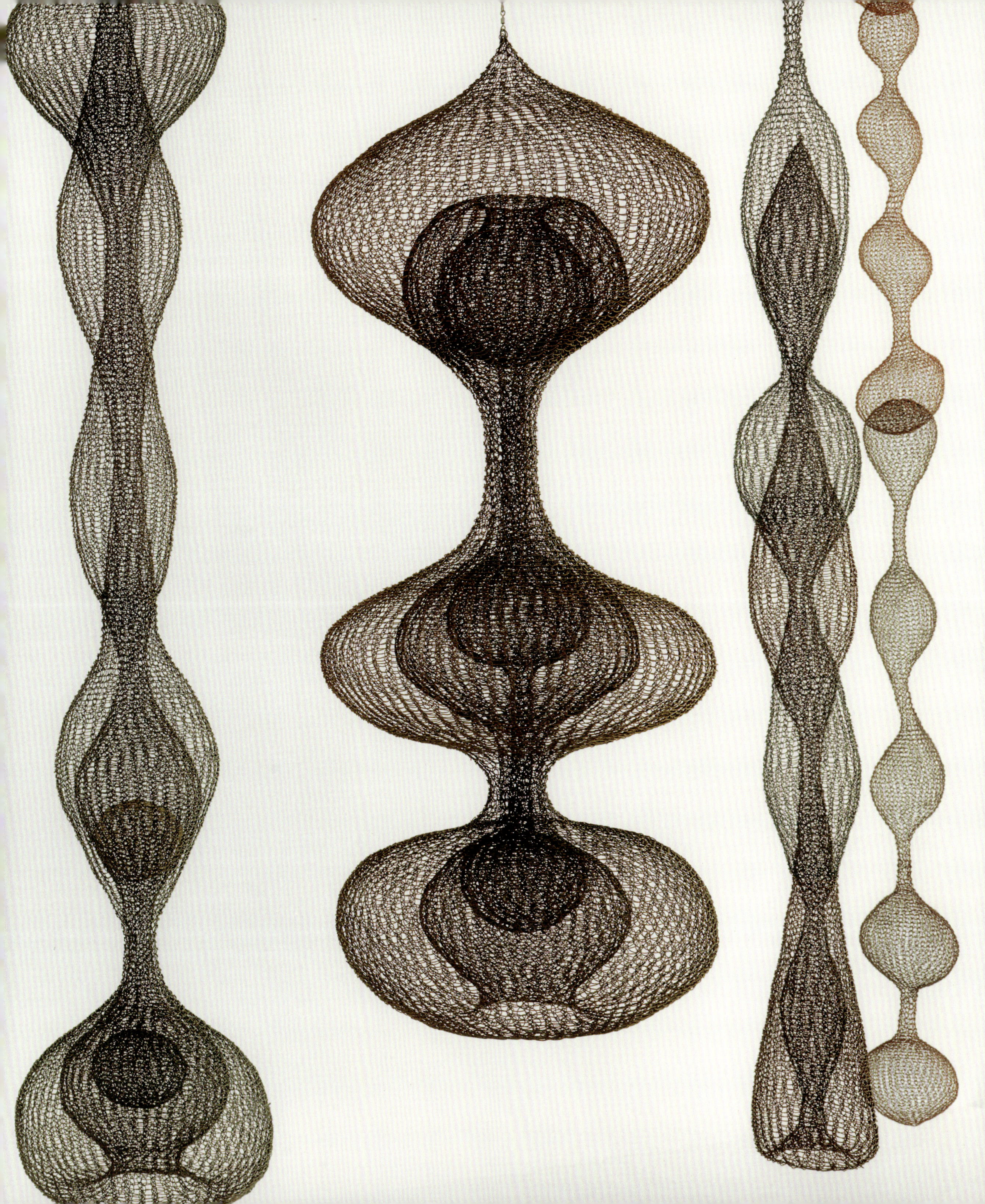

Untitled (S.030, Hanging Eight Separate Cones Suspended through Their Centers), ca. 1952.
Iron wire, 76 × 24 × 24 inches (193 × 61 × 61 cm)

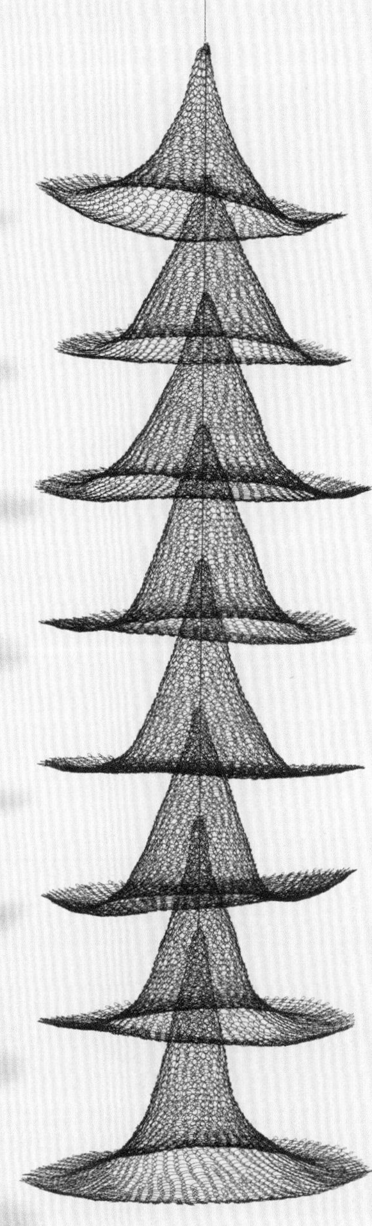

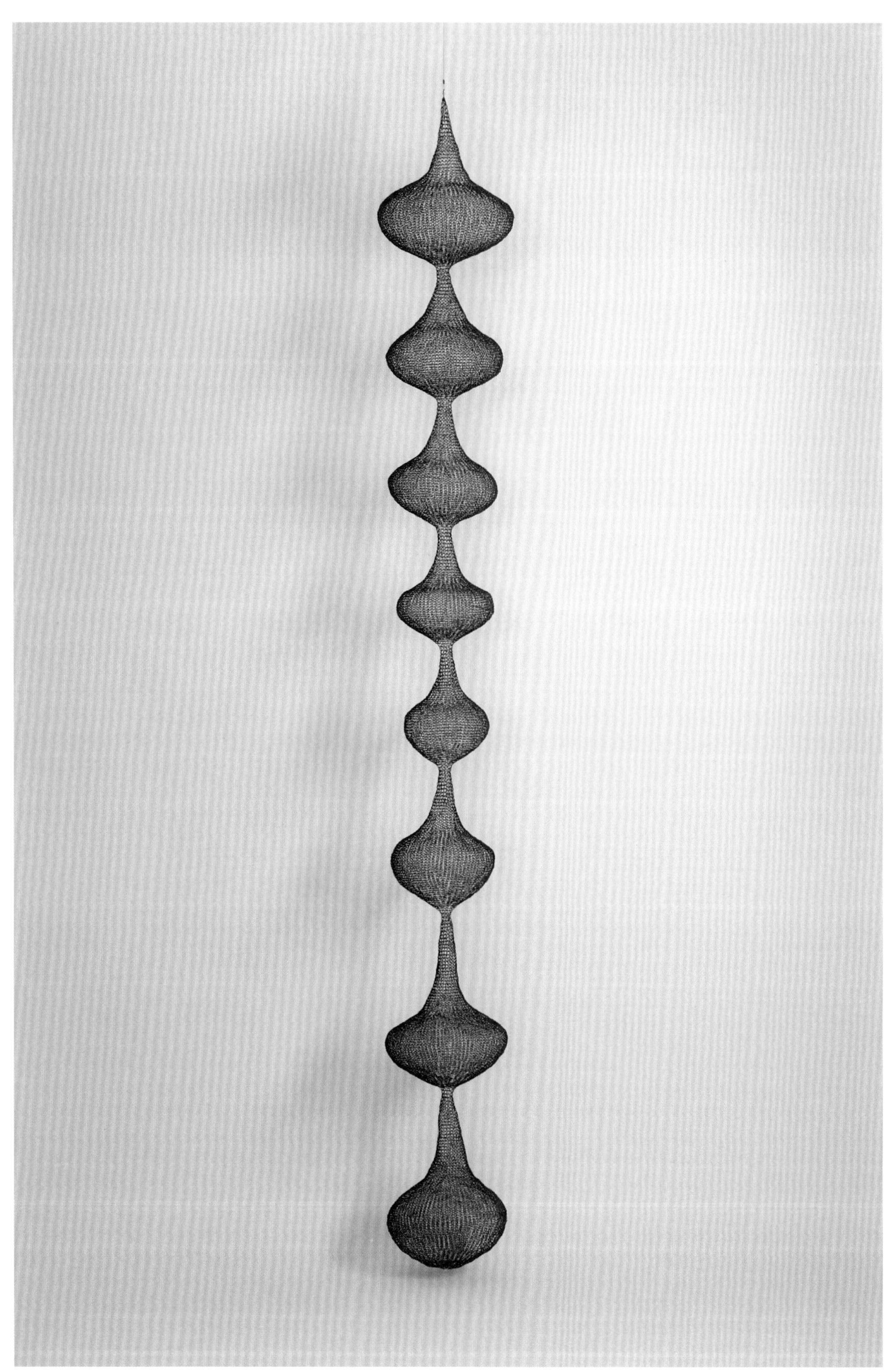

Untitled (S.435, Hanging Eight-Lobed, Single-Layered Continuous Tear-Drop Form), 1952.
Iron wire, 120 × 12 × 12 inches (304.8 × 30.5 × 30.5 cm)

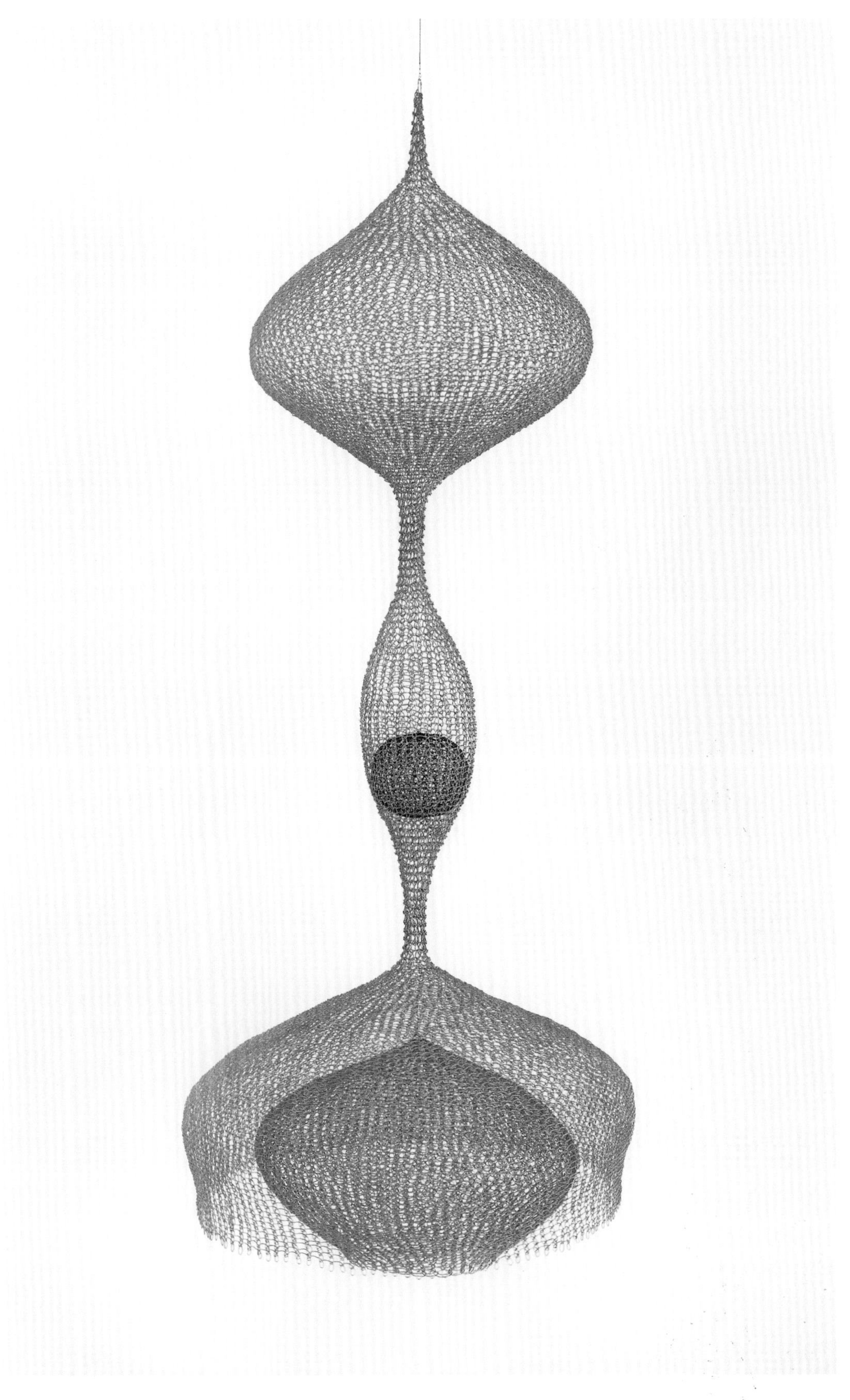

Untitled (S.042, Hanging Three-Lobed Continuous Form, with a Sphere in the Second Lobe, and an Open Sphere Suspended from the Bottom), 1954. Aluminum and brass wire, 90 × 36 × 36 inches (228.6 × 91.4 × 91.4 cm)

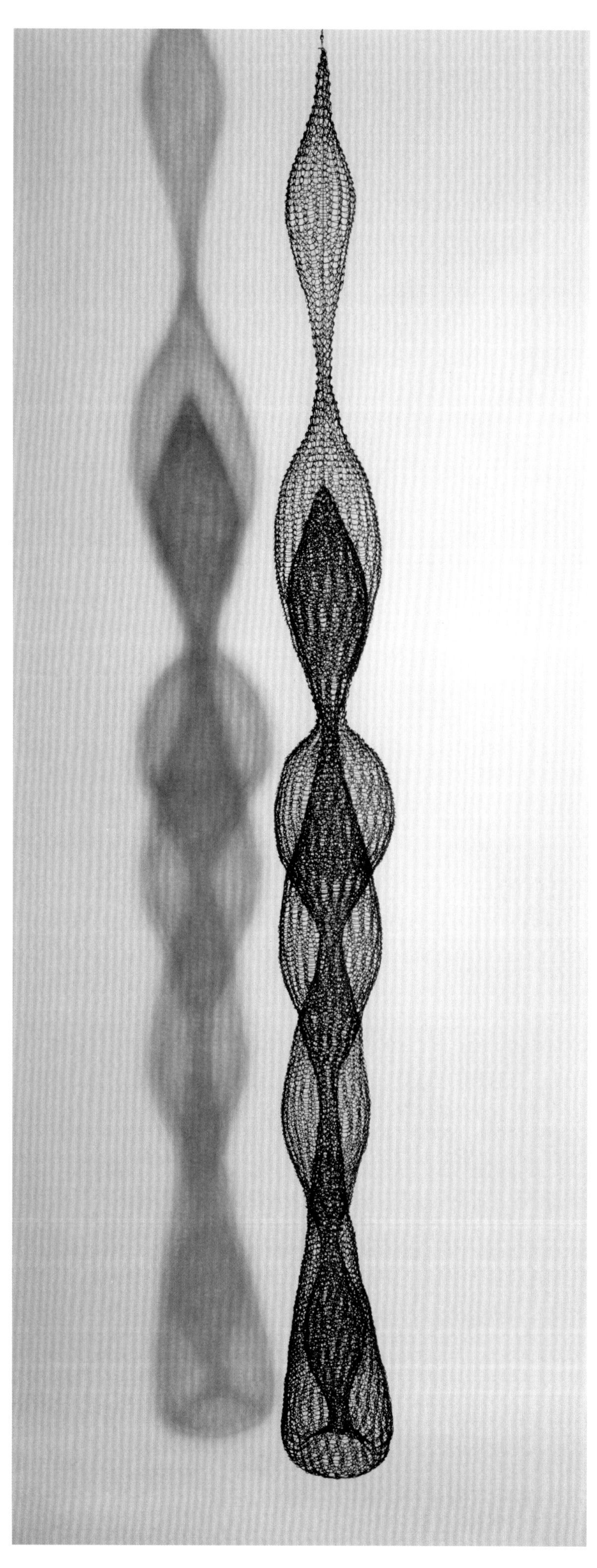

Untitled (S.373, Hanging Six-Lobed, Multilayered Interlocking Continuous Form within a Form), 1954. Enameled and oxidized copper wire, 87 × 8 × 8 inches (221 × 20.3 × 20.3 cm)

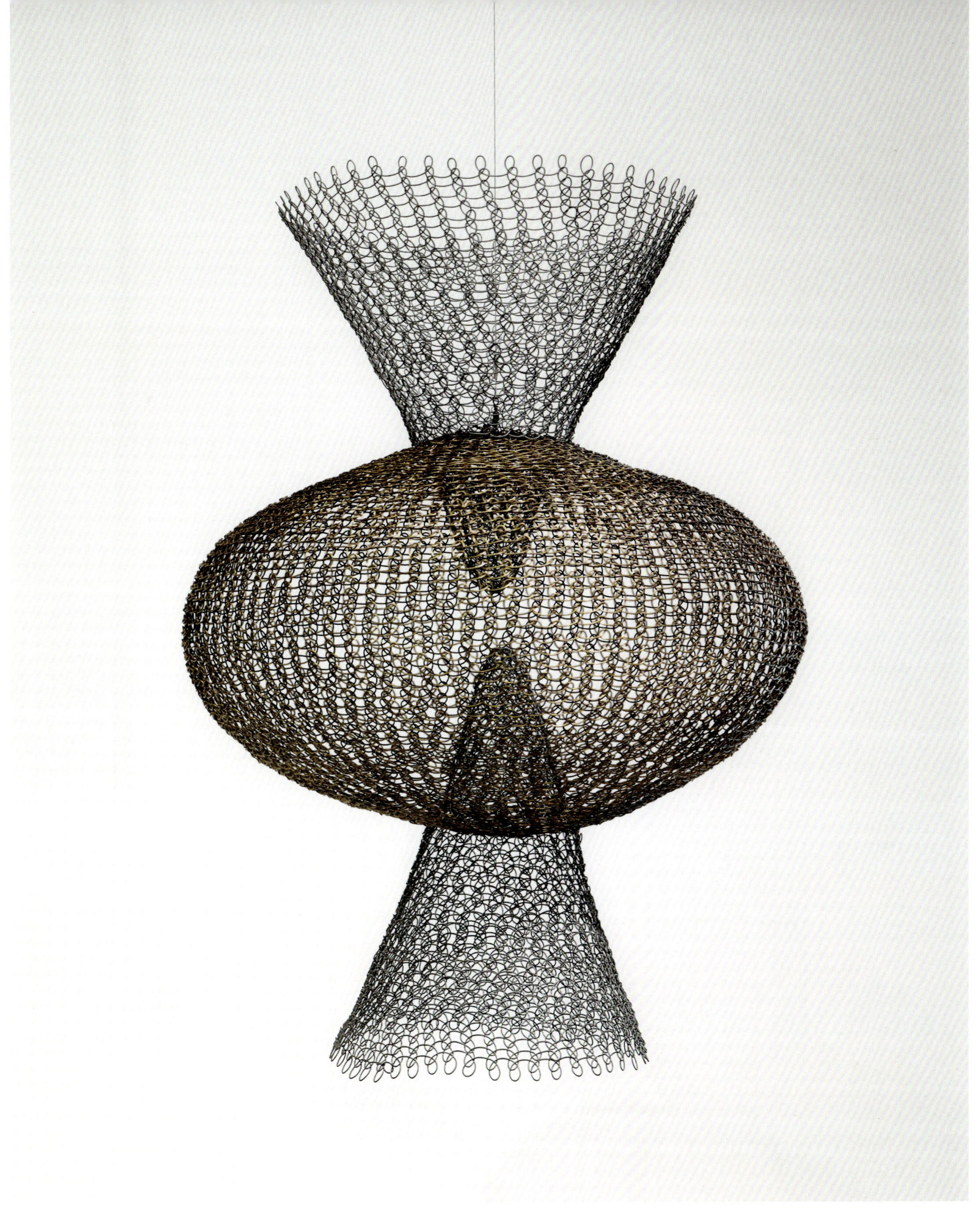

Untitled (S.562, Hanging Sphere with Two Cones that Penetrate the Sphere from Top and Bottom), ca. 1954.
Galvanized steel wire and brass wire, 28 × 18 × 18 inches (71.1 × 45.7 × 45.7 cm)

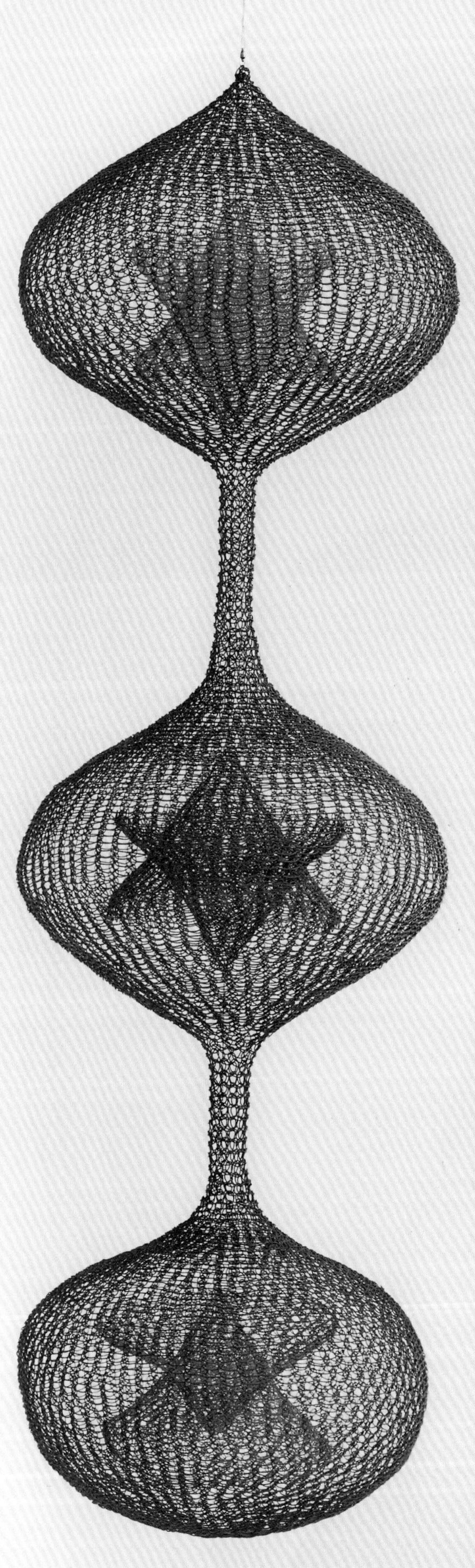

Left: *Untitled* (S.026, Hanging Three-Lobed, Continuous Form with Penetrating Cones within Each Lobe), ca. 1955. Enameled copper wire and brass wire, 60 × 19 × 19 inches (152.4 × 48.3 × 48.3 cm)

Opposite: *Untitled* (S.398, Hanging Eight-Lobed, Four-Part, Discontinuous Surface Form within a Form, with Spheres in the Seventh and Eighth Lobes), ca. 1955. Copper, brass, and iron wire, 104½ × 14½ × 14½ inches (265.4 × 36.8 × 36.8 cm)

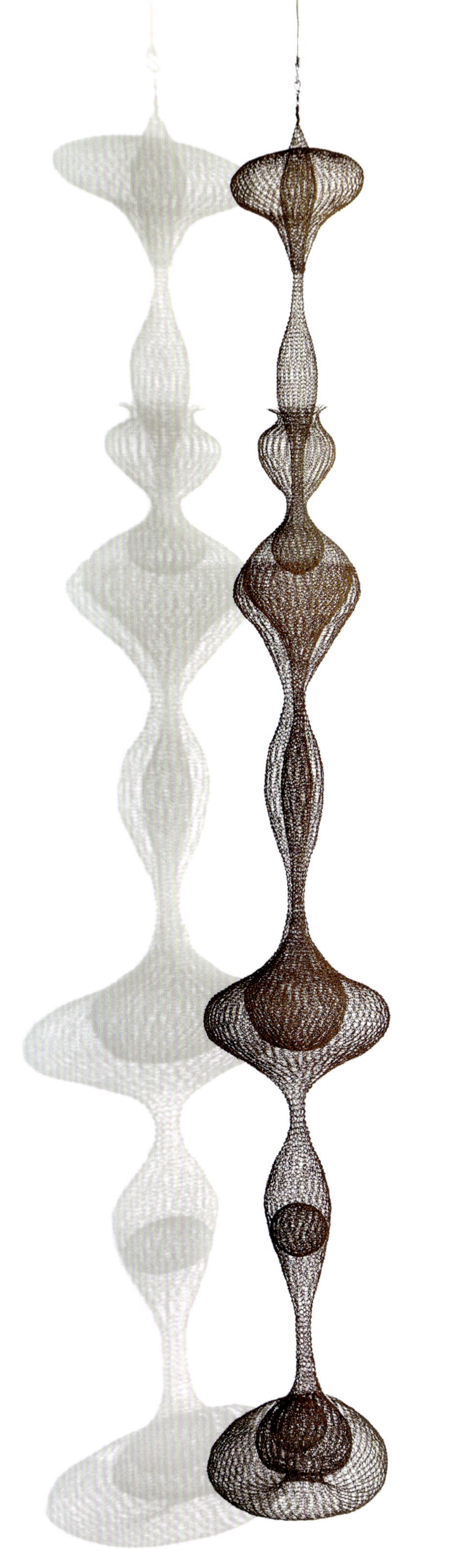

Untitled (S.453, Hanging Three-Lobed, Three-Layered Continuous Form within a Form), ca. 1957–59.
Iron wire, 41¼ × 16½ × 16½ inches (104.8 × 41.9 × 41.9 cm)

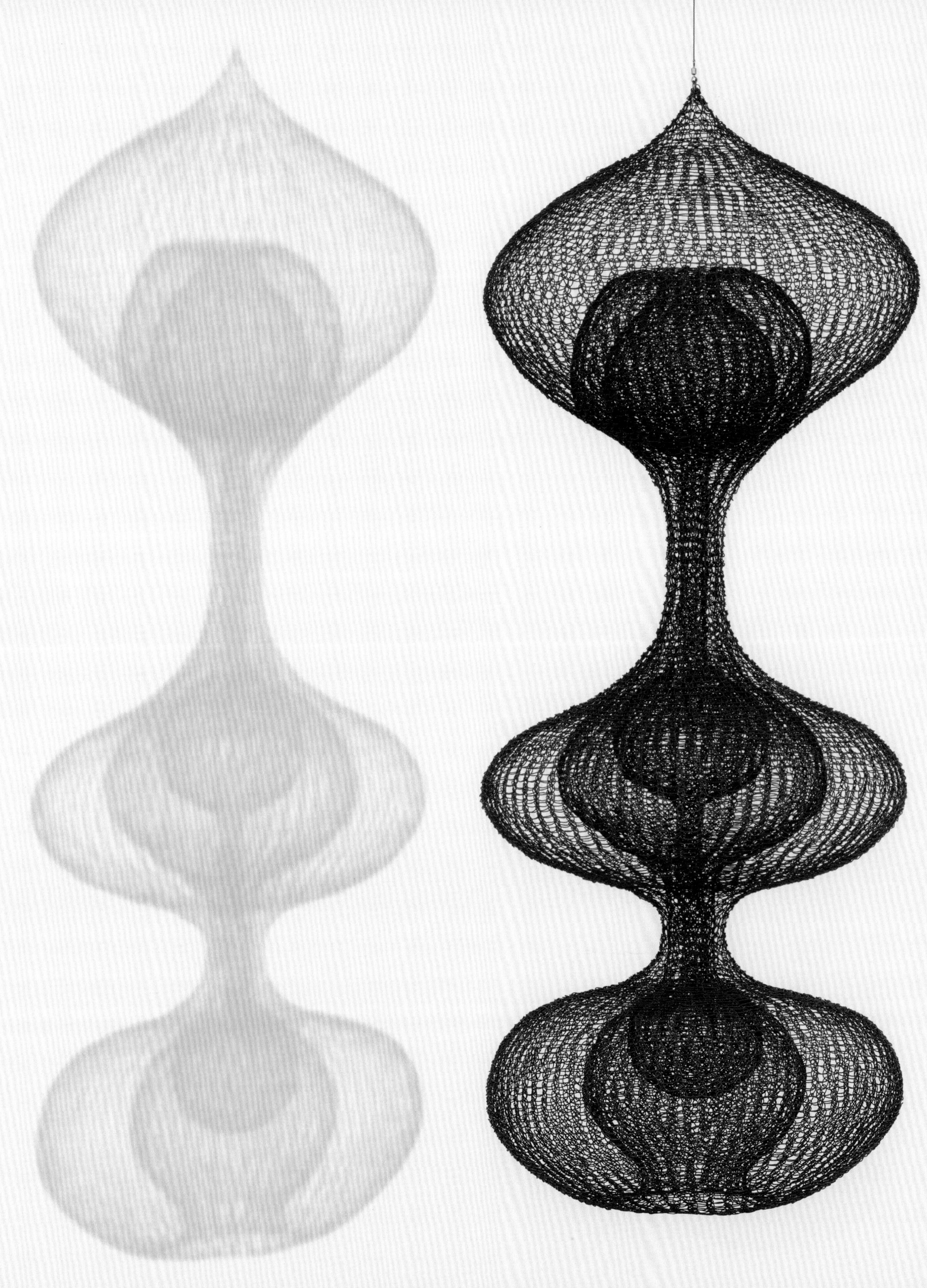

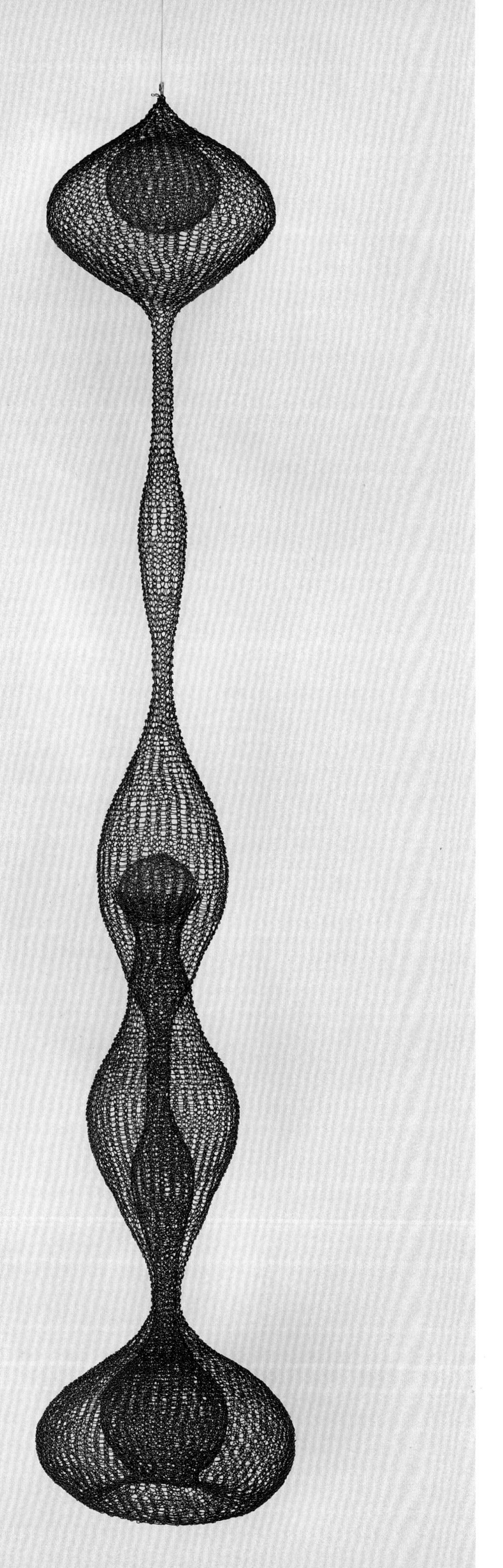

Left: *Untitled* (S.113, Hanging Five-Lobed, Multilayered Continuous Form within a Form with Spheres in the First and Third Lobes), ca. 1958. Copper and brass wire, 90 × 16½ × 16½ inches (228.6 × 41.9 × 41.9 cm)

Opposite: *Untitled* (S.114, Hanging Six-Lobed Continuous Form within a Form with One Suspended and Two Tied Spheres), ca. 1958. Iron, copper, and brass wire, 131 × 22 × 22 inches (332.7 × 55.9 × 55.9 cm)

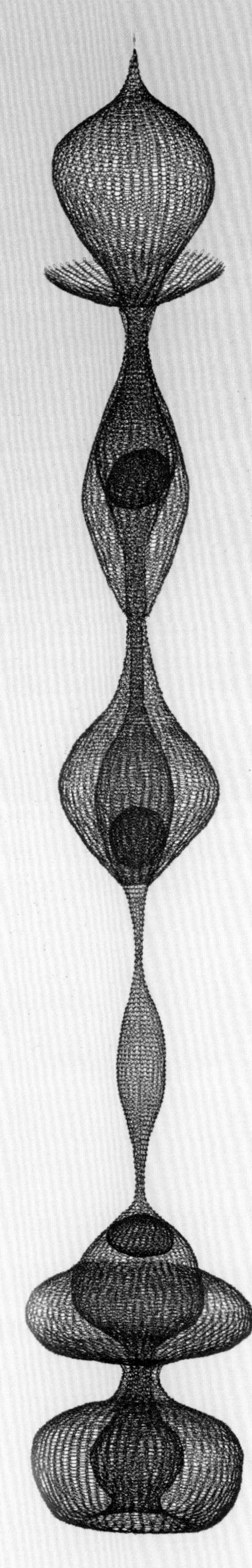

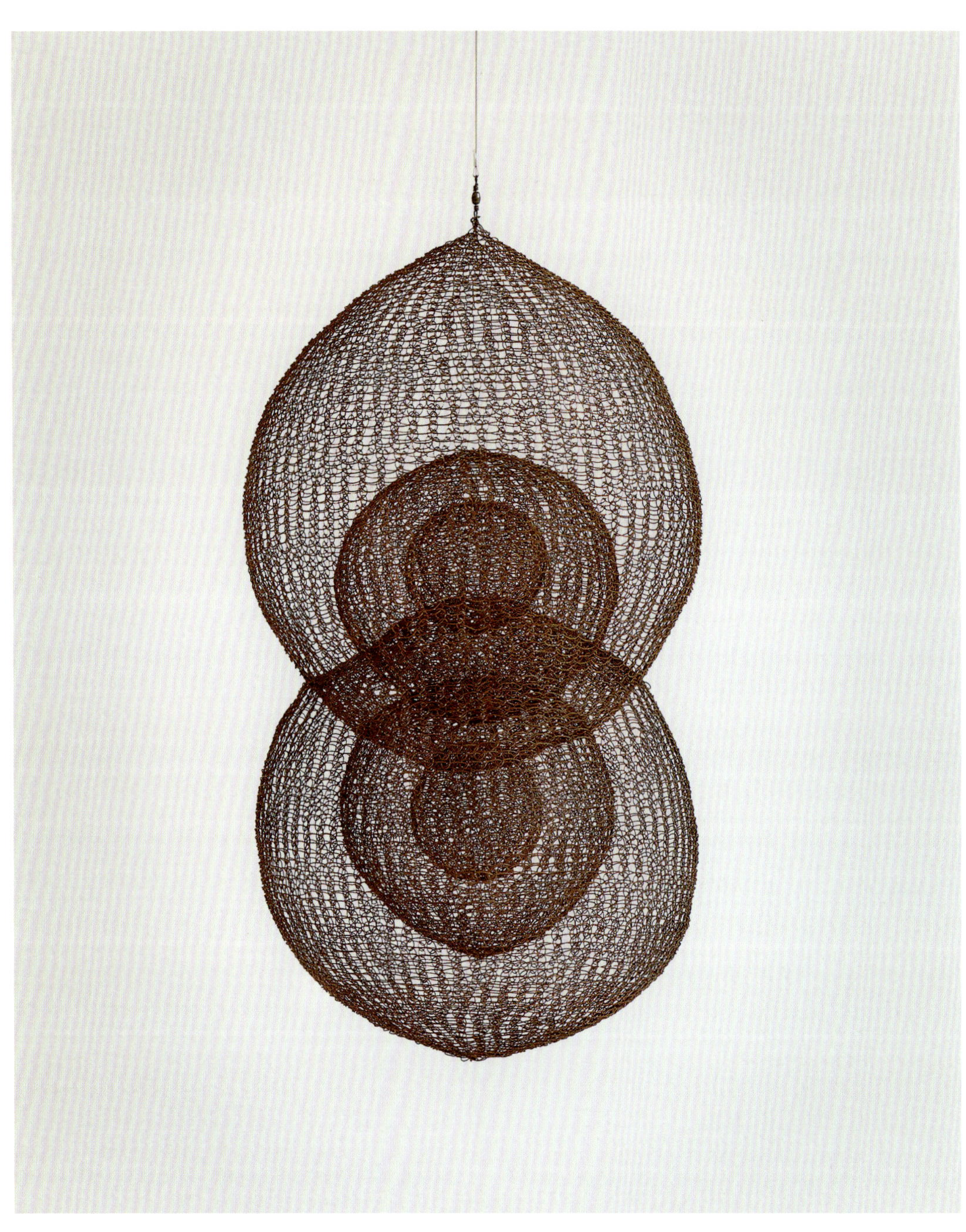

Untitled (S.020, Hanging Miniature Two Interlocked, Three-Layered Spheres), ca. 1978.
Copper wire, 16 × 9 × 9 inches (40.6 × 22.9 × 22.9 cm)

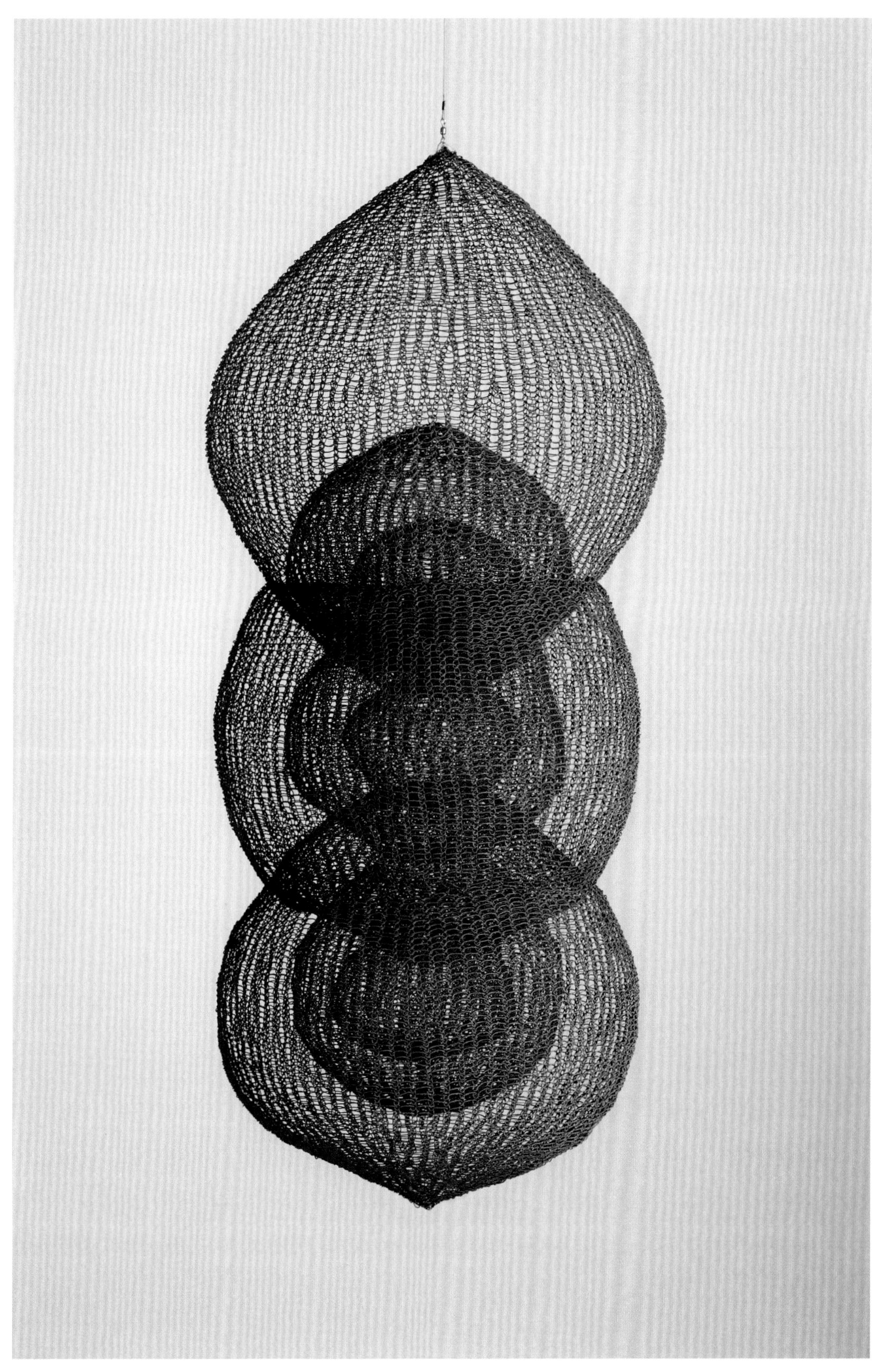

Untitled (S.208, Hanging Three Interlocked, Three-Layered Spheres), 1959–60.
Enameled copper wire, 48 × 22 × 22 inches (121.9 × 55.9 × 55.9 cm)

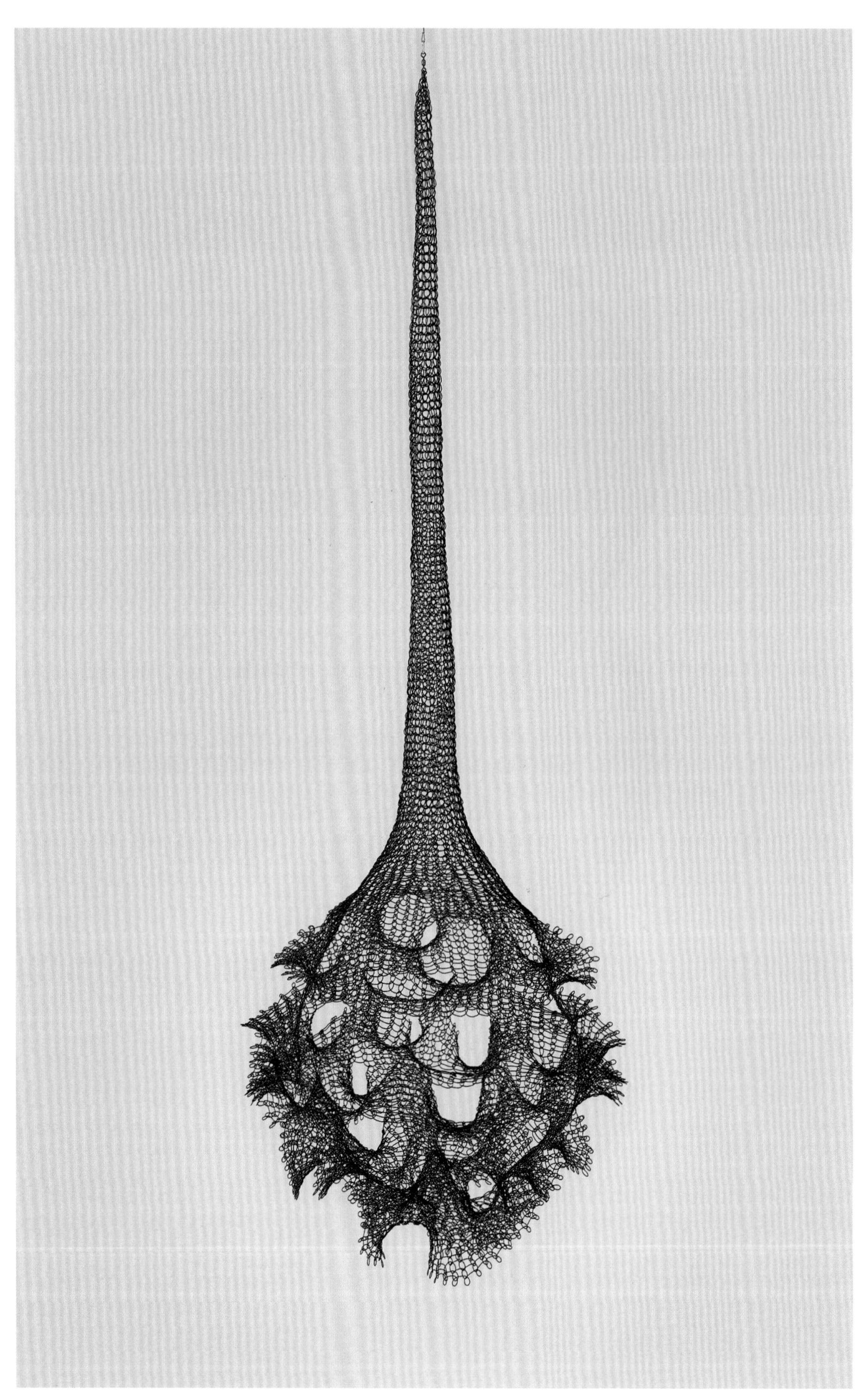

Untitled (S.445, Hanging Single Section, Open Windows Form), ca. 1962.
Copper wire, 56 × 19 × 19 inches (142.2 × 48.3 × 48.3 cm)

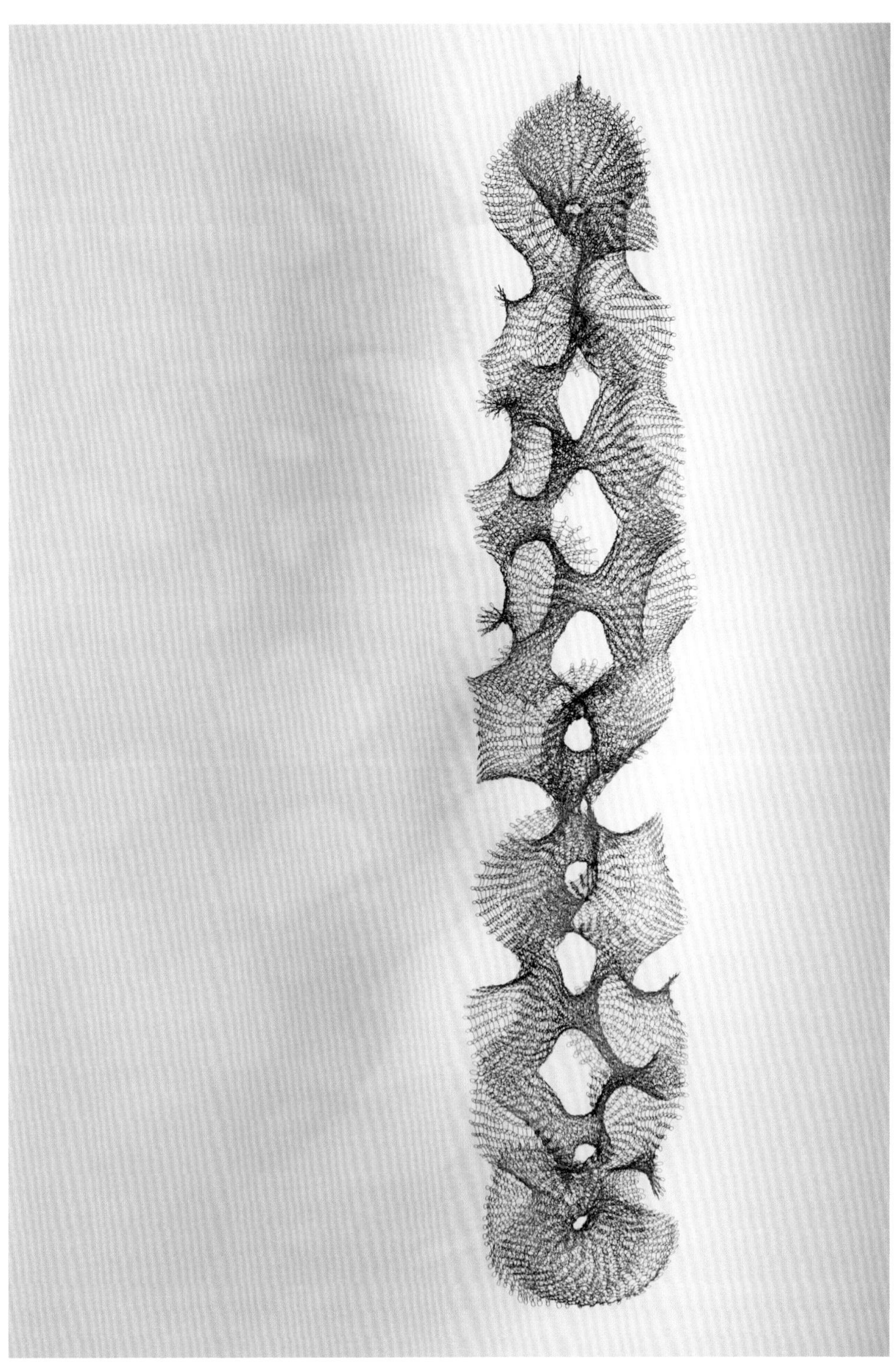

Untitled (S.433, Hanging Nine Open Hyperbolic Shapes Joined Laterally), ca. 1958.
Oxidized copper wire, 76 × 15 × 15 inches (193 × 38.1 × 38.1 cm)

Untitled (AB.004, Waves), late 1950s–early 1961.
 Pen and black ink on tracing paper, 23¾ × 19 inches (60.3 × 48.3 cm)

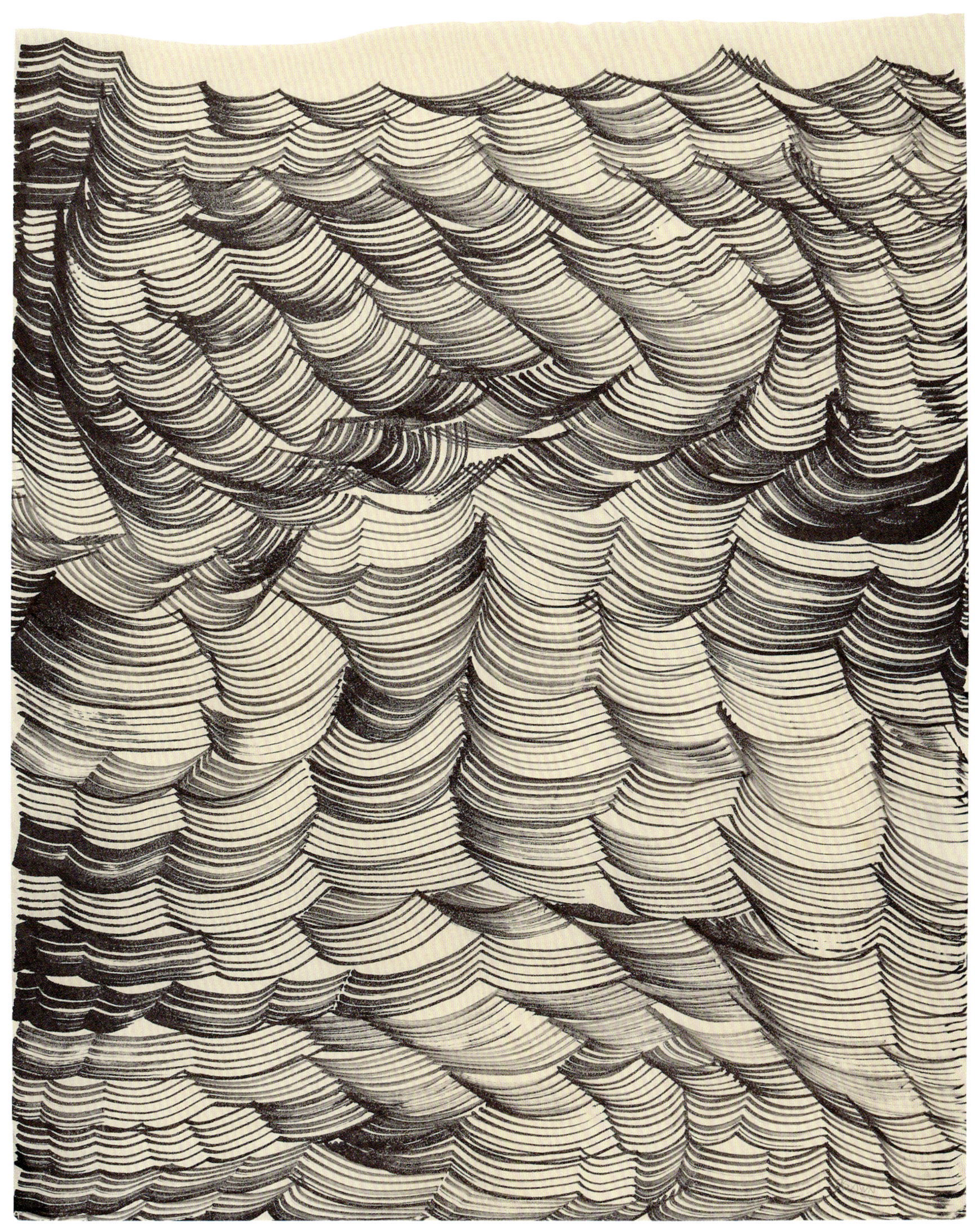

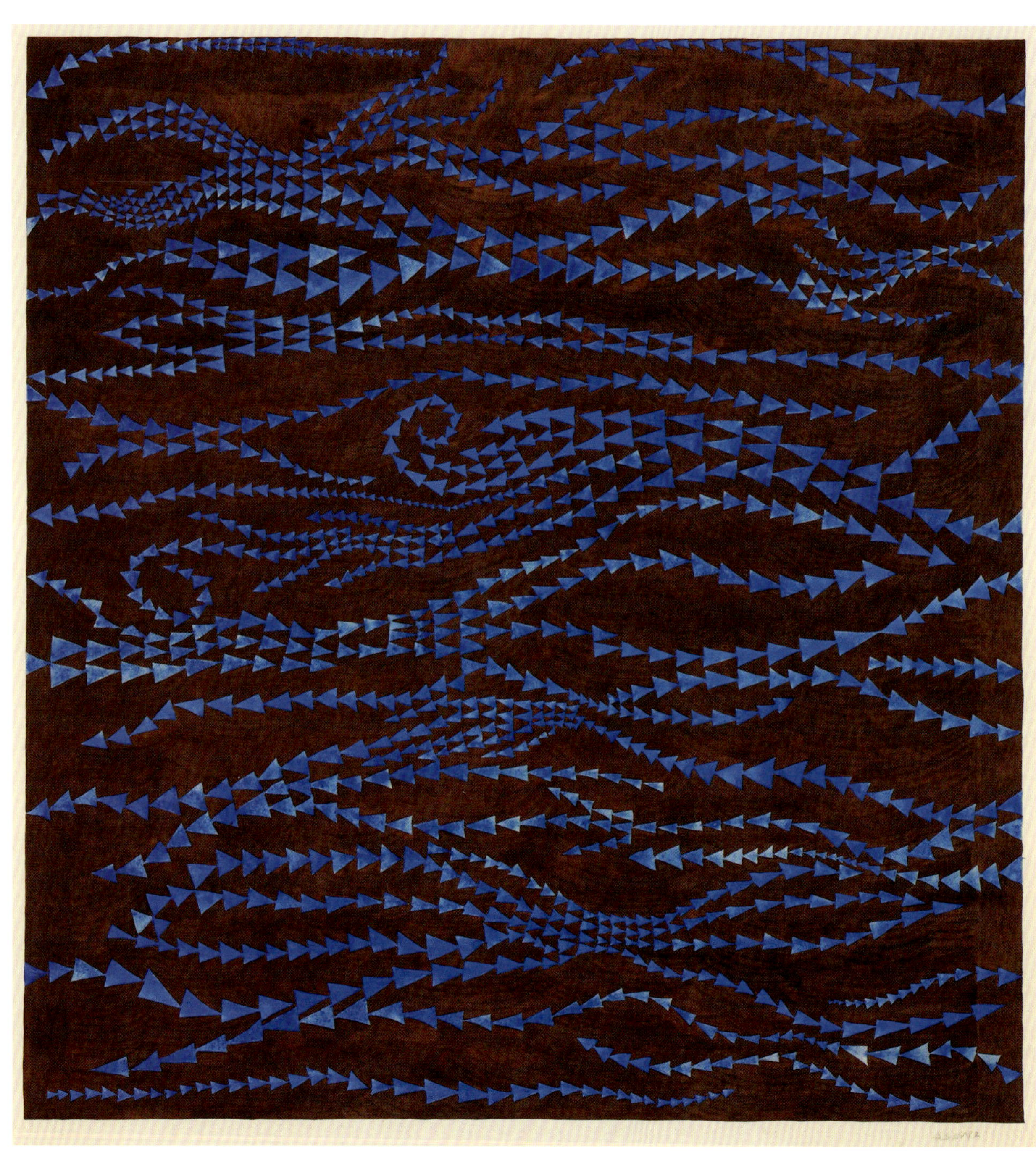

Untitled (SF.030, Blue Triangles on Brown), ca. late 1950s.
Watercolor and tempera paint on matboard, 30 × 28 inches (76.2 × 71.1 cm)

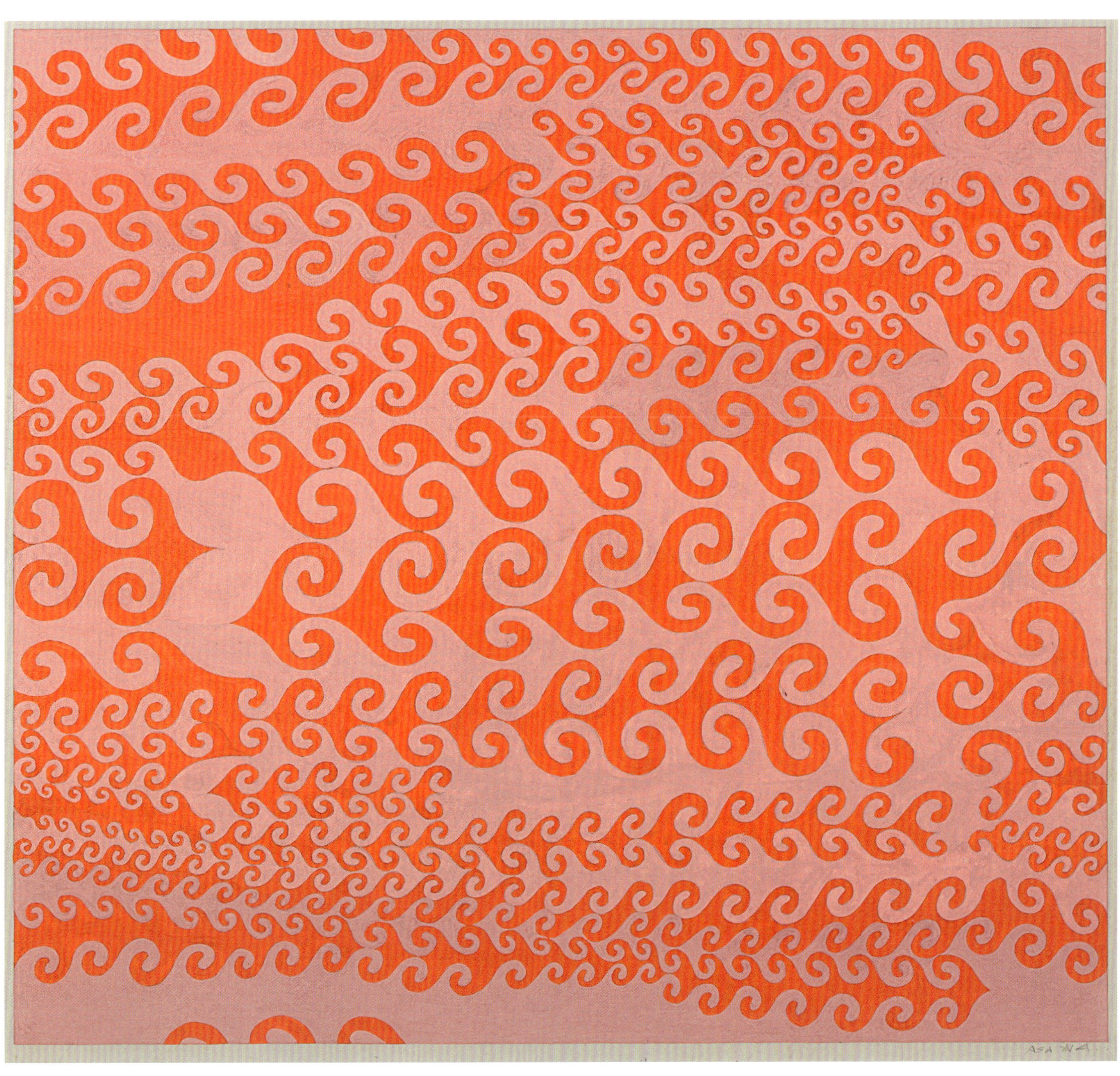

Untitled (SF.031, Red Meander on Pink), ca. late 1950s.
Tempera paint on matboard, 28 × 30 inches (71.1 × 76.2 cm)

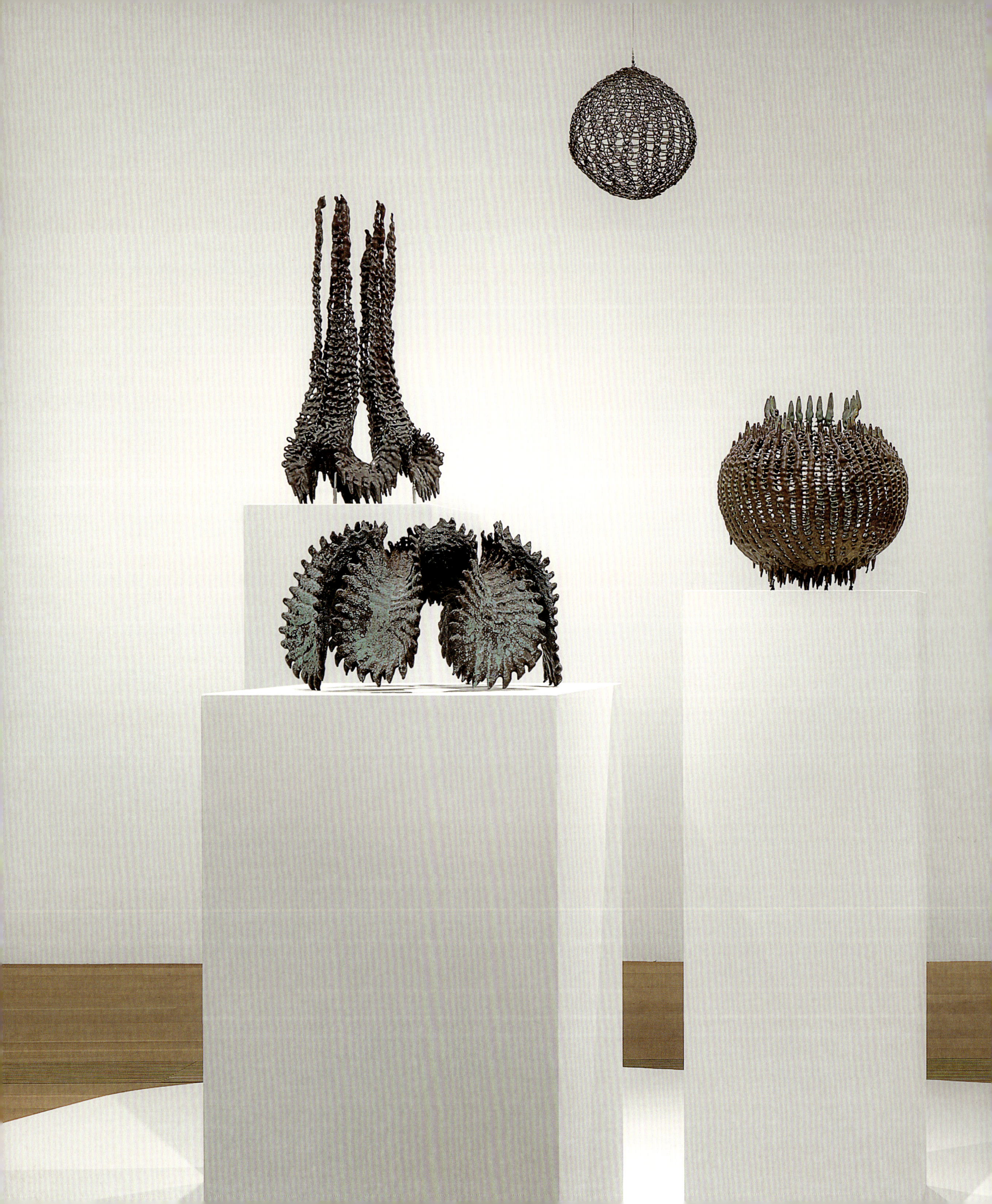

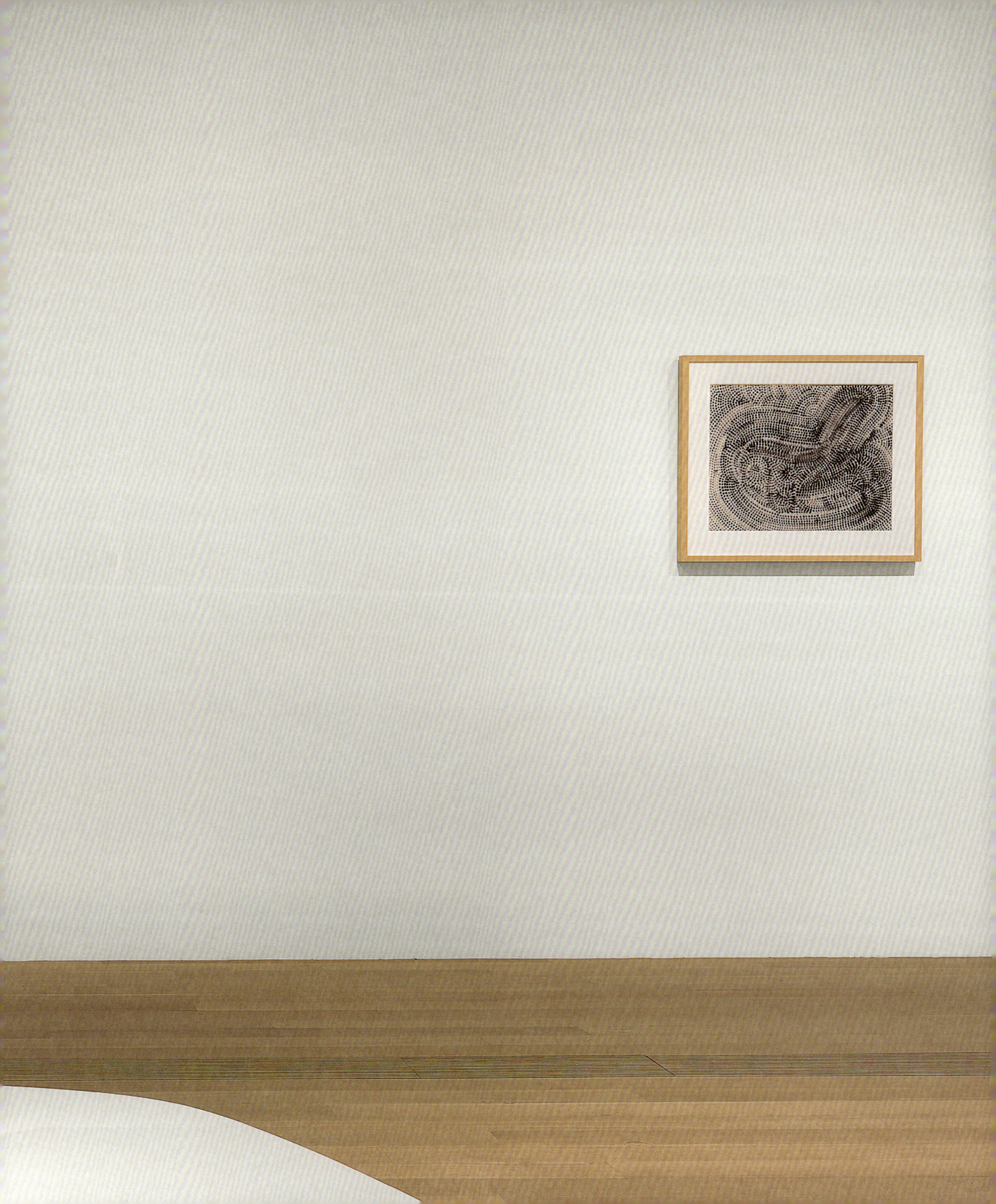

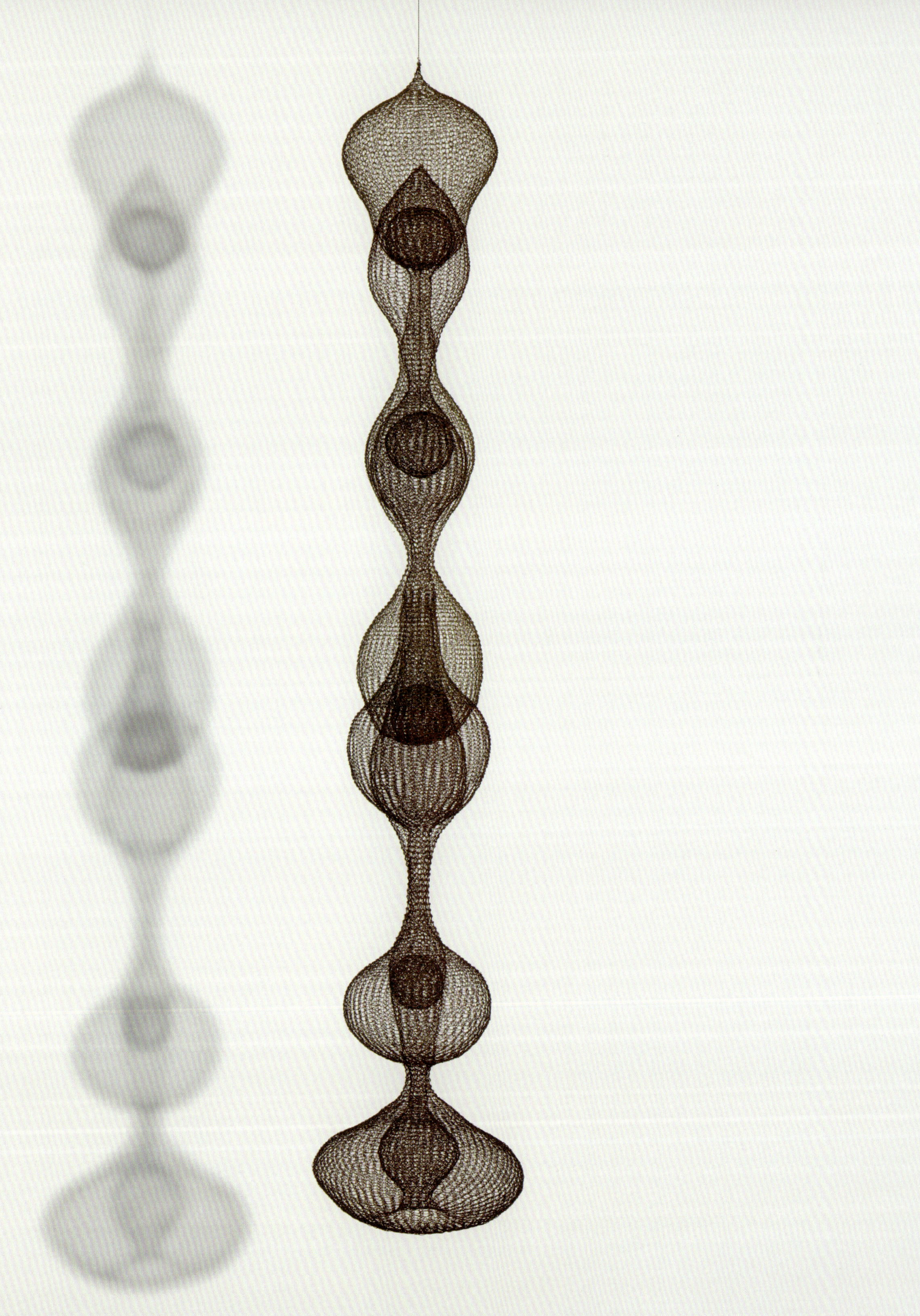

Untitled (S.065, Hanging Seven-Lobed, Multilayered Continuous Form within a Form with Spheres in the Second, Third, Fourth, and Sixth Lobes), ca. 1960–63. Oxidized copper and brass wire, 94 × 17½ × 17½ inches (238.8 × 44.5 × 44.5 cm)

Left to right:

Untitled (S.046 c, a, b & d, Hanging Group of Four, Two-Lobed Forms), 1961.

S.046c (has a single sphere in the bottom lobe). Oxidized copper wire and brass wire, 32 × 13 × 13 inches (81.3 × 33 × 33 cm)

S.046a (has a sphere in the top lobe). Oxidized copper wire and brass wire, 60 × 17 × 17 inches (152.4 × 43.2 × 43.2 cm)

S.046b (has no internal spheres). Brass wire, 21 × 12 × 12 inches (53.3 × 30.5 × 30.5 cm)

S.046d (has two spheres in the top lobe). Copper wire and brass wire, 41 × 16 × 16 inches (104.1 × 40.6 × 40.6 cm)

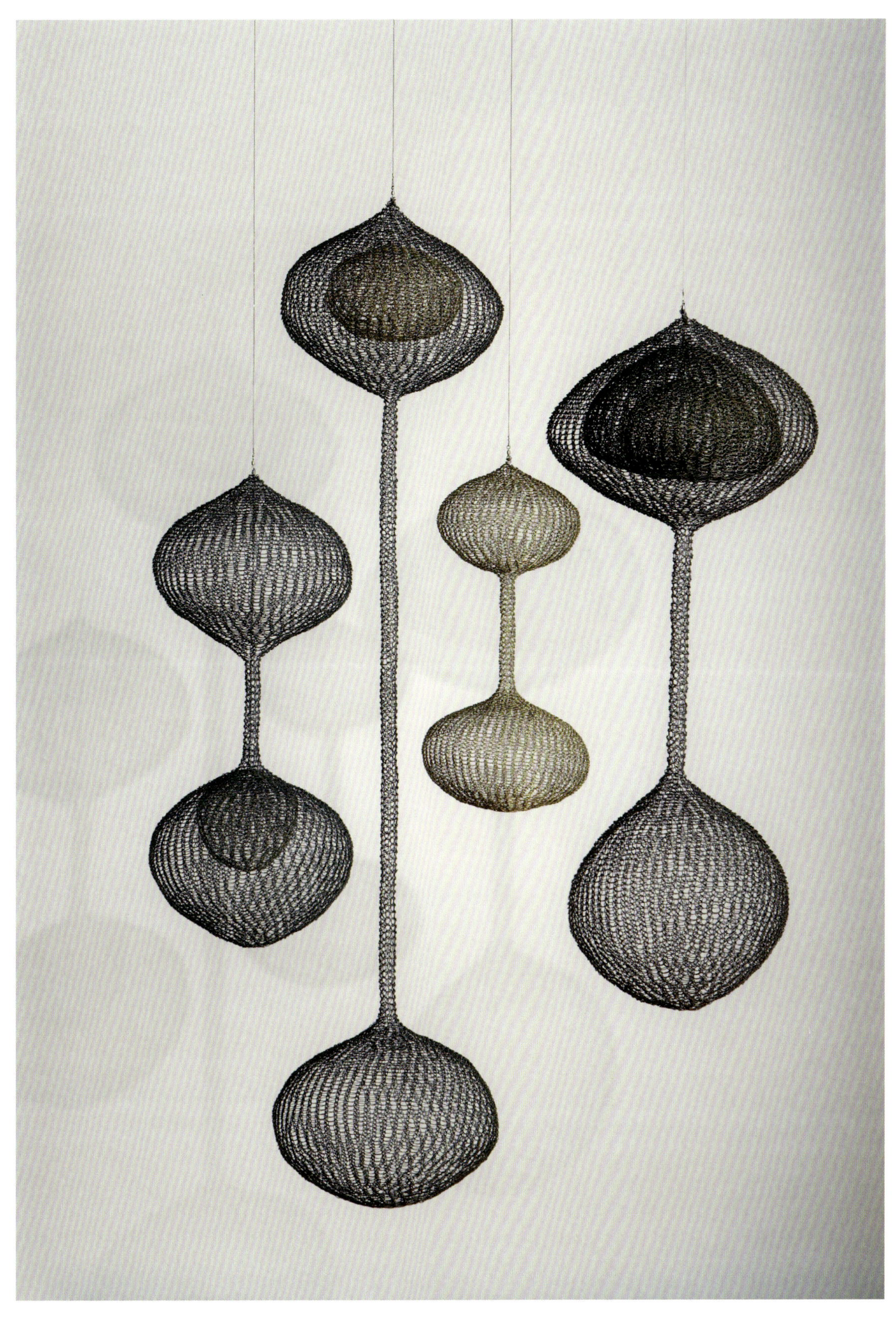

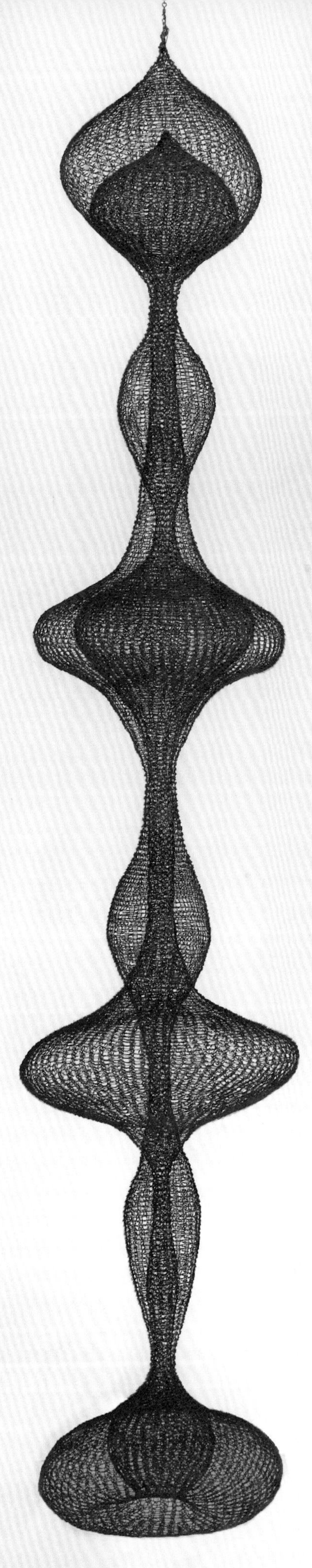

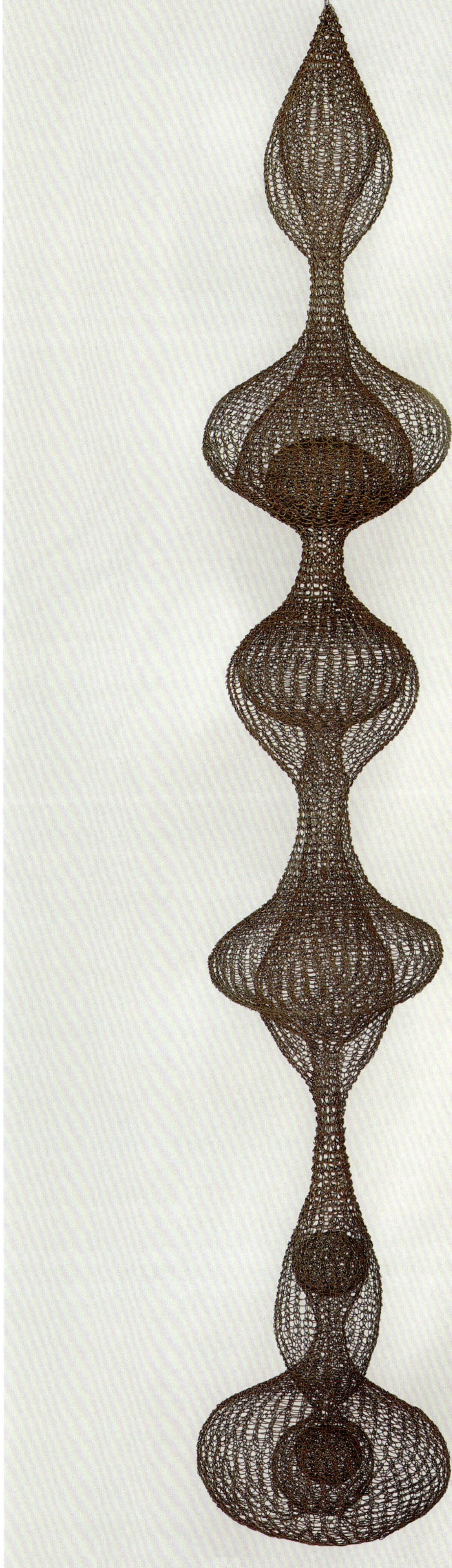

Opposite: *Untitled* (S.266, Hanging Seven-Lobed, Multilayered Interlocking Continuous Form within a Form), 1961. Brass and copper wire, 115 × 22 × 22 inches (292.1 × 55.9 × 55.9 cm)

Right: *Untitled* (S.035, Hanging Six-Lobed, Multilayered Interlocking Continuous Form within a Form with Spheres in the Second, Fifth, and Sixth Lobes), ca. 1962. Brass and copper wire, 88 × 15½ × 15½ inches (223.5 × 39.4 × 39.4 cm)

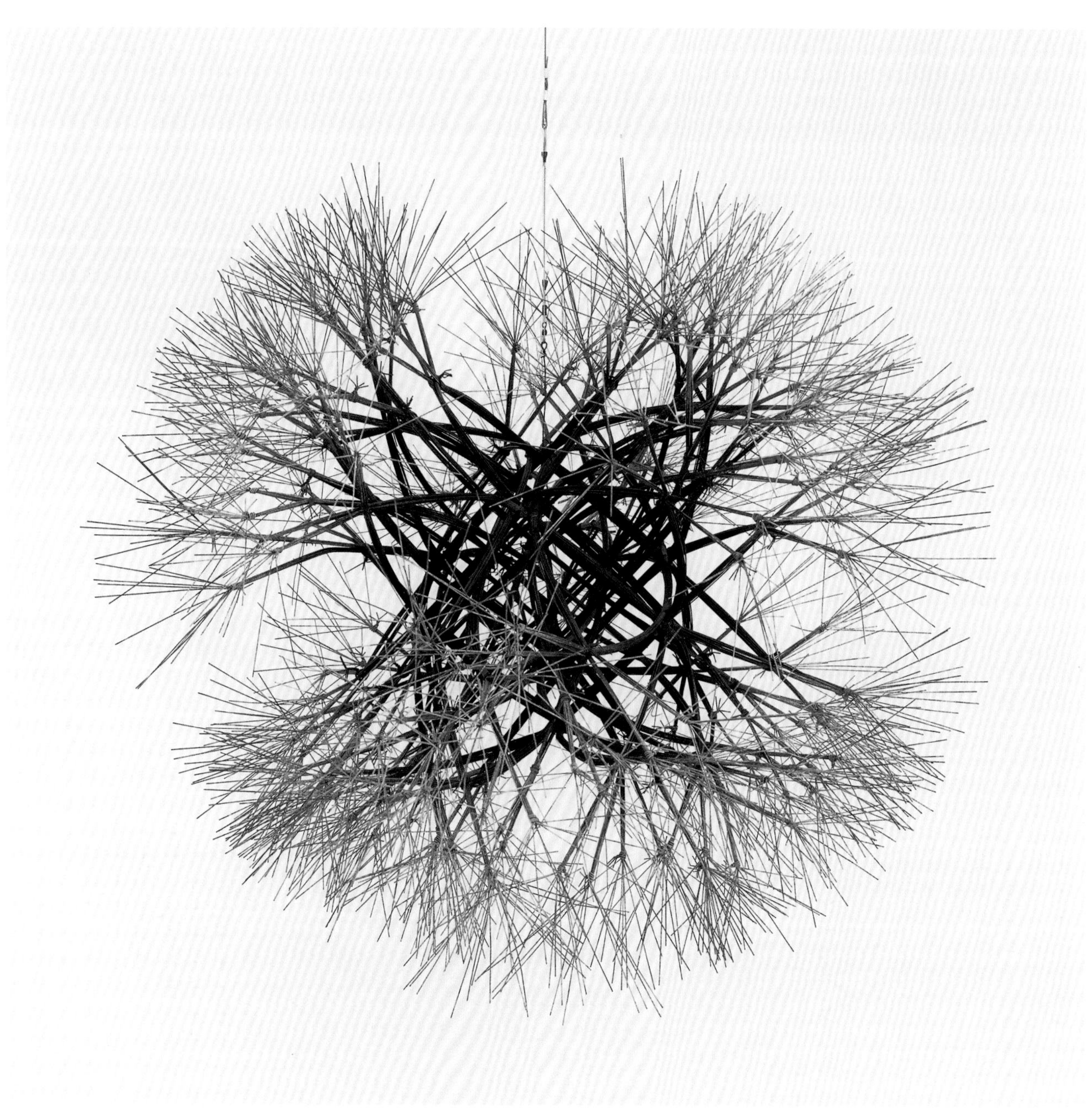

Untitled (S.043, Hanging Tied-Wire, Cubed Open-Center, Multi-Branched Form Based on Nature), ca. 1994.
Bronze wire with green patina, 32 × 32 × 32 inches (81.3 × 81.3 × 81.3 cm)

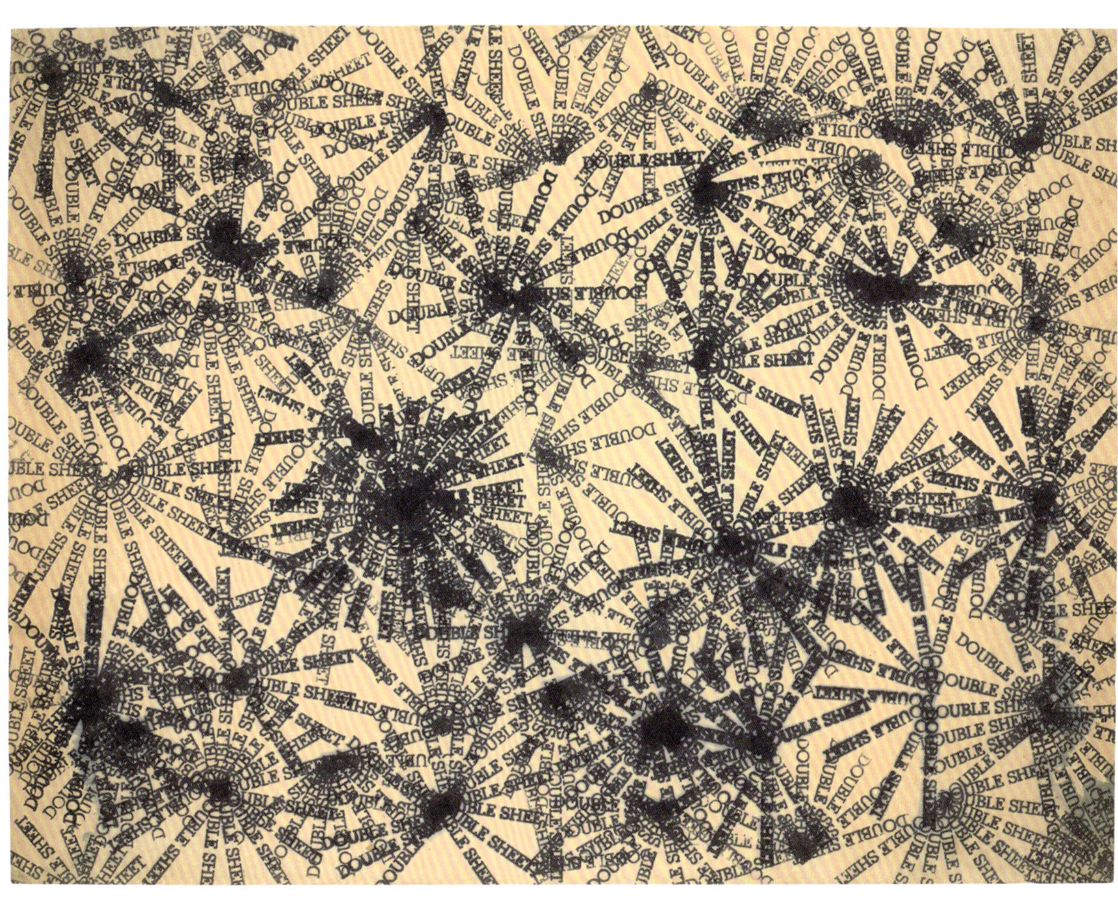

Untitled (BMC.75, Double Sheet Clusters), ca. 1948–49.
Stamped black ink on newsprint, 17¼ × 22 inches (43.8 × 55.9 cm)

Untitled (S.155, Hanging Seven-Lobed, Multilayered Interlocking Continuous Form with a Sphere Suspended in the Top and Fifth Lobes), ca. 1958. Copper and brass wire, 79 × 15½ × 15½ inches (200.7 × 39.4 × 39.4 cm)

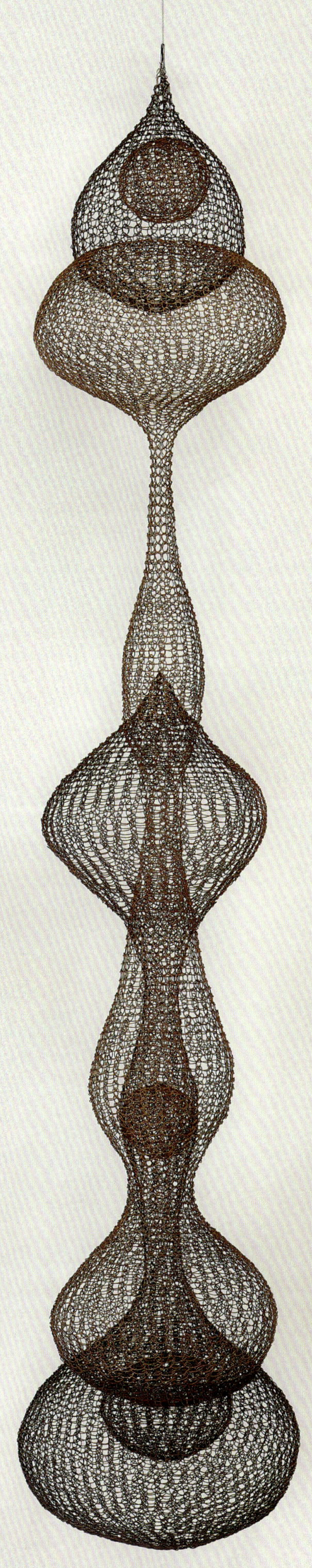

Untitled (PF.1015, Horse's Tail), 1961. Pen and black ink on rice paper mounted on board, 35 × 23 inches (88.9 × 58.4 cm)

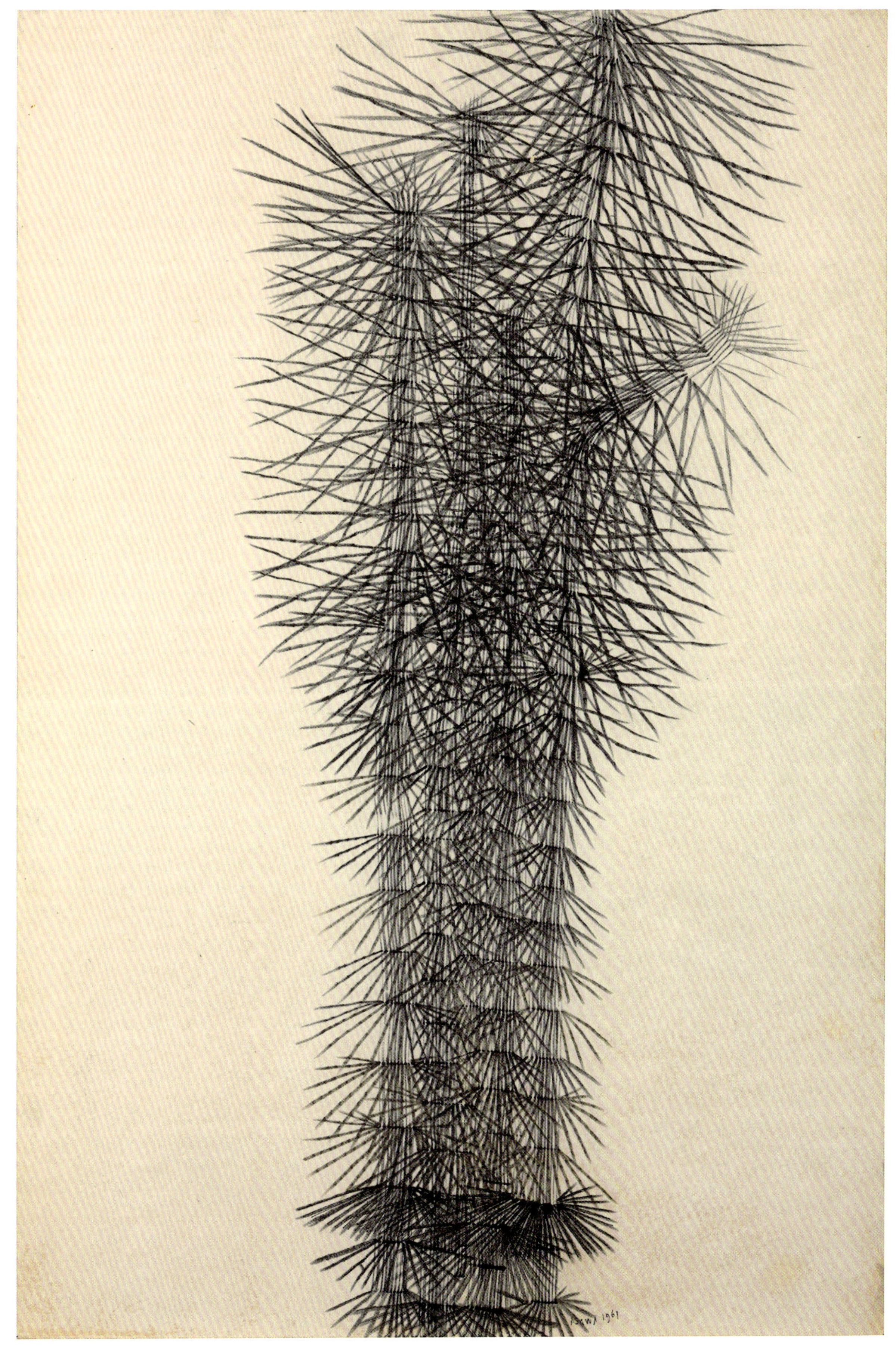

Untitled (S.671, Hanging Tied-Wire, Open-Center, Three-Petaled Form Based on Nature), ca. 1970s.
 Brass wire, 15 × 15 × 8 inches (38.1 × 38.1 × 20.3 cm)

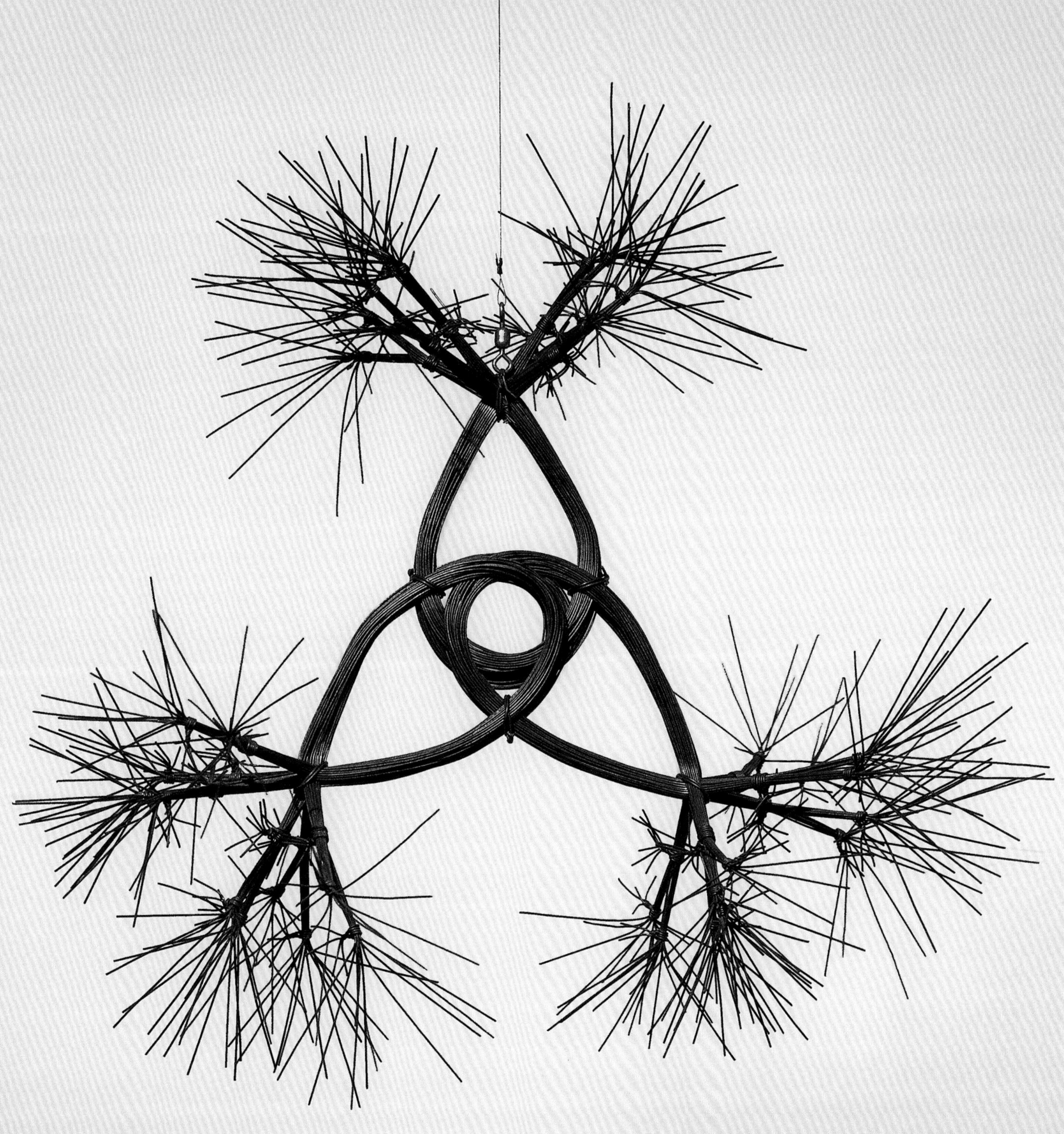

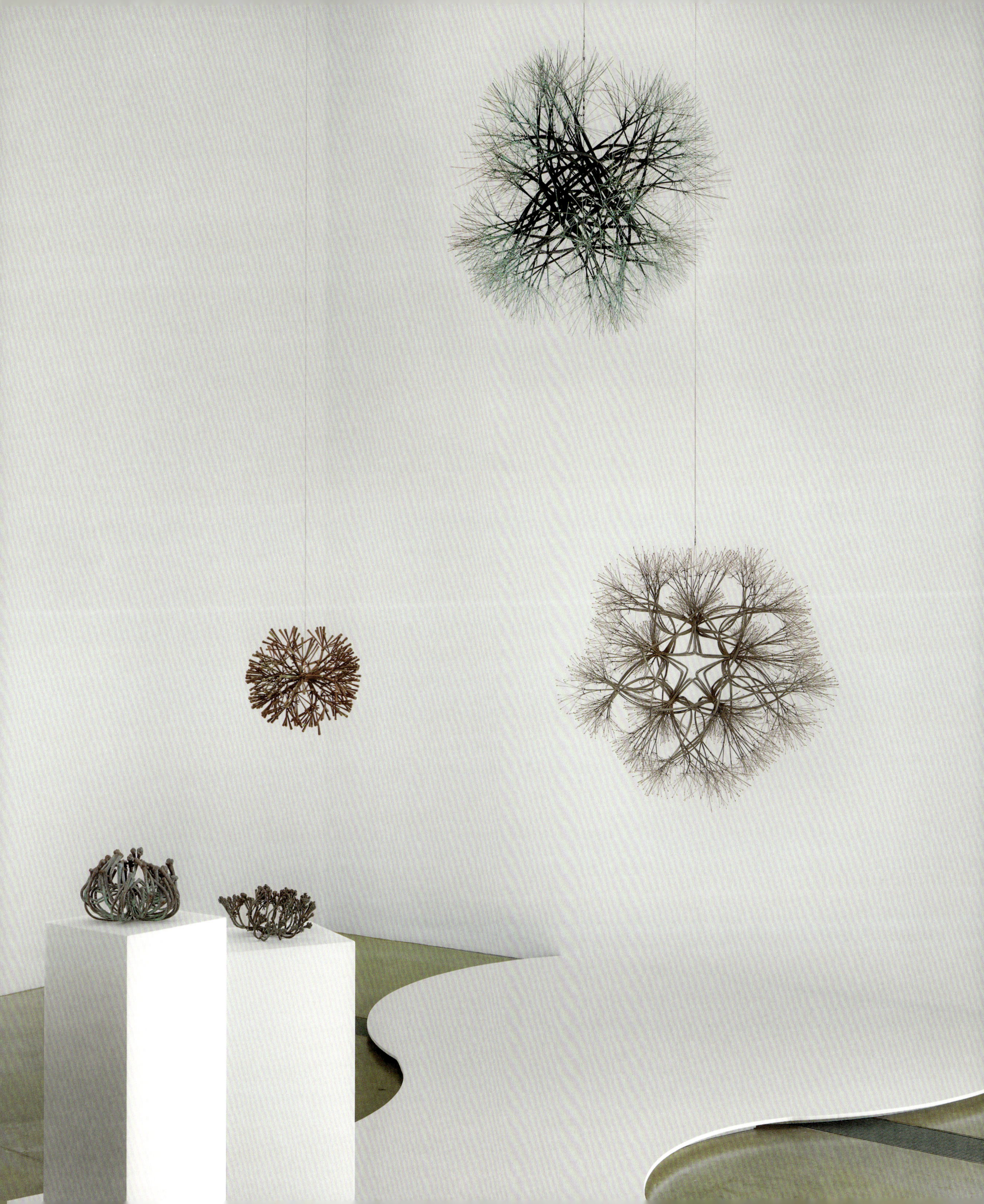

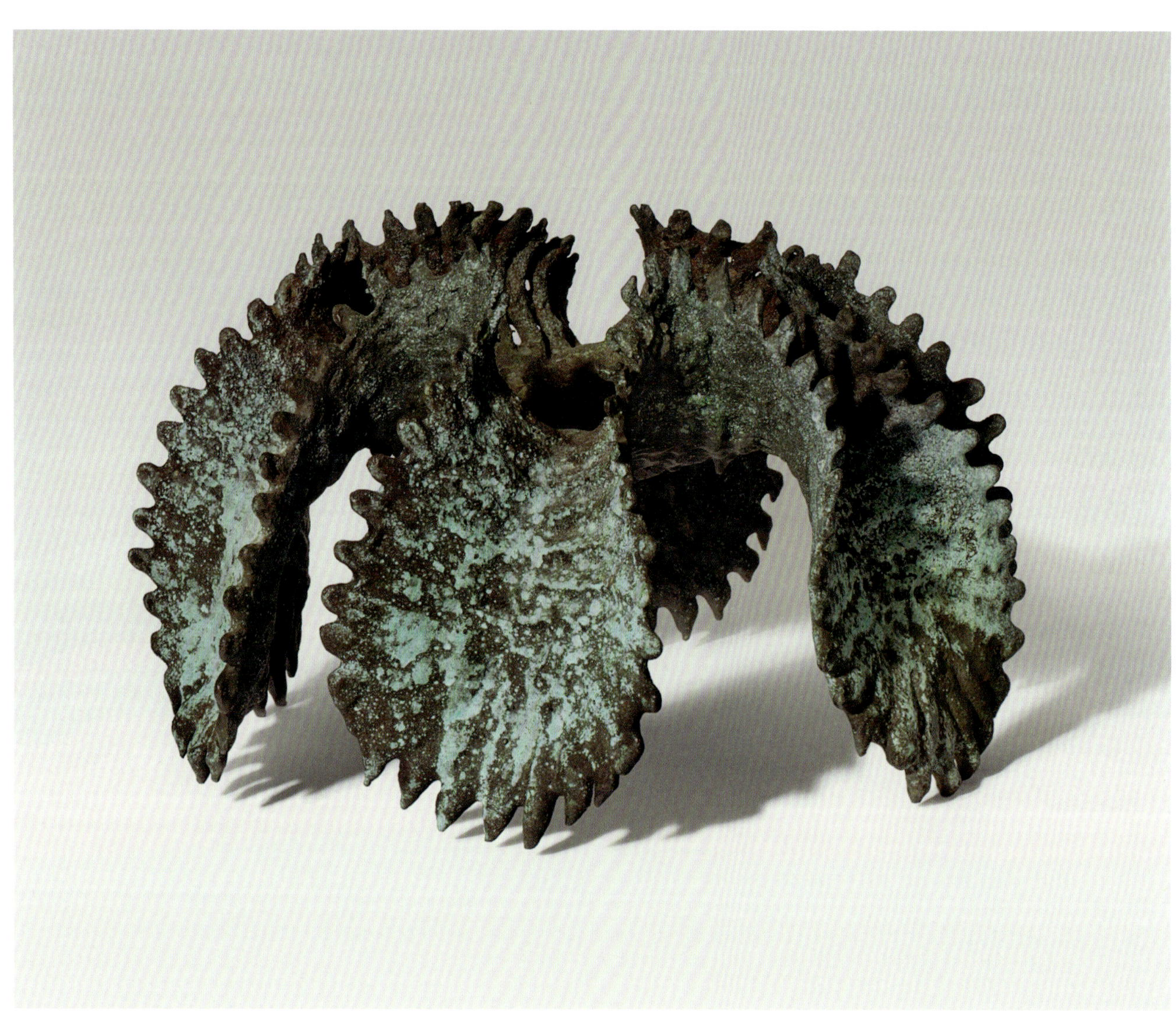

Untitled (S.120, Freestanding Reversible Undulating Form), ca. 1975.
Bronze, natural verdigris, 10 × 18 × 18 inches (25.4 × 45.7 × 45.7 cm)

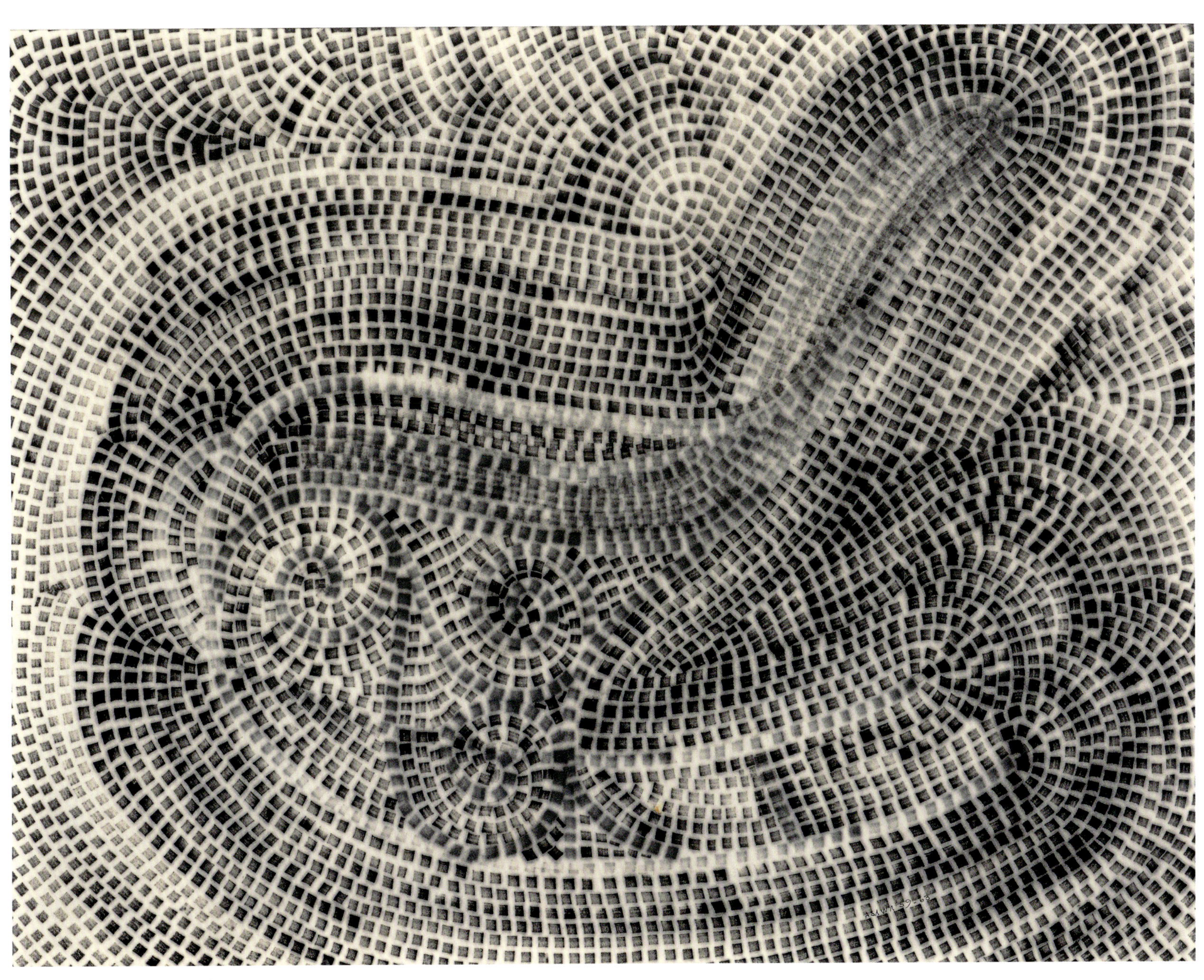

Bentwood Rocker (MI.176), ca. 1959–63. Pen and black ink on paper, 18 × 22¾ inches (45.7 × 57.8 cm)

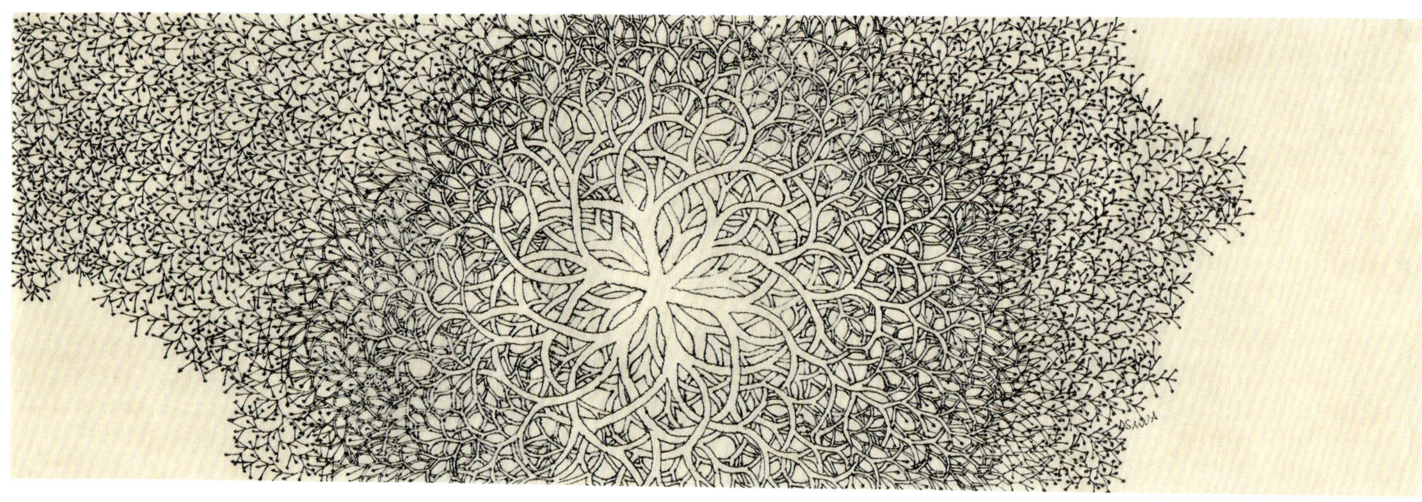

Untitled (SD.263, Tied-Wire Sculpture Drawing with Six-Branch Center and Drops at the Ends), ca. 1963–69. Pen and black ink on Japanese paper, 6 × 17¾ inches (15.2 × 45.1 cm)

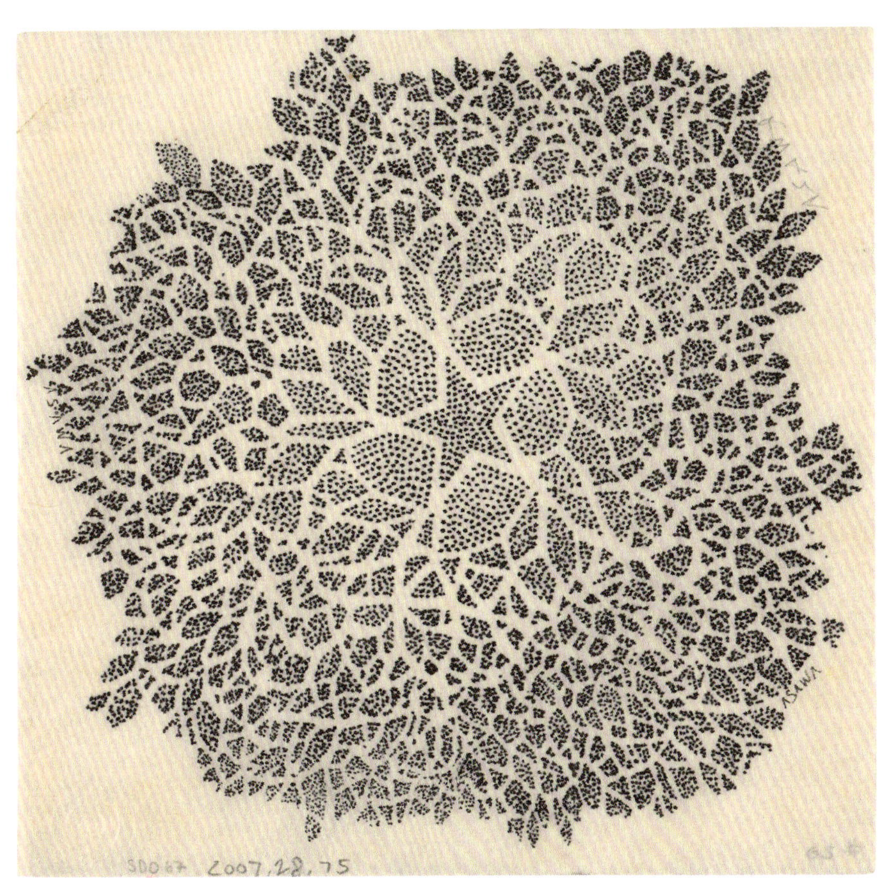

Untitled (SD.067, Tied-Wire Sculpture Drawing with Five-Pointed Star in Center and Asymmetrical Branches), after 1965. Pen and black ink on paper, 6 × 6 inches (15.2 × 15.2 cm)

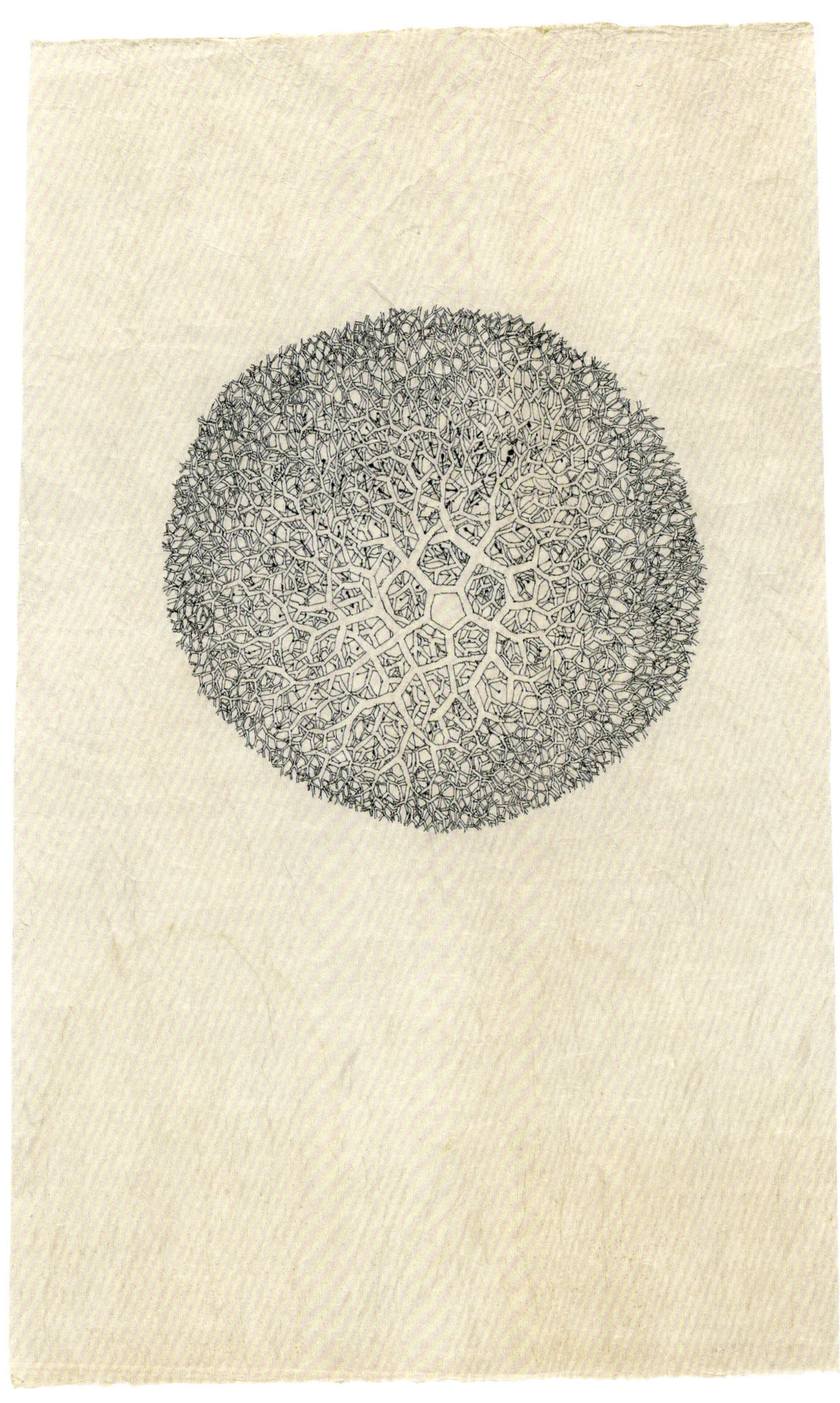

Untitled (SD.139, Tied-Wire Sculpture Drawing with Open Pentagon Center and Branches Enclosed by a Circle), after 1965. Pen and black ink on Japanese paper, 36 × 22 inches (91.4 × 55.9 cm)

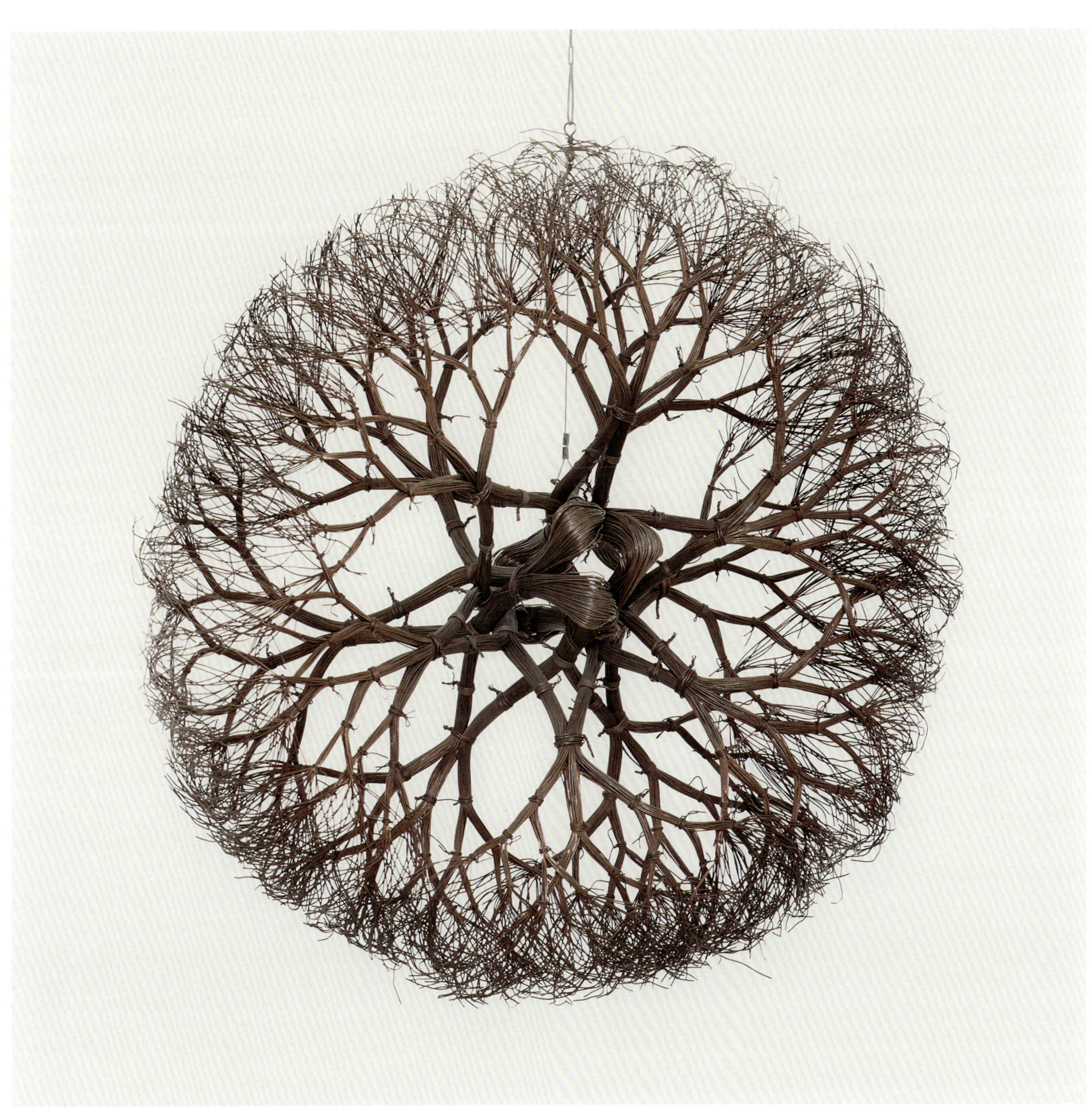

Untitled (S.229, Hanging Tied-Wire, Double-Sided, Open-Center, Multi-Branched Form Based on Nature), 1964. Oxidized copper wire, 20 × 20 × 7½ inches (50.8 × 50.8 × 19.1 cm)

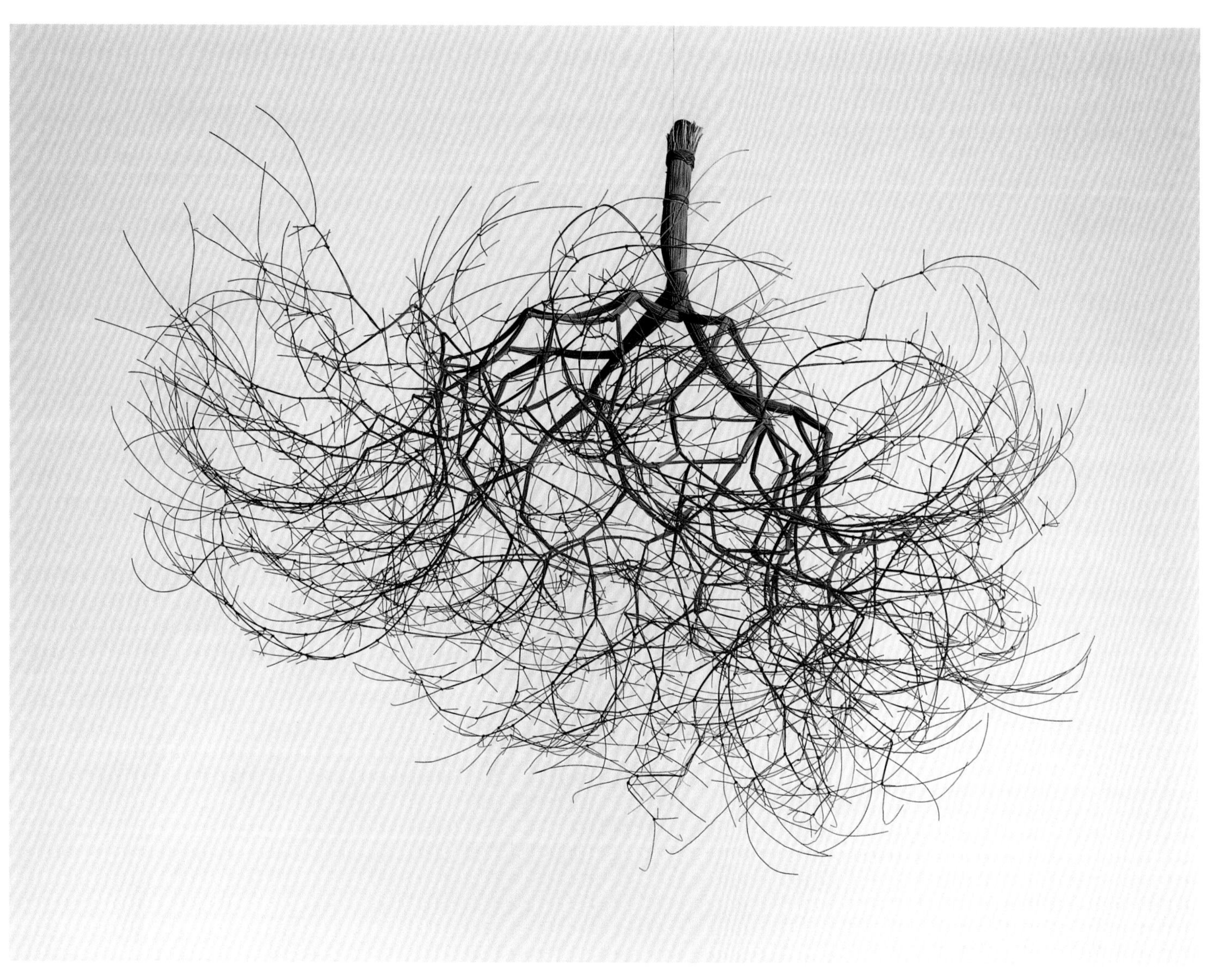

Untitled (S.184, Hanging Tied-Wire, Single-Stem, Multi-Branched Form Based on Nature), ca. 1962.
Galvanized steel wire, 30 × 40 × 40 inches (76.2 × 101.6 × 101.6 cm)

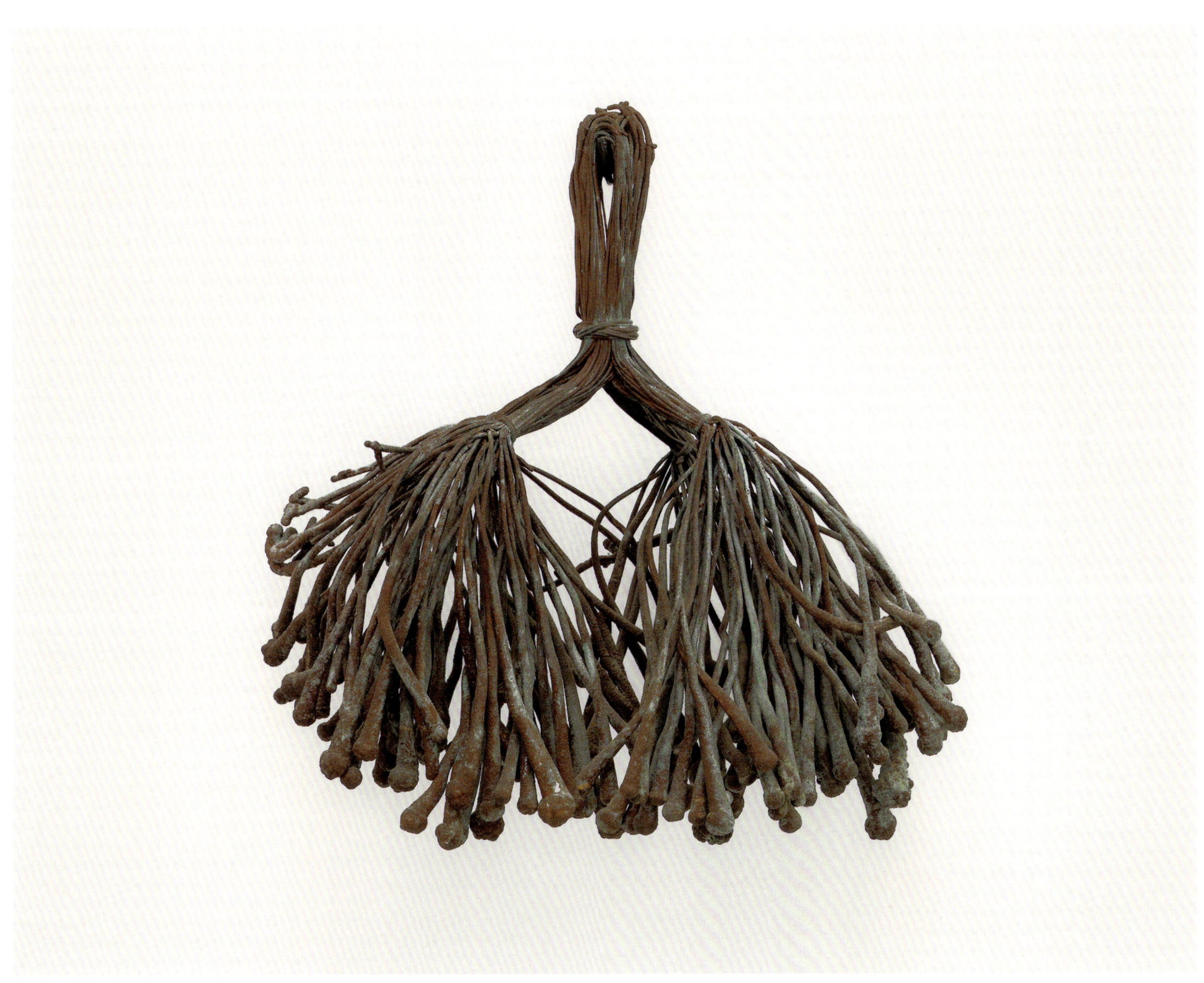

Untitled (S.059, Wall-Mounted Electroplated Tied-Wire, Center-Tied, Four-Branched Form Based on Nature), ca. 1963. Electroplated copper wire, 7⅝ × 8 × 4 inches (19.4 × 20.3 × 10.2 cm)

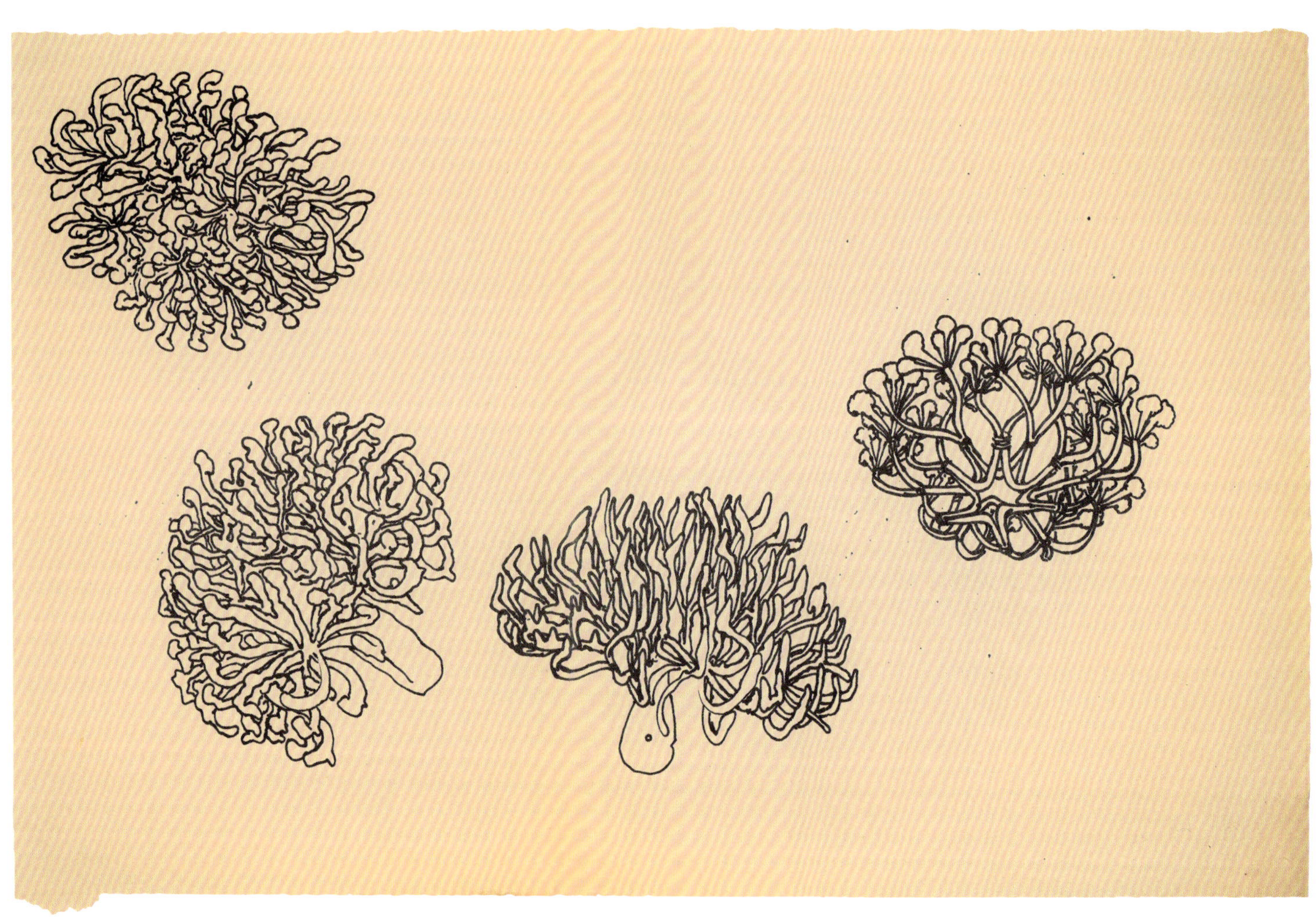

Untitled (SD.041, Three Views of Cast Tied-Wire Sculpture S.768 and One of Electroplated S.136), ca. 1978.
Pen and black ink on newsprint, 20 × 30 inches (50.8 × 76.2 cm)

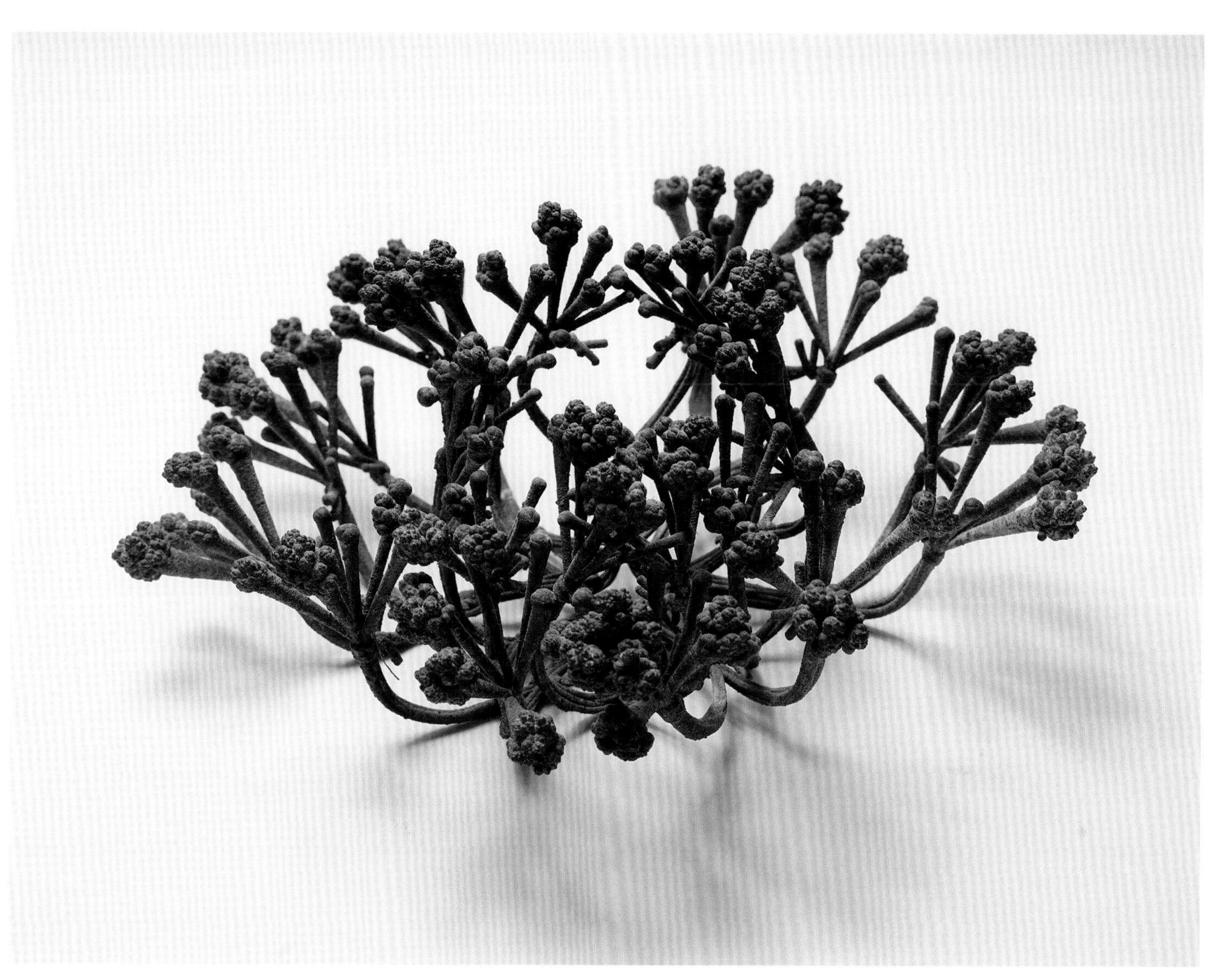

Untitled (S.136, Freestanding Electroplated Tied-Wire, Open-Center, Twelve-Branched Organic Form Based on Nature), 1965. Electroplated copper wire, 4½ × 9¼ × 9¼ inches (11.4 × 23.5 × 23.5 cm)

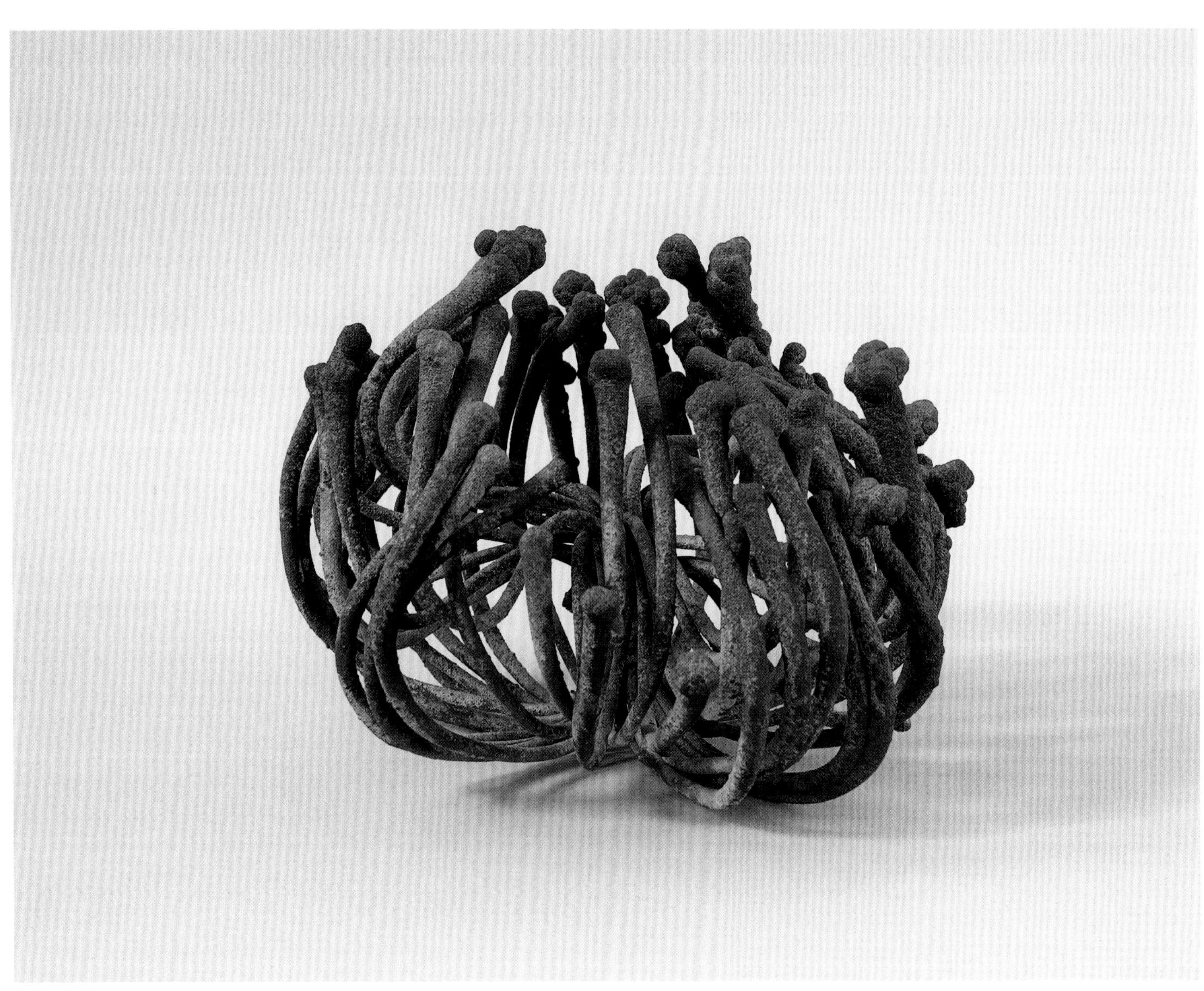

Untitled (S.132, Freestanding Electroplated Tied-Wire, Organic Form Based on Nature), ca. 1963.
Electroplated copper wire, 6½ × 8½ × 8½ inches (16.5 × 21.6 × 21.6 cm)

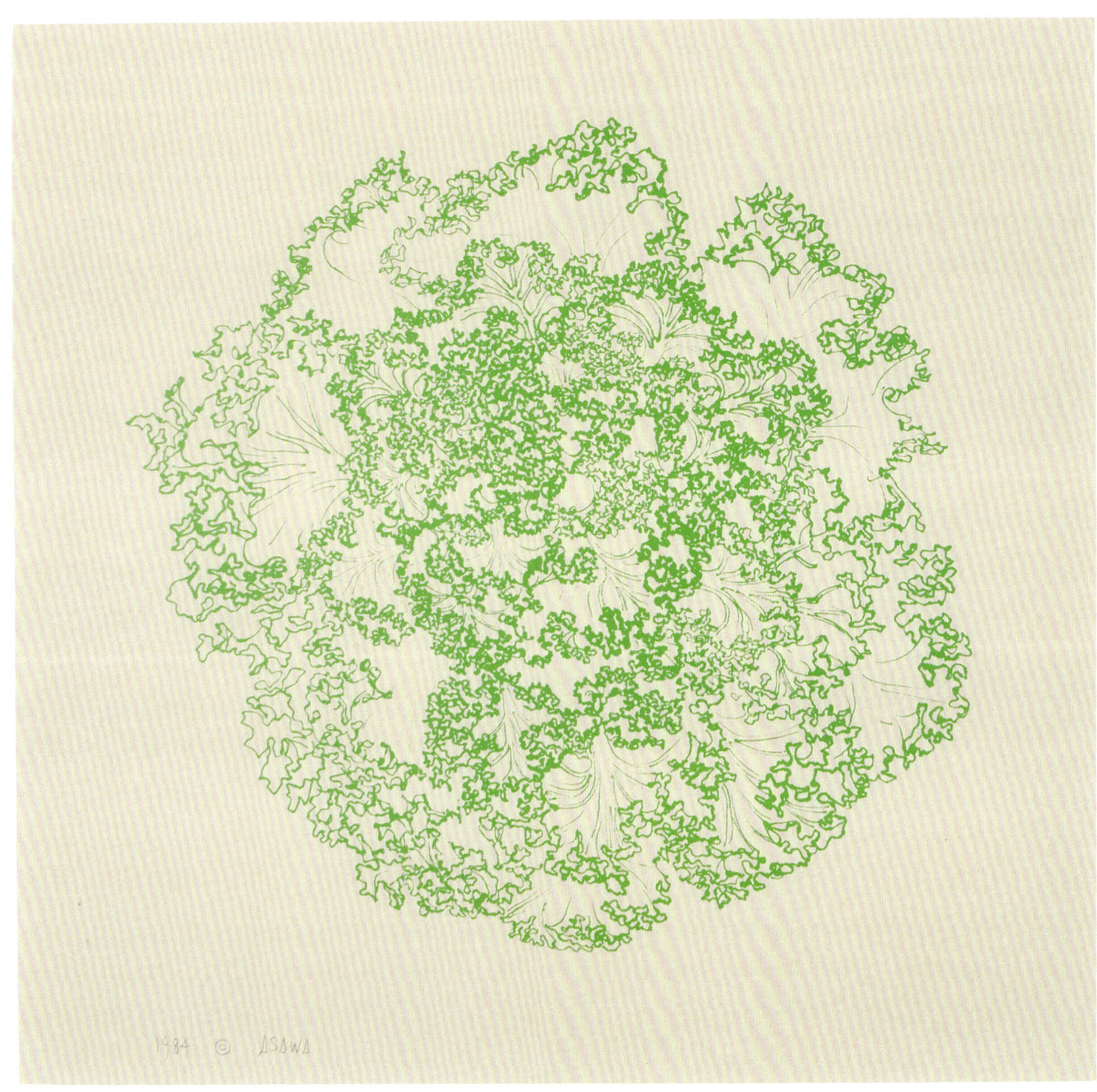

Cabbage (P.021), 1984. Green ink on coated paper, offset lithograph, 9¼ × 9⅜ inches (23.5 × 23.8 cm)

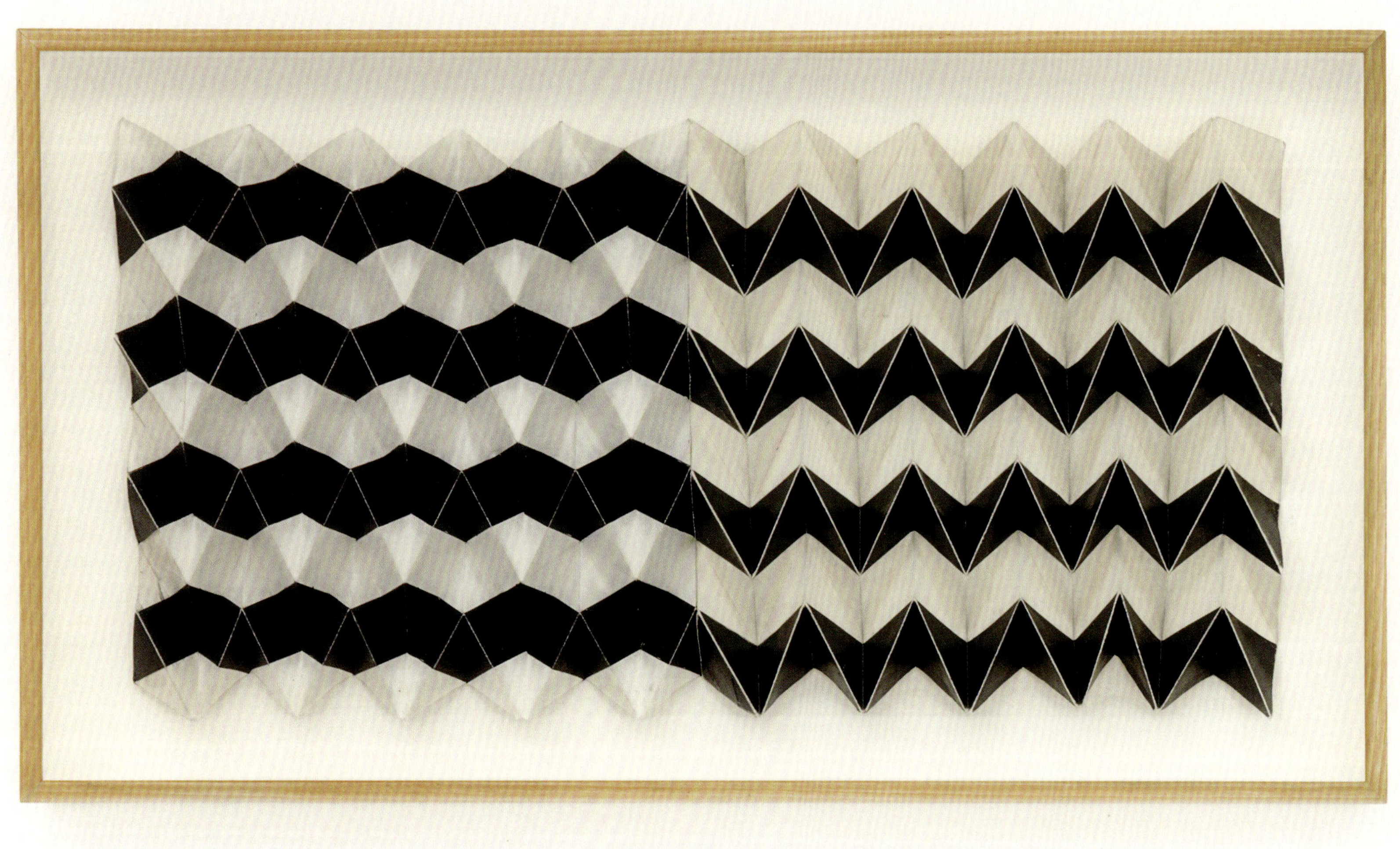

Untitled (S.529, Wall-Mounted Paperfold with Horizontal Stripes), ca. 1970s.
Brushed black ink on paper, 13¾ × 26½ × 1½ inches (34.9 × 67.3 × 3.8 cm)

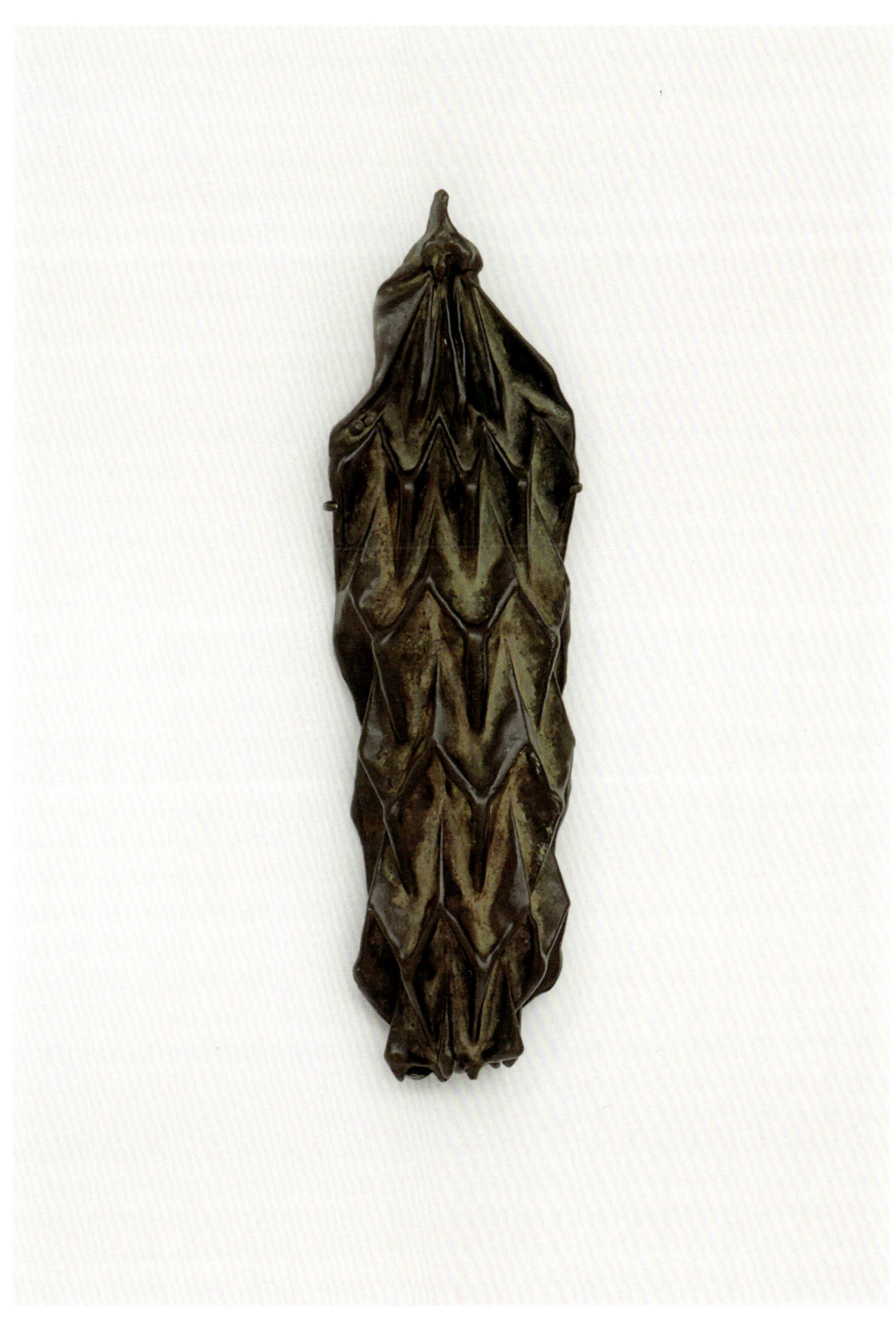

Untitled (S.062, Wall-Mounted Folded Paper Form), ca. 1968–70. Bronze with brown-green patina, 14¾ × 4½ × 2½ inches (37.5 × 11.4 × 6.4 cm)

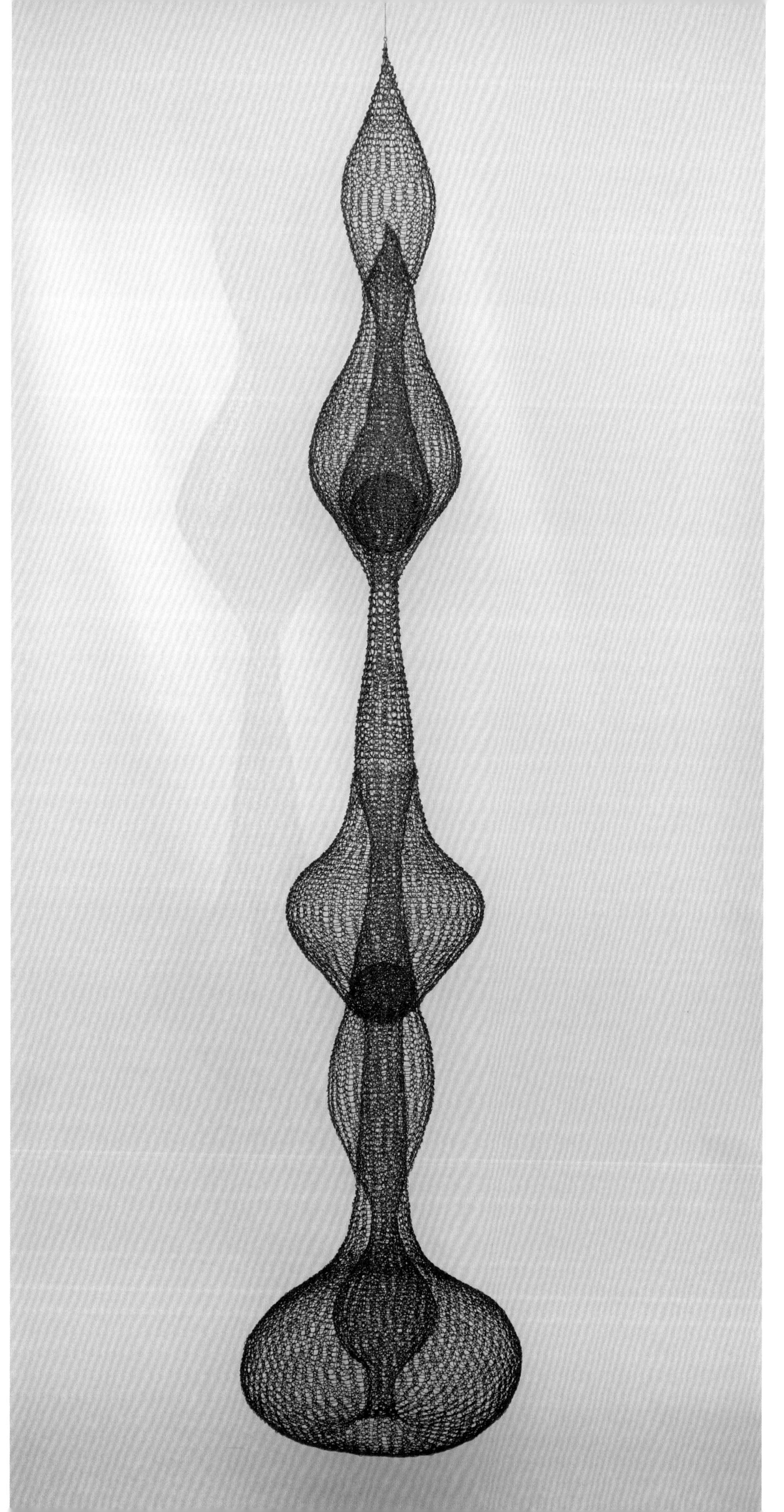

Opposite: *Untitled* (S.315, Hanging Six-Lobed, Multilayered Interlocking Continuous Form within a Form with Spheres in the Second and Fourth Lobes), ca. 1976. Copper and brass wire, 77 × 15 × 15 inches (195.6 × 38.1 × 38.1 cm)

Right: *Untitled* (S.036, Hanging Seven-Lobed, Multilayered Interlocking Continuous Form within a Form with Spheres in the First, Sixth, and Seventh Lobes), 1959. Oxidized copper and brass wire, 137½ × 17 × 17 inches (349.3 × 43.2 × 43.2 cm)

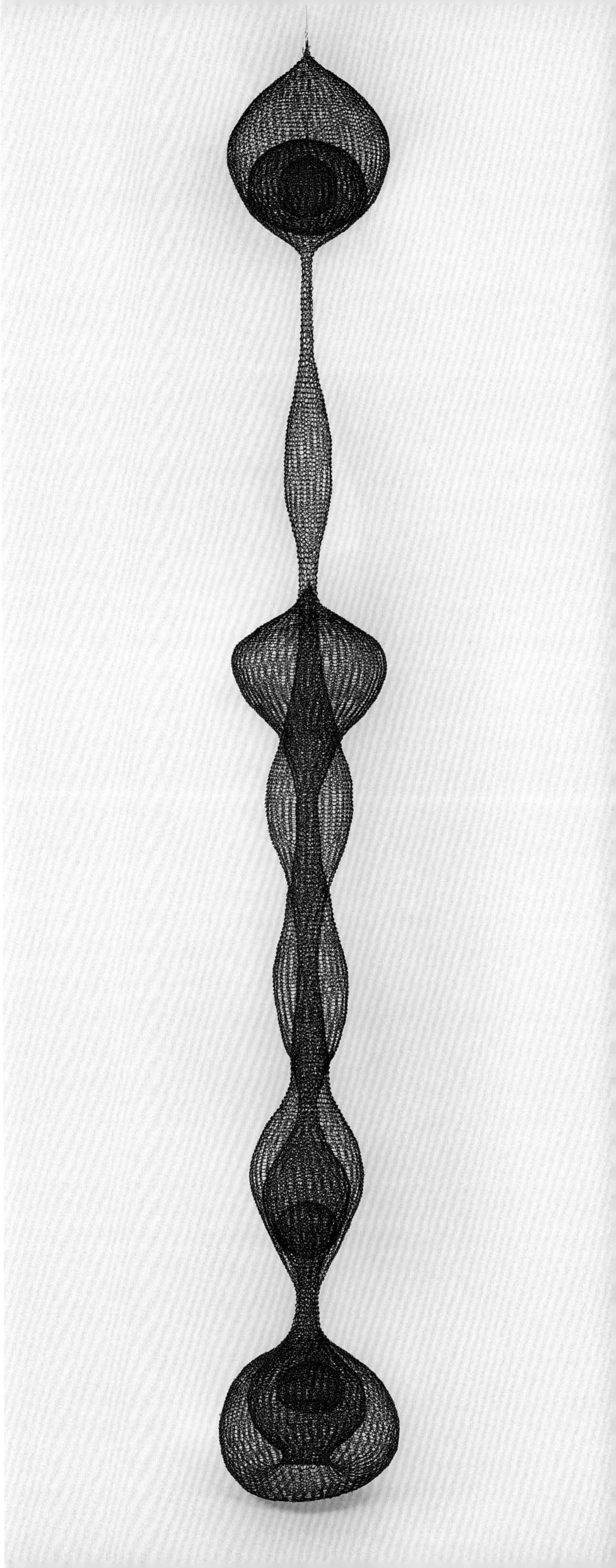

Untitled (S.292, Hanging Miniature Eight-Lobed, Single-Layered Continuous Form), 2000.
Stainless steel wire, 33 × 3¾ × 3¾ inches (83.8 × 9.5 × 9.5 cm)

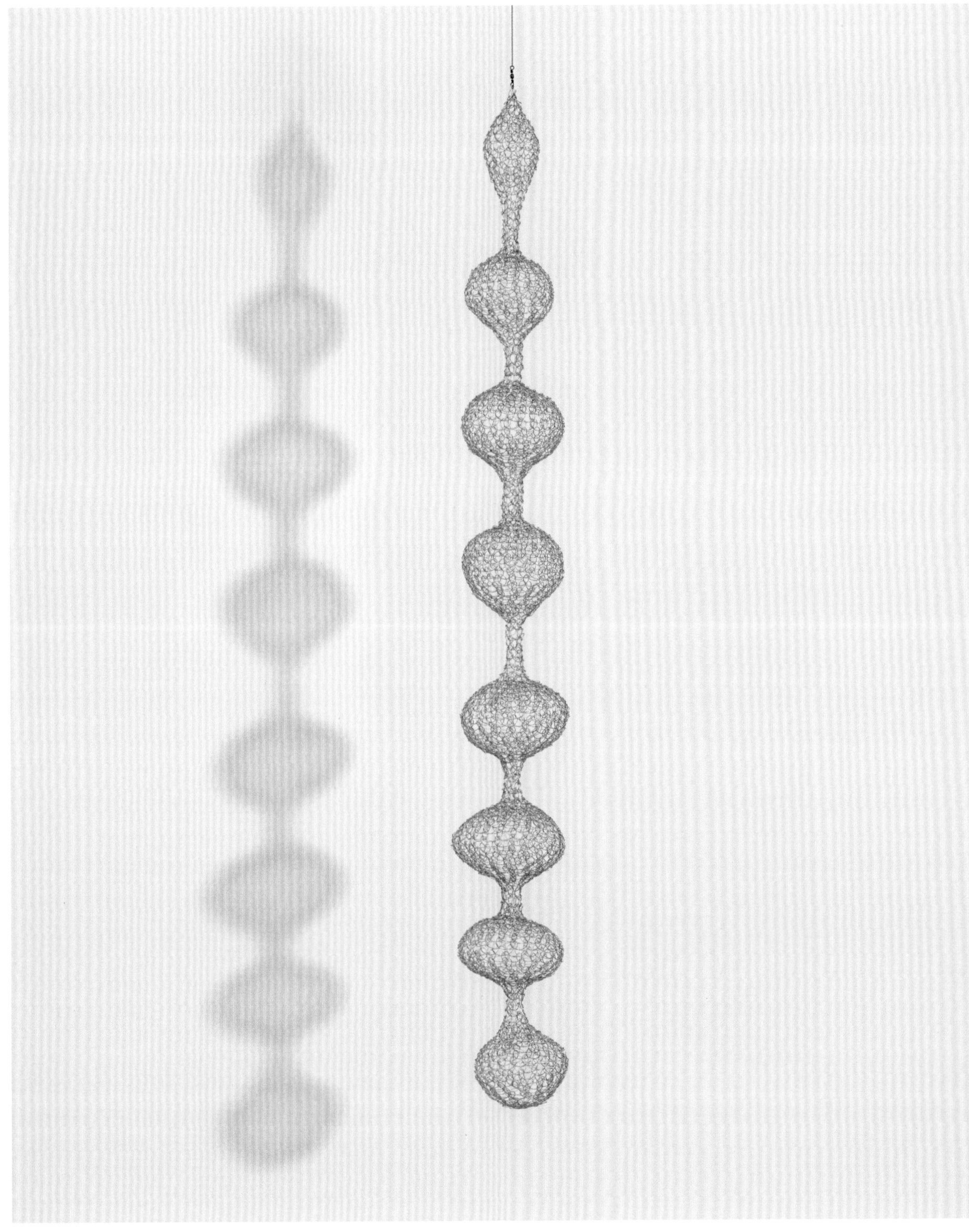

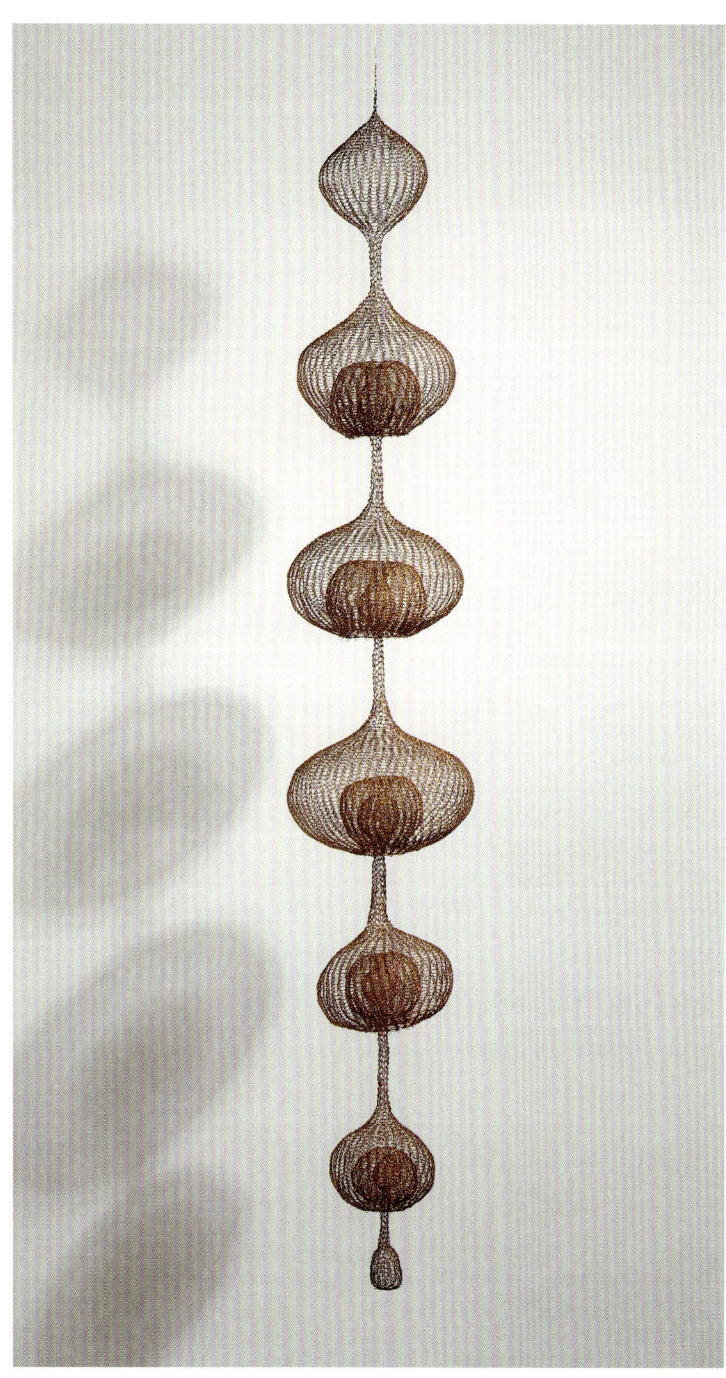

Untitled (S.077, Hanging Miniature Seven-Lobed Continuous Form within a Form), ca. 1978.
Copper wire, 33 × 5½ × 5½ inches (83.8 × 14 × 14 cm)

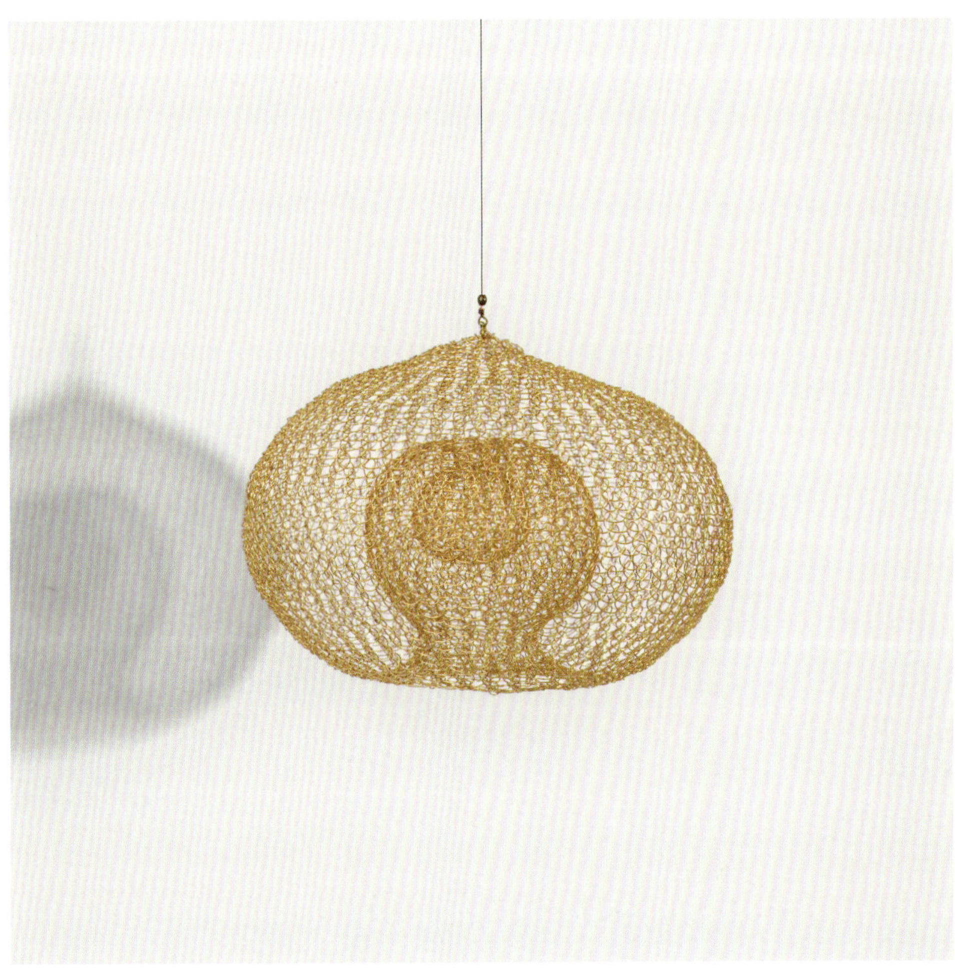

Continuous (S.340, Hanging Miniature Single-Lobed, Three-Layered Continuous Form within a Form), ca. 1981–82. Gold-filled wire, 3½ × 4½ × 4½ inches (8.9 × 11.4 × 11.4 cm)

Untitled (S.041, Hanging Four Layers of Hourglass Forms Surrounding a Bud-Shaped Center with an Intersecting Disk in Top), ca. 1962. Galvanized steel and iron wire, 29 × 31 × 31 inches (73.7 × 78.7 × 78.7 cm)

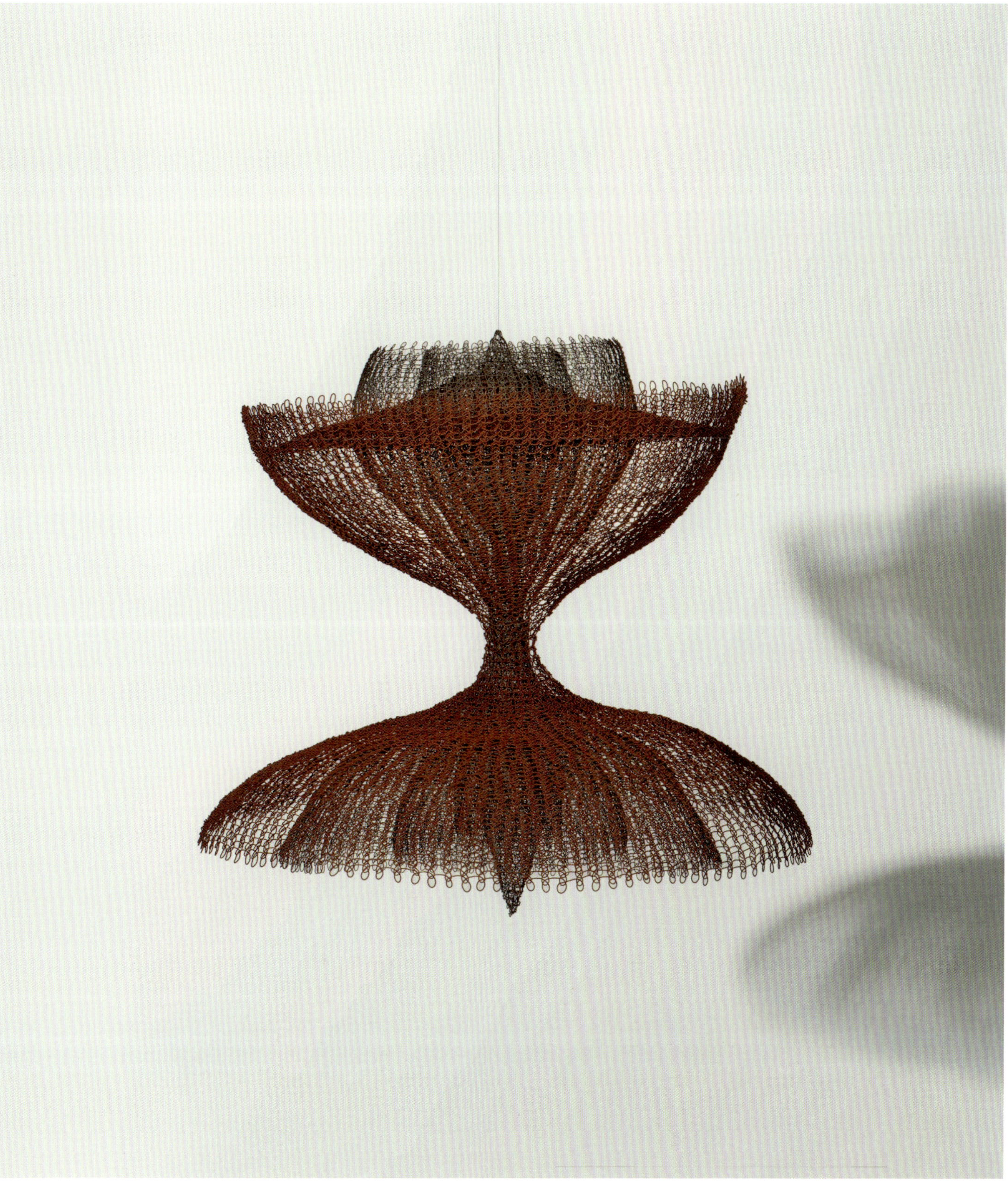

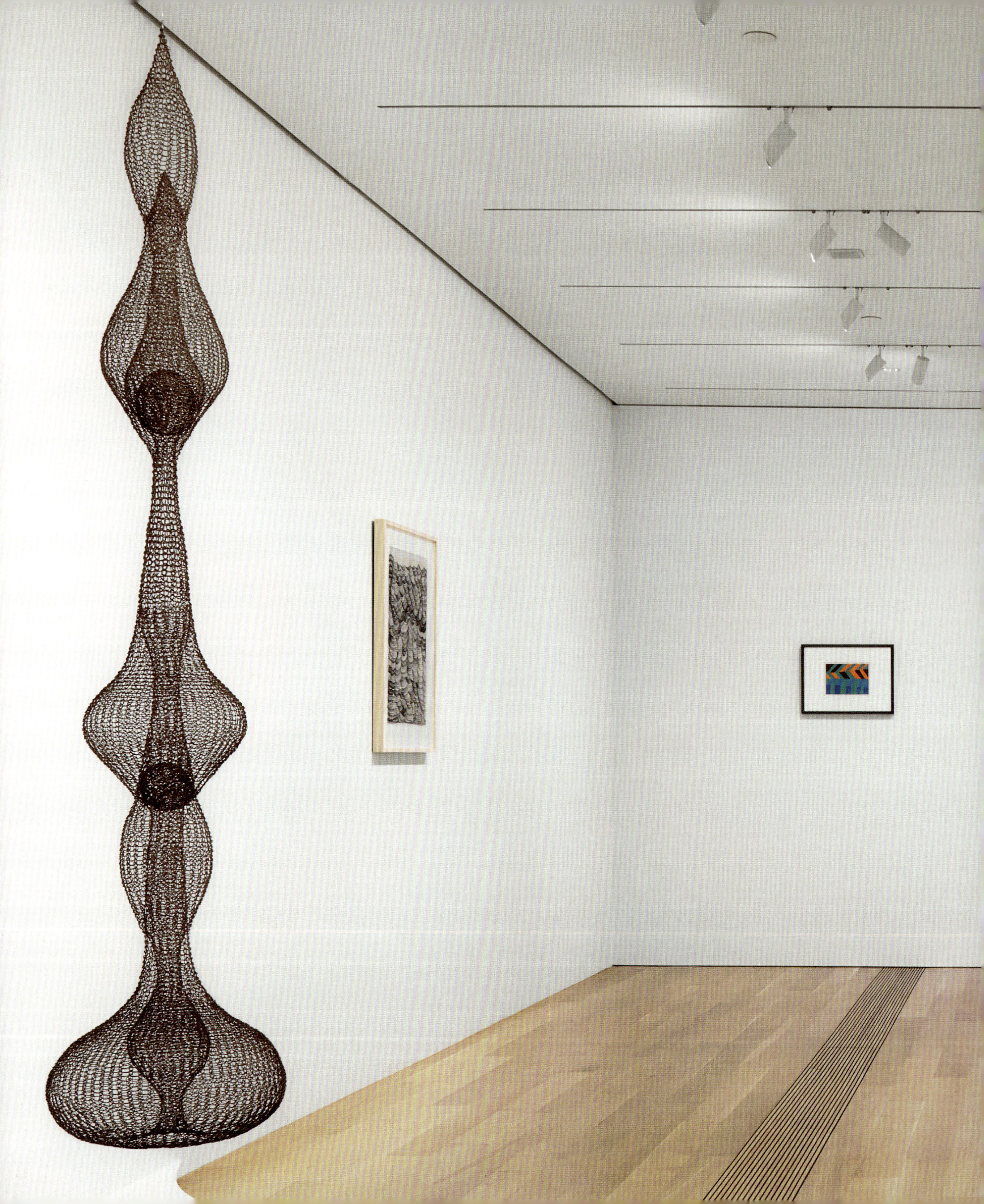

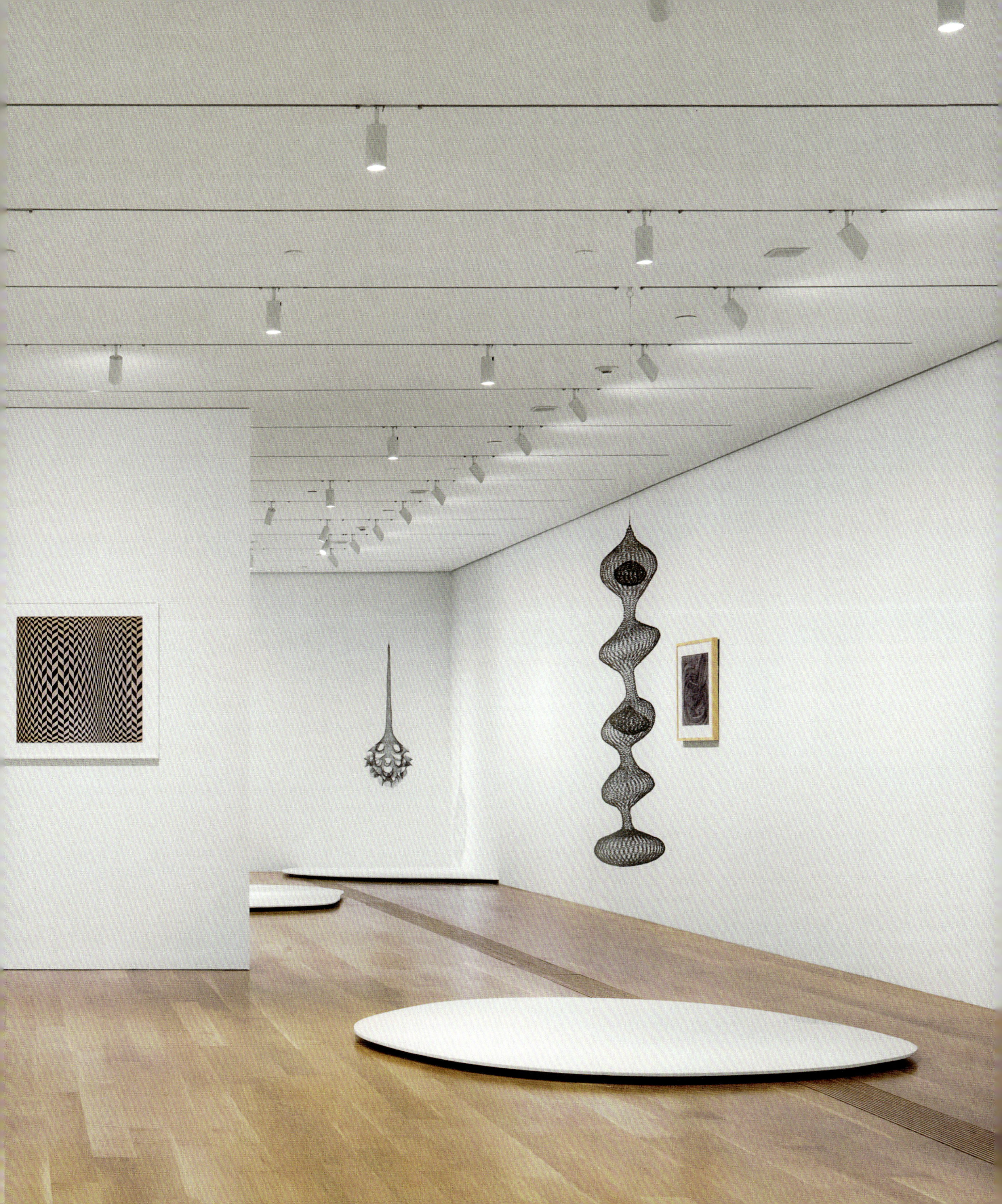

Evolution of Form

Aiko Cuneo, Addie Lanier, and Tamara H. Schenkenberg

By the late 1940s, Ruth Asawa extended her exploration of line into sculpture with wire as her primary medium. Over the ensuing decades, she devoted a major part of her practice to taking this material through its paces, exploring the diversity of expression that she could derive from it. Asawa's approach became increasingly methodical, resulting in two bodies of sculptural work—looped-wire and tied-wire sculptures—each based on the technical manipulation of the material. Asawa's experiments eventually propelled these two distinct groupings into new, though closely related, subcategories, each named for the process in which the works were created. Chemically treated tied-wire works resulted in electroplated sculptures, and most of her cast bronze sculptures began as looped-wire pieces. Taken together, the looped-wire, tied-wire, electroplated, and cast sculptures attest to how Asawa achieved innovation through iteration.[1]

Asawa worked with wire of various color and material composition. These materials often changed over time, as is the nature of most metallic surfaces. Asawa accepted and embraced this and viewed the organic patination of her sculptures as an inevitable and beautiful facet in the life of her works.

We openly acknowledge that with this first-ever attempt to classify Asawa's sculptural works, our intention is not to conclusively summarize her oeuvre with a rigid chronological timeline. Rather, we offer this section as a resource for initiating new dialogue around Asawa's contribution to the field of sculpture, and to lay the groundwork for future scholarship.

The categories on the following pages derive from terminology that Asawa developed with the help of her husband, Albert Lanier, and curatorial consultant Paula B. Freedman. In 1999, these three attempted to describe her work and capture information that Asawa felt was relevant to her process. When possible, we have also included the approximate dates when Asawa first developed these discrete forms; however, the artist's process was not linear. She regularly revisited and reworked existing forms and in different combinations throughout her five-decade career.

1. It should be noted that in addition to wire, Asawa also created sculpture in paper, wood, ceramic, plaster, and baker's clay (which she also used for her work in public schools and her public commissions).

Looped-Wire Sculptures

While visiting Toluca, Mexico, in the summer of 1947, Asawa became fascinated with wire egg baskets that she saw in local markets. With the help of a local craftsman, she learned and translated his craft-based technique into this unique body of work. "Looping" is the most accurate term to describe Asawa's application of this method because it describes the act of coiling the wire around a wooden dowel to achieve a series of loops—which Asawa described as a "string of e's"[1]—that she used to build her forms by hand.

Baskets

Asawa's first looped-wire sculptures took the form of open baskets [S.364].

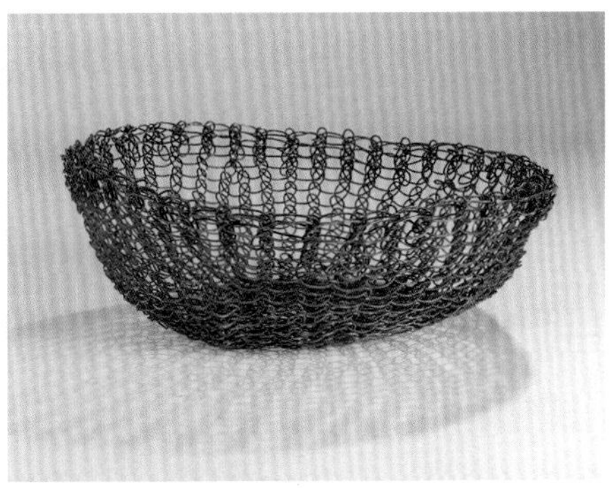

S.364*

Full caption information for works listed with an asterisk (*) can be found on page 144.

Single-Lobed Spheres

By 1949, she closed up the top and by 1950 started creating single spheres that hang from a chain [S.793].

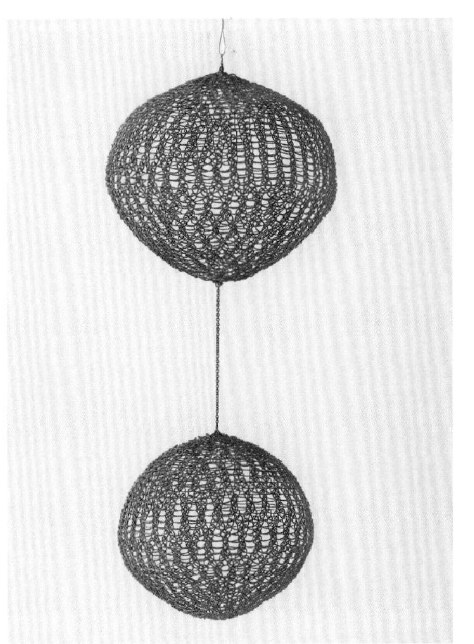

S.793 (p. 19 right)

Single-Lobed Layered Spheres

Asawa eventually nested spheres within spheres to create transparent overlapping layers [S.461]. These spherical forms are connected by chain, and there is no direct contact between the layers.

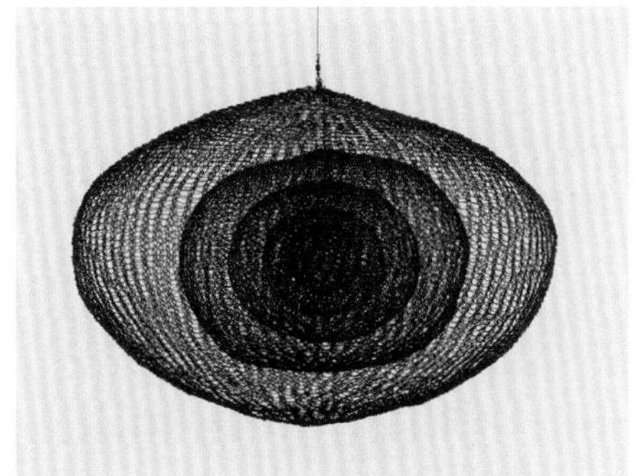

S.461 (p. 20)

Multi-Lobed, Single-Layered Forms

Works in this category, which Asawa began developing circa 1949, have more than one lobe and consist of a single layer of wire [S.264].

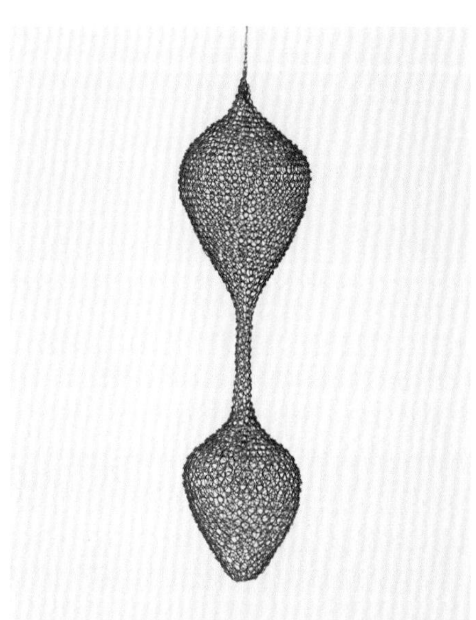

S.264 (p. 19 left)

Asawa created symmetrical and asymmetrical examples of this type of construction [S.435].

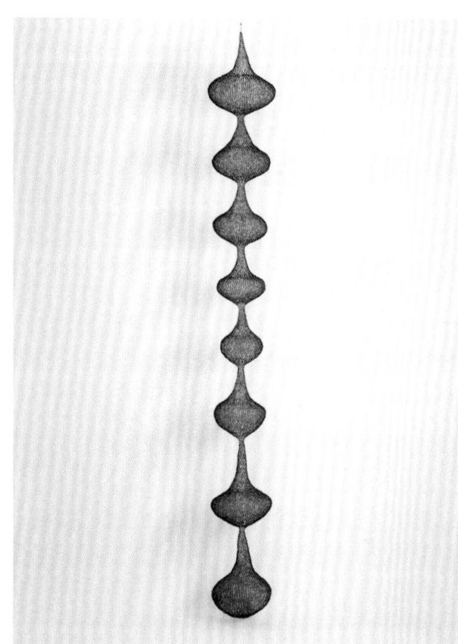

S.435 (p. 70)

Asawa later enclosed spheres suspended within single-layer, multi-lobed forms [S.042, S.541].

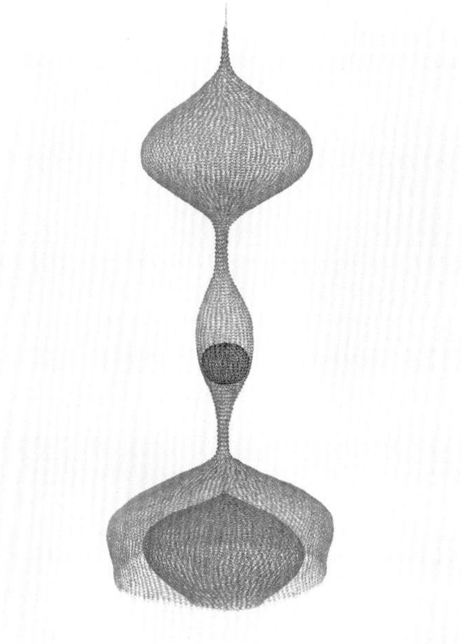

S.042 (p. 71)

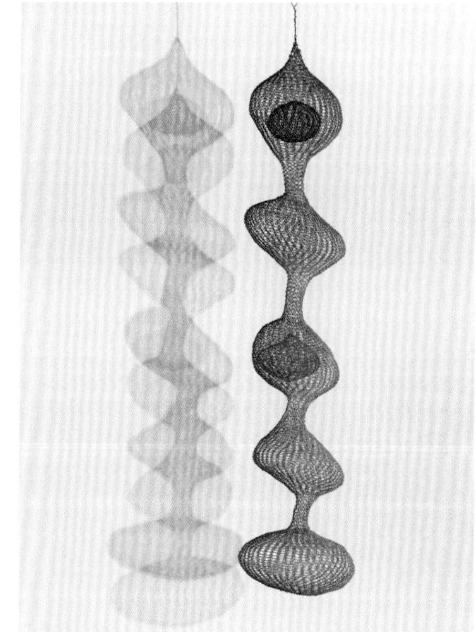

S.541 (p. 24)

Multi-Lobed Forms within Forms

Circa 1951, Asawa began constructions of sculptures that involve interior forms developing into the exterior forms. These sculptures may begin with an interior form that descends to the bottom, inverts to its exterior and ascends upward to close at the top [S.535].

These works may also be made from different, discrete sections that are joined by barbell-like connectors or have partial lobes that sit on top of other lobes [S.267]. These constructions show Asawa experimenting with the layering of form, but she had not yet developed the complex interlocking of a sculpture's interior and exterior surfaces. They do, however, show Asawa introducing different types of wire, resulting in contrasts of color.[2]

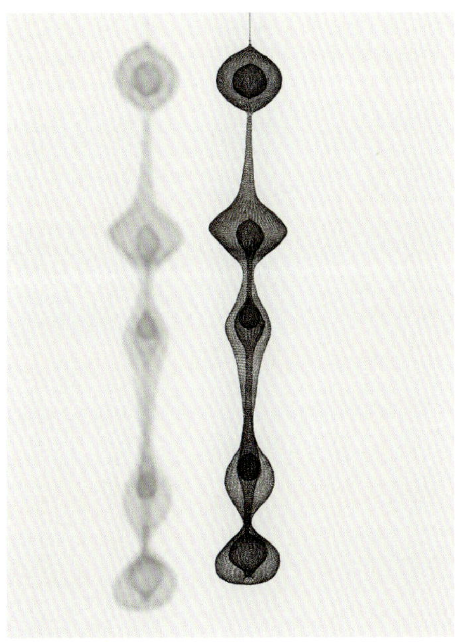

S.535 (p. 61)

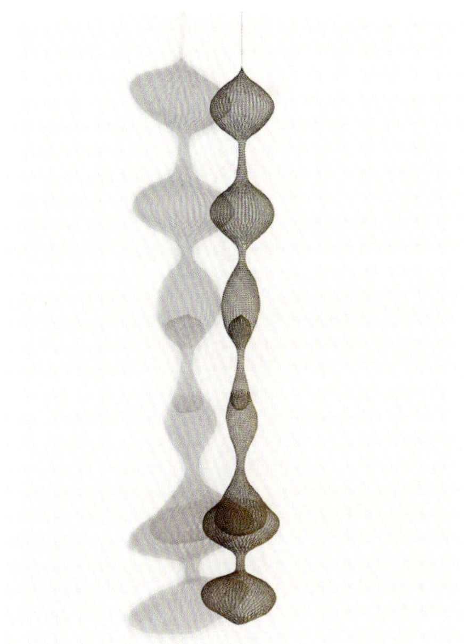

S.267*

Conical and Hyperbolic Forms

This category, first developed circa 1951, shows Asawa moving away from the sphere to explore conical forms. It features cone-like constructions linked by chain [S.030], as well as cones that intersect at oblique angles, which Asawa described as "interpenetrating" [S.166]. These sculptures are often made from the same wire and are therefore monochromatic.

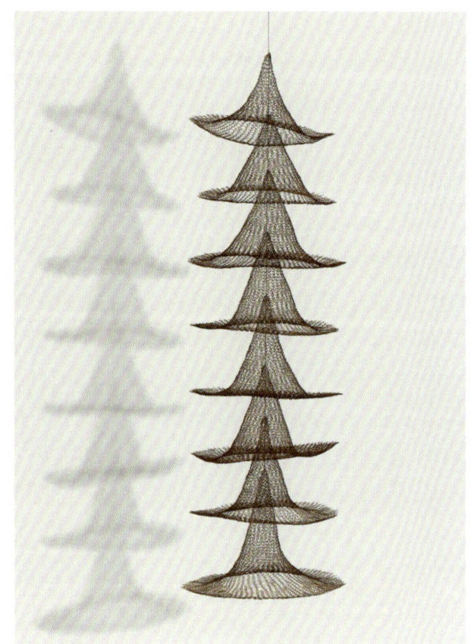

S.030 (p. 69)

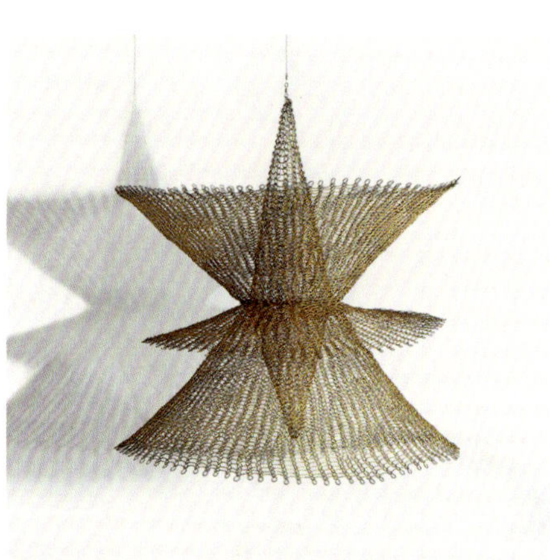

S.166 (p. 22)

By contrast, and concurrent to her multi-lobed forms within forms, Asawa used different types of wire to achieve color variations in her "hyperbolic" sculptures, which are an interlocking extension of her conical constructions [S.040]. Asawa concluded her experiments with this form by 1960.

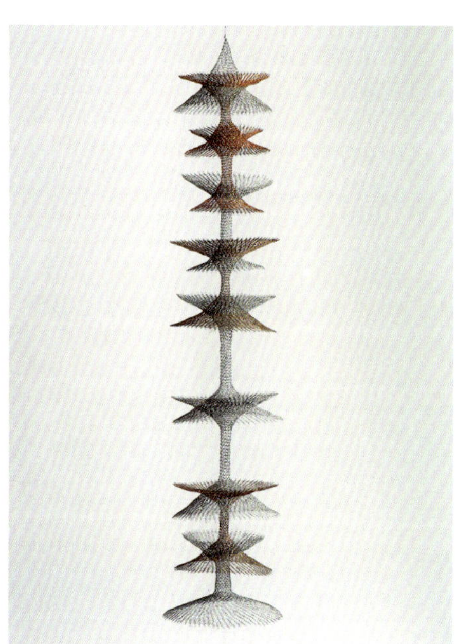

S.040 (p. 23 left)

Continuous Form within a Form

Circa 1951 Asawa began experimenting with continuous forms within forms,[3] which refers to constructions created in a series of overlapping layers that start with the innermost (or the smallest) sphere and are connected to the outermost (or the largest) sphere in graduating layers that progress from interior to exterior in a continuous surface from beginning to end. These sculptures may be single-lobed [S.095] or multi-lobed [S.453]. Asawa considered this construction to be one of her most important innovations.

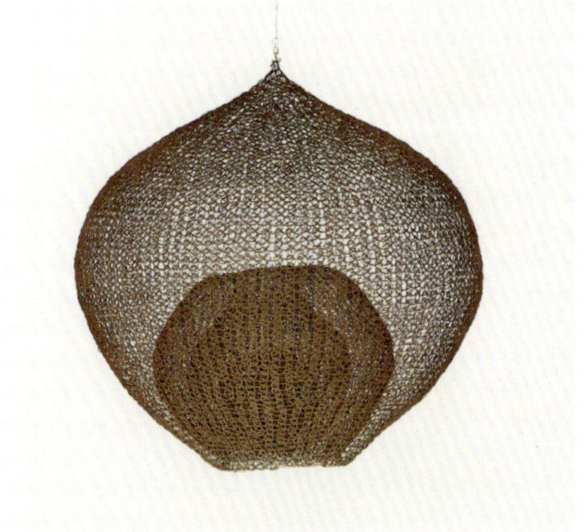

S.095 (p. 10)

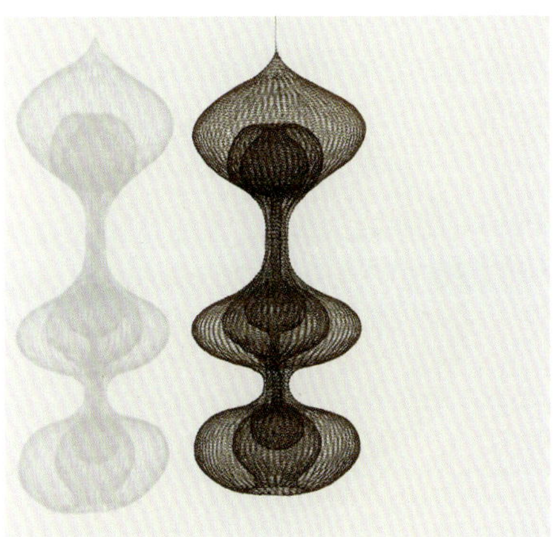

S.453 (p. 77)

In the 1980s Asawa experimented with leaving the outermost layer open [S.722].

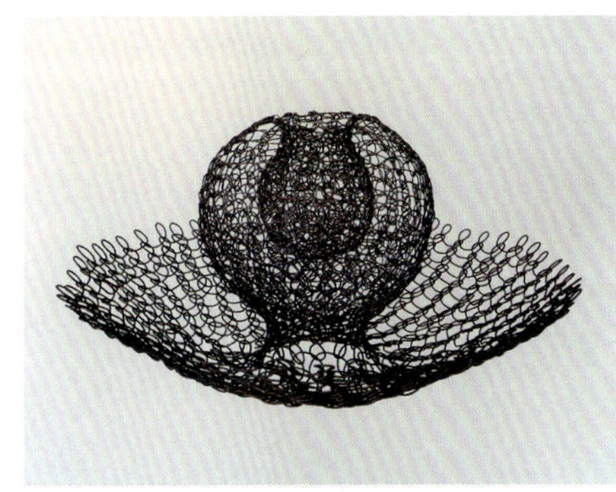

S.722*

In the 1990s, she began creating interlocking continuous form-within-a-form spheres, which are her most dense and complex interlocking forms [S.158].

Asawa also made miniature form-within-a-form constructions during the 1970s, '80s, and in 2000 (see S.077 on p. 124).

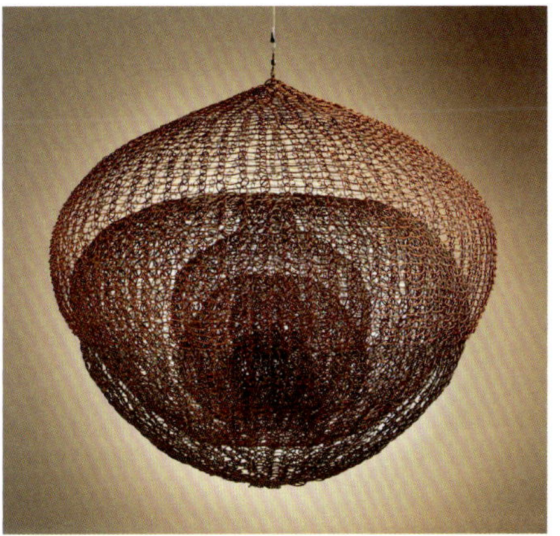

S.158*

Multilayered, Interlocking Forms within Forms

These works, developed during the mid- to late 1950s, represent the culmination of Asawa's various experiments in looped wire. She now applied the interlocking technique she developed from the interpenetrating cones to her multilobed, spherical structures. These are created by working on at least two forms at the same time, constructing an interior form that passes through the exterior layer to become the outside/outermost surface, while passing the exterior layer through the interior form to turn it into the inside/innermost surface. These complex sculptures are often colorful from the use of different wire, such as black iron, red copper, and yellow brass [S.036].

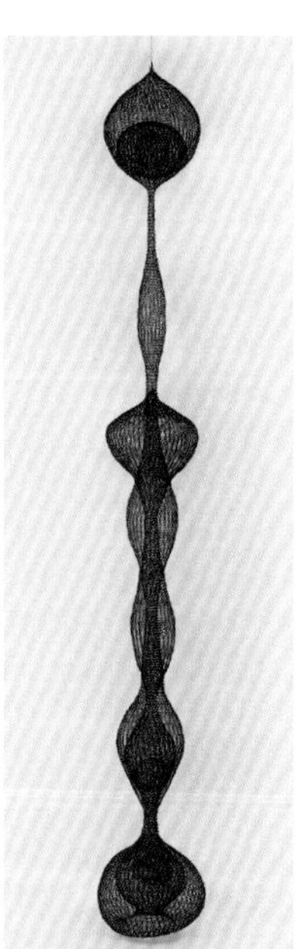

S.036 (p. 121)

Asawa created increasingly complex permutations of this form throughout the 1960s [S.065].

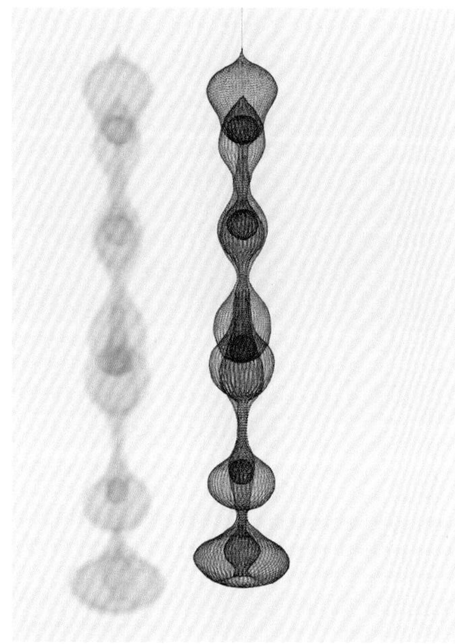

S.065 (p. 90)

In the 1960s and early '70s Asawa's experiments became more elaborate as she began to loop with multiple strands of wire coiled together, then separating three strands to two to one and then building back to three strands again. The switching between one, two, and three strands creates subtle differences in the perceived densities of the sculptures [S.035, S.634].

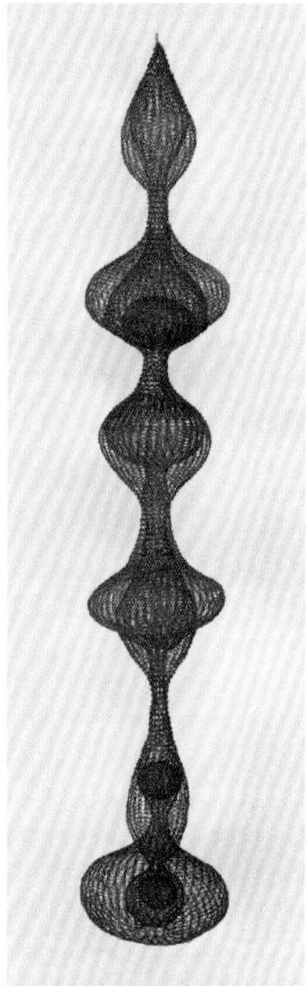

S.035 (p. 95)

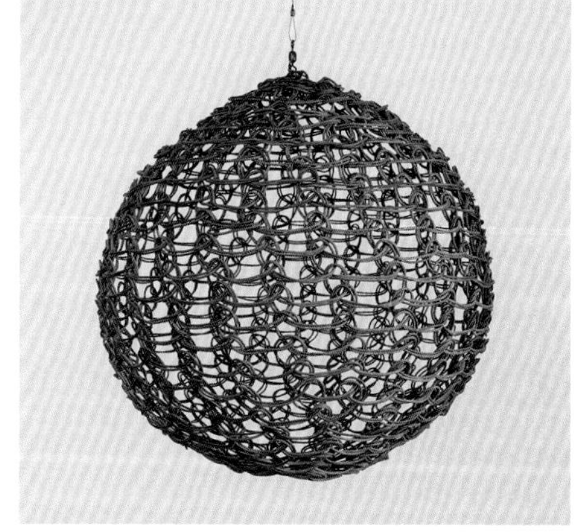

S.634 (p. 25)

Interlocking Forms

The formal challenge Asawa addressed in this category, beginning circa 1954, was how to interlock different forms, including spheres, cones, and other unique shapes. She studied how one form could be attached to, or penetrated by, another. Sculptures executed in this category are often smaller in scale [S.562, S.089].

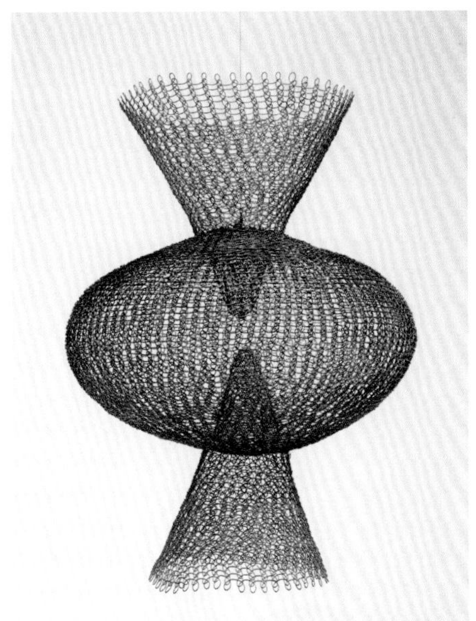

S.562 (p. 73)

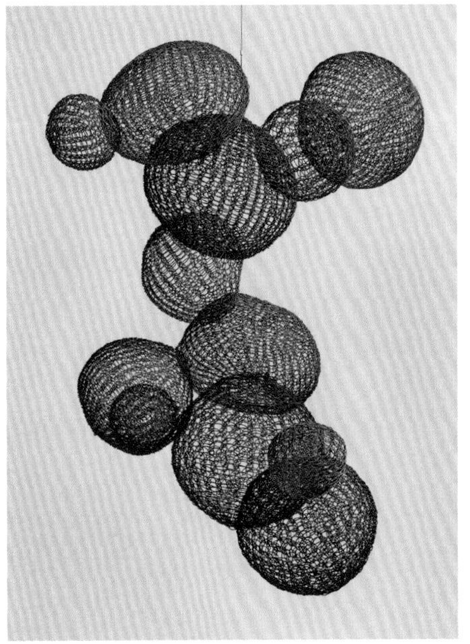

S.089 (p. 64)

Interlocking Multilayered Spheres

Some of Asawa's most complicated interlocking constructions feature three, three-layered interlocking spheres [S.208]. She created miniature variations of this form during the 1980s.

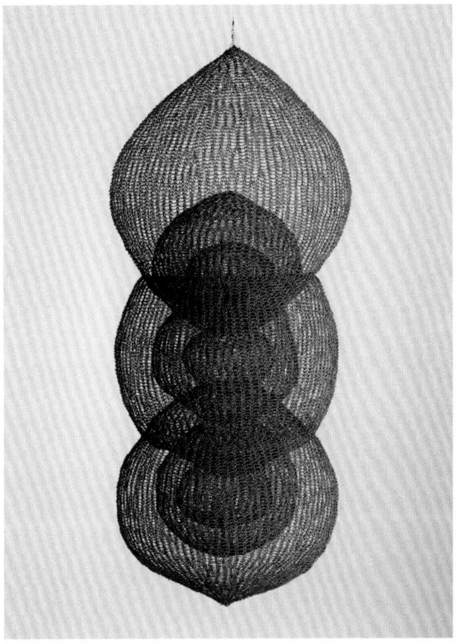

S.208 (p. 81)

Window Forms

This construction accidentally came about when Asawa cut open a looped work to correct a mistake. When split apart, the weight of the metal caused the sculpture to twist and spread open into an "open window" shape [S.659]. These forms first appeared in 1954, and were initially described as "pine cones." During 2000, Asawa made miniature examples of this construction.

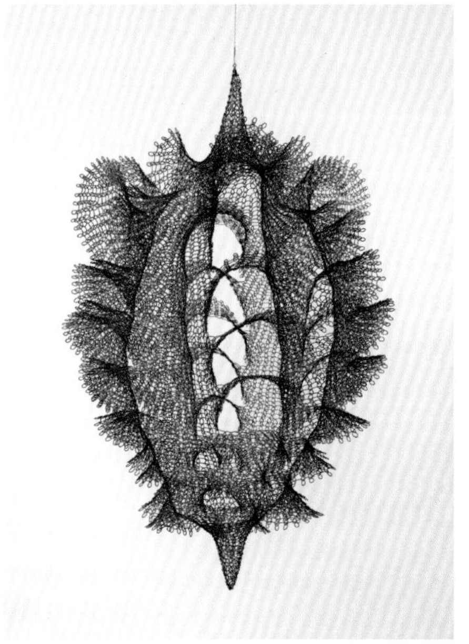

S.659 (p. 23 right)

Open Forms

Sculptures in this broad category are composed of open forms that fall outside the basket category and tend to be experimental and often playful expressions of Asawa's ideas.

These include crowns, Möbius strips, and other undulating forms [S.183].

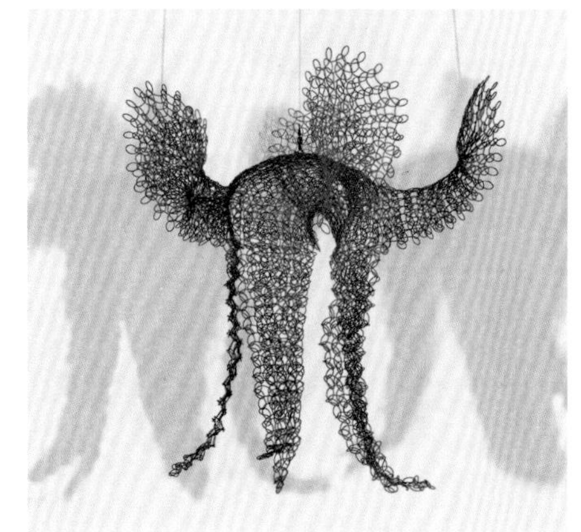

S.183*

Trumpet Forms

The trumpet form, which Asawa began articulating circa 1958, represents one of the most complex interlocking forms. It is also the final formal innovation she achieved through her looped-wire technique.

This construction intrigued Asawa because, once interlocked, the inside surface of the work became the outside surface. She continued to make this form into the 1970s and '80s, including miniatures [S.306].

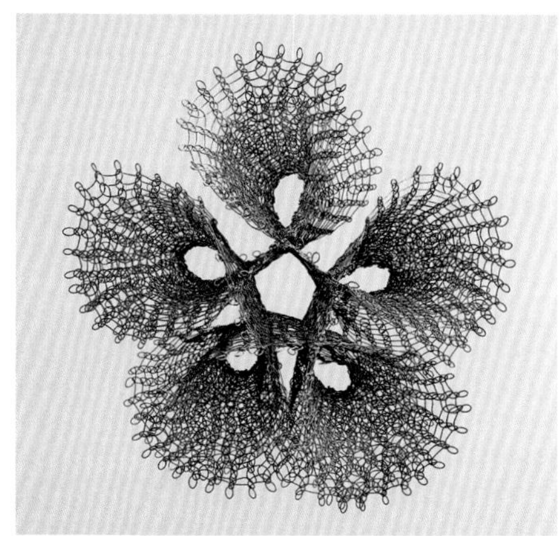

S.306 (p. 62)

Cast Bronze Sculptures

Cast bronze sculptures evolved from Asawa's attempts to accurately render the mermaid's tail for her 1968 *Andrea* fountain at Ghirardelli Square in San Francisco. In an effort to create a rough, scale-like surface, she looped the tail out of heavy aluminum wire, bent it into a sinuous curve, coated it in wax, invested it in plaster, and finally cast it in bronze [S.218]. Though traditional casting methods were used, all works are unique.

Additional looped-wire constructions that Asawa later cast into bronze include baskets, windows, and undulating open forms. The casting process required the works to be dipped in wax; the pendulous drips added yet another expression to this form [S.120, S.130].

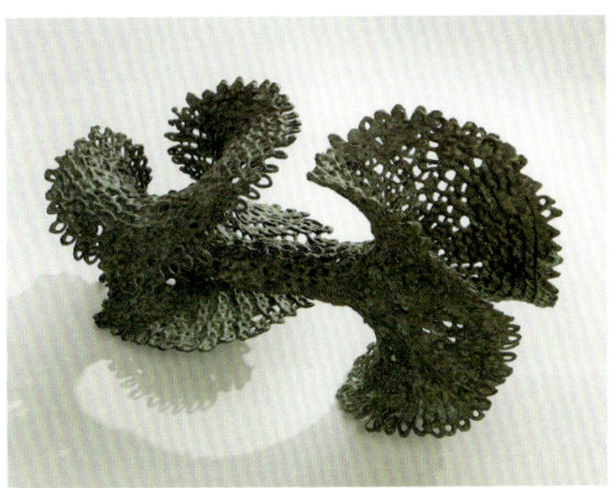

S.218*

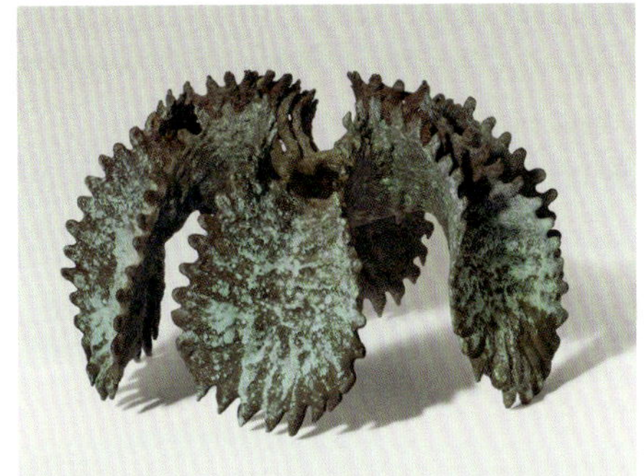

S.120 (p. 106)

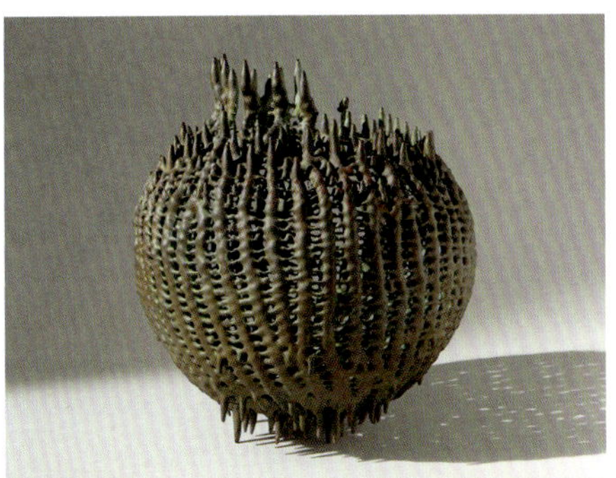

S.130 (p. 32)

Tied-Wire Sculptures

Inspired by the skeleton of a desert plant she received from Paul and Virginia Hassel in 1962, Asawa attempted to draw its form, but was unable to do so to her satisfaction. She then constructed the plant in wire, which enabled her to draw its form on paper. Tied-wire sculptures are a direct outgrowth of this specific exercise with the desert plant. For this new technique Asawa gathered wire into bundles, then shaped, divided, and tied them into branching forms.

Single-Stem Form

Asawa's first efforts with the tied-wire technique date to 1962. She constructed these earlier works with wire that was gathered and tied into a single stem and then branched out into a tree-like formation. Her materials were soft brass and copper wire cut to length from spooled wire. This particular kind of wire's pliability lent itself to constructions that were irregular, gnarled, and soft-edged [S.058].

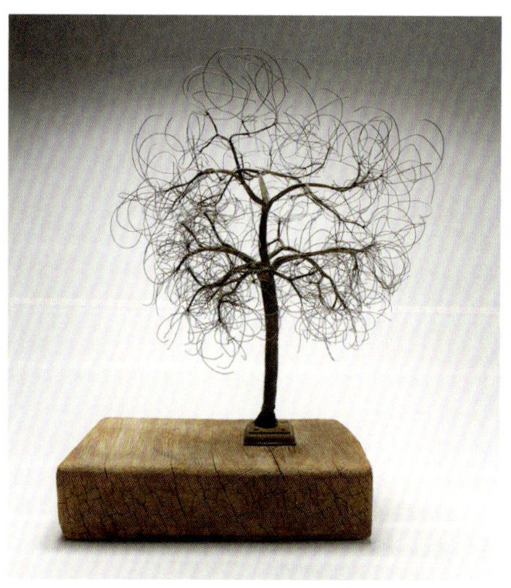

S.058*

The first tied-wire sculptures were freestanding, but Asawa quickly inverted the form, suspending her works from the ceiling [S.184]. She also began using stronger galvanized steel wire from precut lengths, which she divided into radiating, straight branches [S.178].

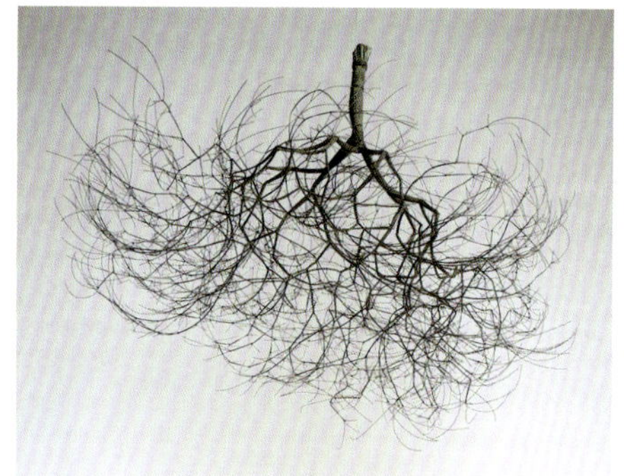

S.184 (p. 112)

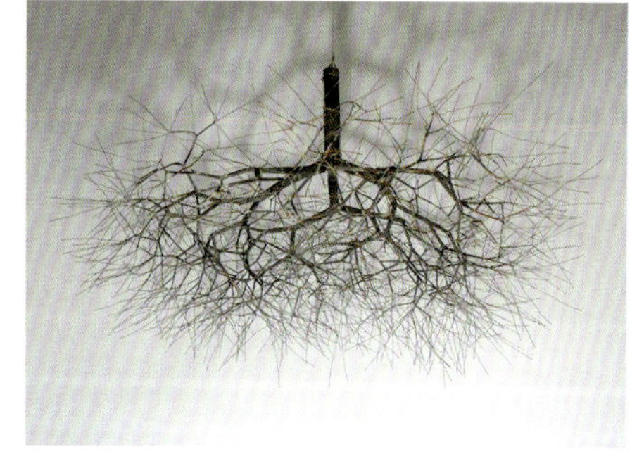

S.178*

Hanging, Center-Tied Forms

Asawa developed this form in 1962–63, concurrently with the Single-Stem Form, by tying a single bundle of wire at midpoint and branching it into opposing directions. Trees served as the inspiration for this type of construction, with root systems mirroring and even equaling the above-ground canopies [S.177].

Pushing this idea further, Asawa began spreading out denser configurations of wire from a tied midpoint, which she clustered into radiating, spherical formations.

She occasionally treated the tips of these sculptures with resin or beads to create glistening effects similar to the raindrops she noticed on the pine tree needles in her garden after rain [S.479]. Works in this category can be either suspended or mounted on stands, and viewed from all sides.

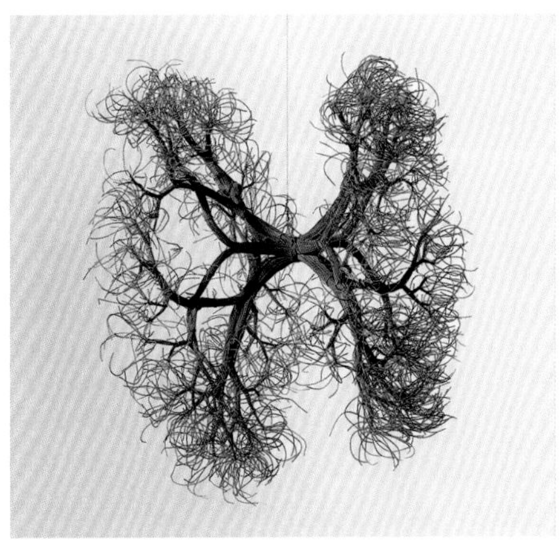

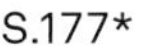

S.177*

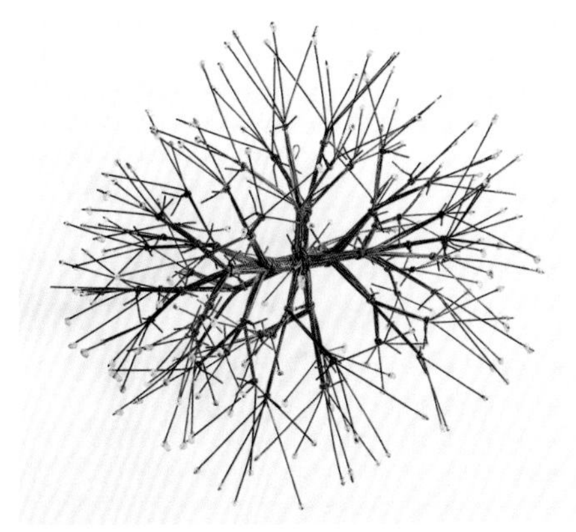

S.479*

Hanging, Double-Sided Forms

Asawa's evolving interest in how the arrangement of wires emanating from a midpoint affects, and even determines, the construction of the branching forms, is the line of inquiry that led to sculptures in this category. She made these works by creating two centered and symmetrical structures that interlock and lead to complex and increasingly elaborate offshoots [S.229]. Unlike the hanging, center-tied forms, these sculptures have definite fronts and sides.

Included in this category are a few stained-glass sculptures that Asawa made in collaboration with glass artist Bruce Sherman in the 1970s.

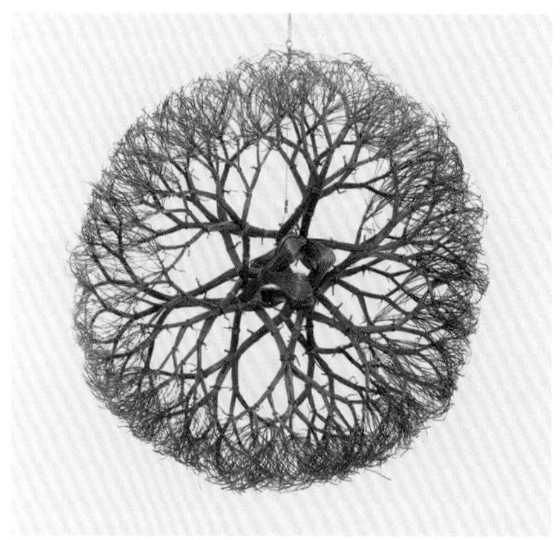

S.229 (p. 111)

Wall-Mounted Petal Forms

This mode of construction developed from Asawa's ongoing efforts to understand how the arrangement of the center of a sculpture affects the form that the work eventually takes. In 1965 she started to construct works in this category by gathering straight wires into separate bundles, which she then formed into individual "petals," before finally tying them together in a geometric pattern. The branching begins where the petal forms end [S.557].

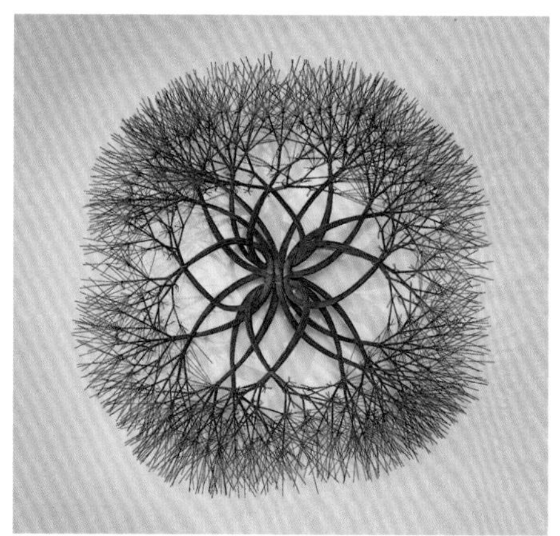

S.557 (p. 27)

Asawa experimented with different arrangements of the petal centers, configuring them in spirals as well as interlocking and overlapping them [S.238]. Asawa flattened the sculptures for wall-mounted presentations.

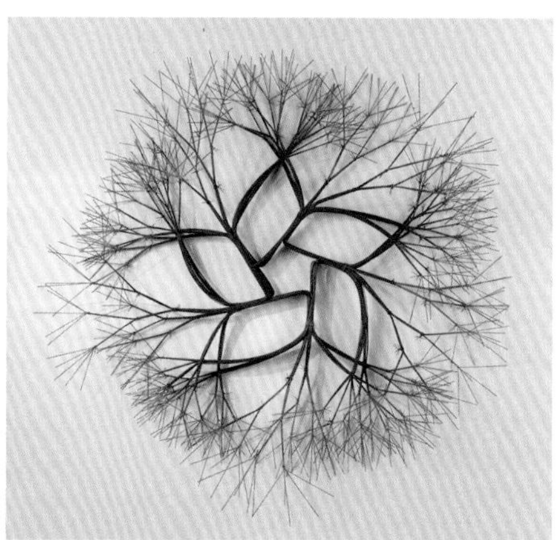

S.238*

Wall-Mounted Branching Form

In the mid-1960s, close to the development of the open petal form, Asawa began using straight bundles of wire to create a myriad of open centers. The centers are often formed into five- or six-pointed stars, but they can also be pentagons and crosses. Asawa constructed them from either intersecting or v-shaped bundles of wire that are tied adjacent to each other, with branches that divide and terminate in single strands [S.242, S.145].

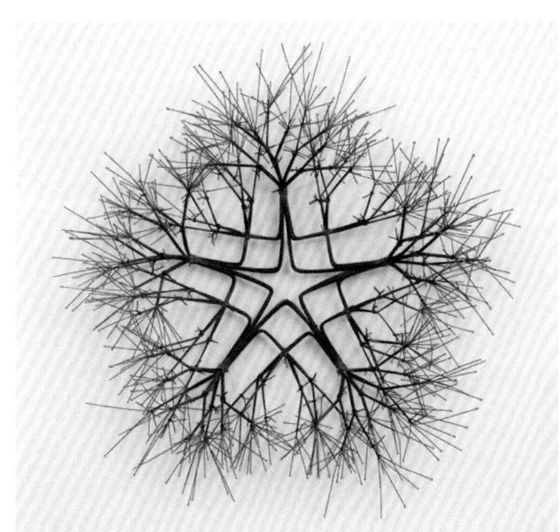

S.242*

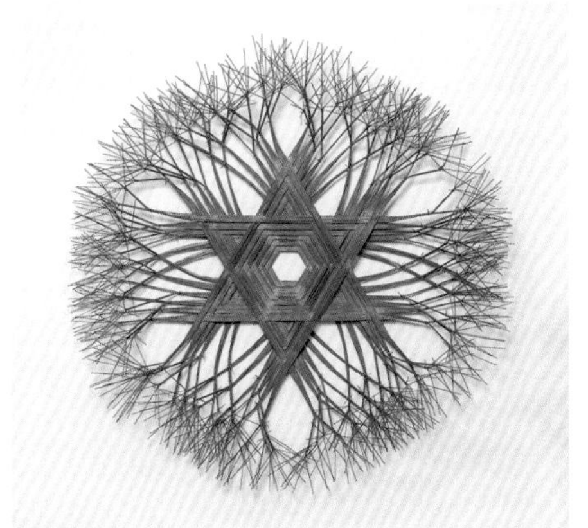

S.145*

Electroplated Sculptures

This body of work emerged from Asawa's friendship with Cyril "Mac" MacDonald, an industrial plater who helped her clean and oxidize her looped-wire sculptures beginning around 1957. In his shop, Mac used an electroplating process to restore car bumpers. The process involved submerging copper bars into an electrically charged sulfuric acid bath, which caused the impurities from the bumpers to latch onto the copper bars, creating crusty growths. Intrigued by this electroplating process, Asawa studied how she could repurpose it to her explorations in tied wire.

All electroplated sculptures started as tied-wire sculptures in copper wire, which Asawa would soak in an acid bath for about three weeks to grow the rough surface she wanted. She experimented with different gauges of wire, soaking times, and forms, including wire she wrapped around glass bottles. In 1965, after experimenting for about two years, Asawa stopped creating electroplated sculptures, having concluded that the end result was too fragile [S.059, S.136, S.021].

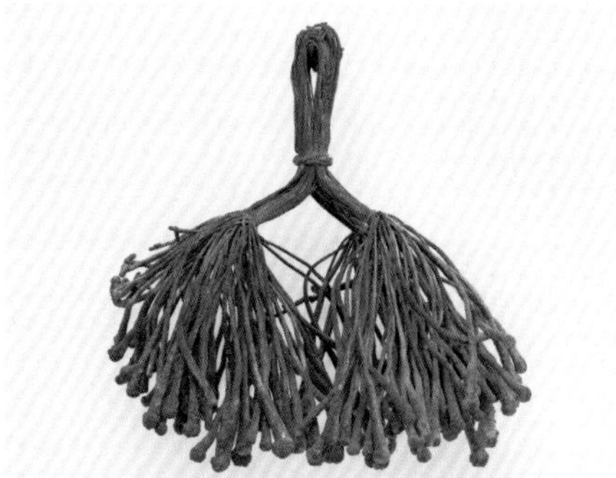

S.059 (p. 113)

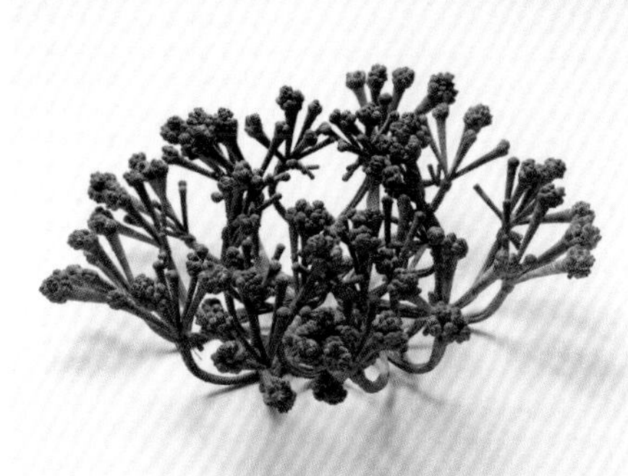

S.136 (p. 115)

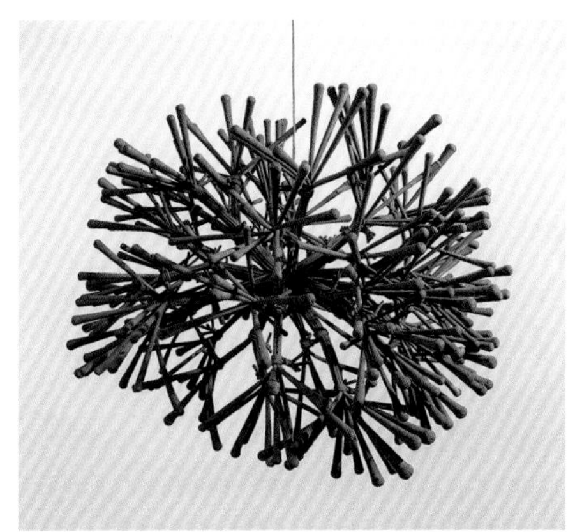

S.021 (p. 29)

Evolution of Form captions for starred (*) works

Page 131
Untitled (S.364, Freestanding Basket), ca. 1948–49. Copper wire, 2¼ × 6½ × 6½ inches (5.7 × 16.5 × 16.5 cm)

Page 133, right
Untitled (S.267, Hanging Six-Lobed, Four-Part, Discontinuous Surface, with Interior Forms in the Third, Fourth, and Fifth Lobes), ca. 1952. Brass wire, 85 × 13 × 13 inches (215.9 × 33 × 33 cm)

Page 135, center
Untitled (S.722, Hanging Single-Lobed, Two-Layered Continuous Form within a Form, with a Collar Forming a Partial Third Layer), ca. 1990s. Copper wire, 4 × 7½ × 7½ inches (10.2 × 19.1 × 19.1 cm)

Page 135, right
Untitled (S.158, Hanging Two Interlocked, Three-Layered Continuous Form within a Form Lobes), ca. 1996. Oxidized copper wire, 20 × 19 × 19 inches (50.8 × 48.3 × 48.3 cm)

Page 138, center
Untitled (S.183, Hanging Open Form with Five Upward Ears and Five Downward Tails), ca. 1954. Galvanized steel wire, 17 × 14 × 14 inches (43.2 × 35.6 × 35.6 cm)

Page 139, left
Study for Mermaid's Tail, *Andrea*, Ghirardelli Square Fountain (S.218, Freestanding Reversible Undulating Form), ca. 1967. Bronze, natural patina, 16½ × 29½ × 19 inches (41.9 × 74.9 × 48.3 cm)

Page 140, left
Untitled (S.058, Freestanding Tied-Wire Tree Form), 1962. Naturally oxidized brass wire mounted on a driftwood base, 18 × 13¾ × 12¼ inches (45.7 × 34.9 × 31.1 cm)

Page 140, bottom right
Untitled (S.178, Hanging Tied-Wire, Single-Stem, Multi-Branched Form Based on Nature), 1962. Galvanized steel wire, 24 × 39 × 39 inches (61 × 99.1 × 99.1 cm)

Page 141, left
Untitled (S.177, Hanging Tied-Wire, Double-Sided, Center-Tied, Six-Branched Form Based on Nature), ca. 1962. Copper wire, naturally oxidized, 27 × 27 × 19 inches (68.6 × 68.6 × 48.3 cm)

Page 141, right
Untitled (S.479, Hanging Tied-Wire, Closed-Center, Double-Sided, Multi-Branched Form Based on Nature), 1963. Brass and copper wire with glass beads and resin, 11 × 12 × 11 inches (27.9 × 30.5 × 27.9 cm)

Page 142, right
Untitled (S.238, Wall-Mounted Tied-Wire, Open-Center, Five-Petaled Form Based on Nature), mid to late 1970s. Bronze wire with natural verdigris, 42 × 42 × 8 inches (106.7 × 106.7 × 20.3 cm)

Page 143, top left
Untitled (S.242, Wall-Mounted Tied-Wire, Open-Center, Five-Branched Form Based on Nature), ca. 1965–69. Bronze wire with resin coated tips, 21 × 21 × 6 inches (53.3 × 53.3 × 15.2 cm)

Page 143, bottom left
Untitled (S.145, Wall-Mounted Tied-Wire, Open-Center, Six-Branched Form Based on Nature), ca. 1968. Galvanized steel wire, 44 × 44 × 8 inches (111.8 × 111.8 × 20.3 cm)

Notes

1. Jacqueline Hoefer, "Ruth Asawa: A Working Life," in *The Sculpture of Ruth Asawa: Contours in the Air*, ed. Daniell Cornell (San Francisco: Fine Arts Museums of San Francisco; and Berkeley: University of California Press, 2006), 16.
2. In a letter dated December 1, 1951, Asawa's husband, Albert Lanier, wrote to his parents, describing how she had made a sculpture of "enameled copper wires varying in color from a red-rust through purple and a blue black. The wire came from the electrical coils of smashed-up slot machines that were recently outlawed here [San Francisco]."
3. Ray Johnson's description of one of her sculptures he saw in New York in 1952 probably gave Asawa the terminology "form within form." In a letter to her he wrote, "My favorite is the one I saw at Laverne's of forms within forms within forms."

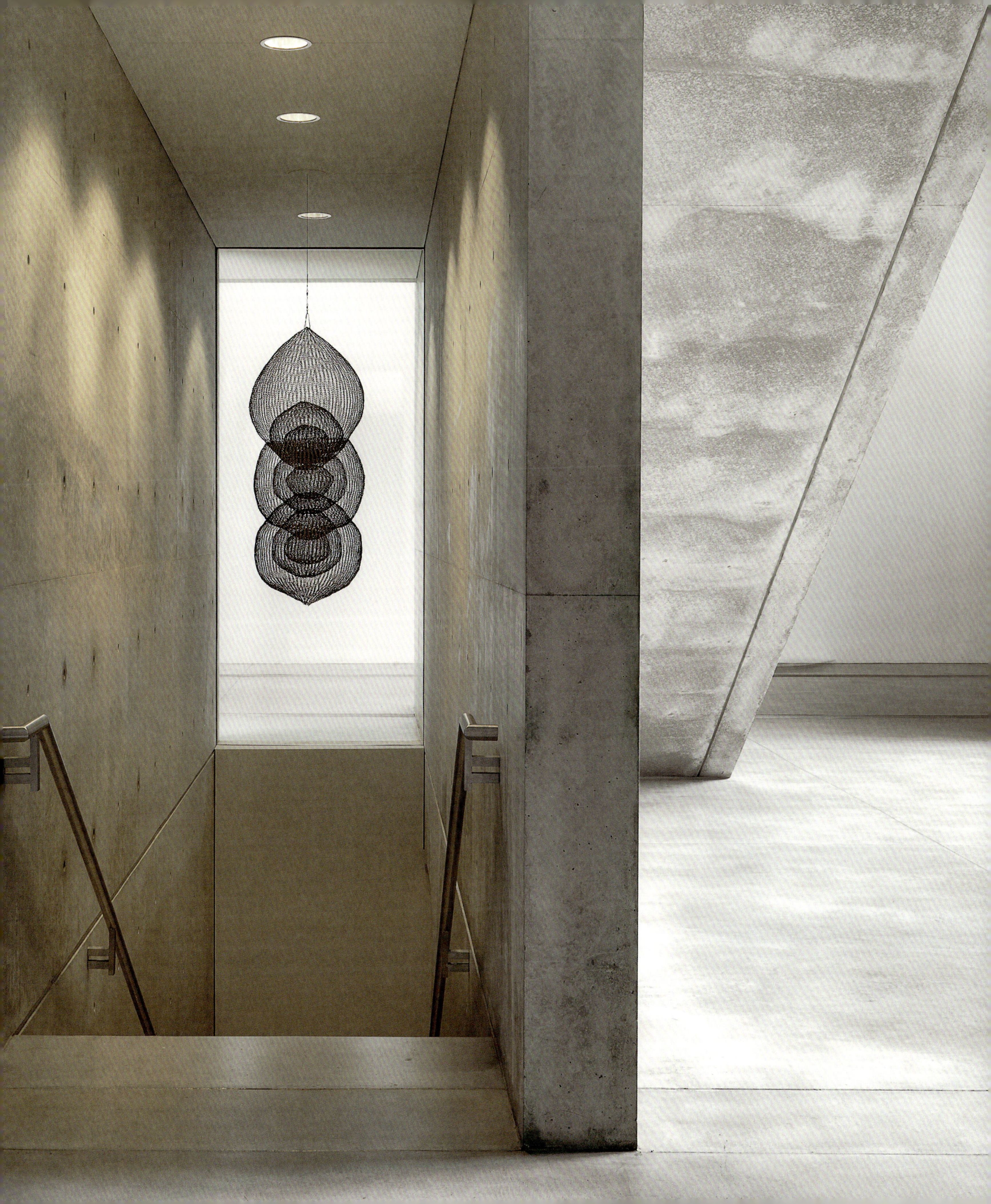

Exhibition Checklist

All works listed chronologically; most are untitled and include inventory numbers and descriptions using a terminology developed in collaboration with the artist.

Untitled (BMC.119, Early Organic Biomorphic Forms), ca. 1946–49
Cut coated papers in brown and white on plywood
14¹⁵⁄₁₆ × 27¹⁵⁄₁₆ inches (38 × 71 cm)
Harvard Art Museums/Busch-Reisinger Museum; Gift of Josef Albers, BR49.406
p. 53

Untitled (BMC.124, Meander Black and Red), ca. 1946–49
Black and red ink with graphite on tracing paper
17 × 22 inches (43.2 × 55.9 cm)
Harvard Art Museums/Busch-Reisinger Museum; Gift of Josef Albers, BR49.387
p. 15

Untitled (BMC.66, Stem with Leaves: "Background" Painting), ca. 1948–49
Watercolor over graphite on paper
19¾ × 16 inches (50.2 × 40.6 cm)
Fine Arts Museums of San Francisco; Gift of the artist
p. 54

Untitled (BMC.75, Double Sheet Clusters), ca. 1948–49
Stamped black ink on newsprint
17¼ × 22 inches (43.8 × 55.9 cm)
Fine Arts Museums of San Francisco; Gift of the artist
p. 97

Untitled (BMC.83, Dogwood Leaves), ca. 1948–49
Oil and watercolor on paper
9½ × 8¼ inches (24.1 × 21 cm)
Private collection
p. 56

Untitled (BMC.96, In and Out), ca. 1948–49
Oil paint on paper
6½ × 9¼ inches (16.5 × 23.5 cm)
Fine Arts Museums of San Francisco; Gift of Aiko and Laurence Cuneo
p. 58

Untitled (BMC.117, BMC Laundry Stamp on Newsprint), ca. 1948–49
Stamped black ink on newsprint
16½ × 22 inches (41.9 × 55.9 cm)
Harvard Art Museums/Busch-Reisinger Museum; Gift of Josef Albers, BR49.390
p. 59

Untitled (BMC.143, Dancer), ca. 1948–49
Oil paint on paper
6¾ × 5½ inches (17.2 × 14 cm)
Fine Arts Museums of San Francisco; Gift of the artist
p. 60

Untitled (BMC.144, Dancers), ca. 1948–49
Blue colored pencil and watercolor on tracing paper
8 × 10½ inches (20.3 × 26.7 cm)
Fine Arts Museums of San Francisco; Gift of the artist
p. 39

Untitled (S.264, Hanging Two-Lobed Continuous Form), 1949
Oxidized copper wire
16 × 4 × 4 inches (40.6 × 10.2 × 10.2 cm)
Private collection
p. 19

Untitled (S.535, Hanging Five-Lobed Continuous Form within a Form with Two Interior Spheres and One Teardrop Form), 1951
Iron and brass wire
87 × 12½ × 12½ inches (221 × 31.8 × 31.8 cm)
Collection of Chuck and Kathy Harper
p. 61

Untitled (S.541, Hanging Five-Lobed Continuous Form, with Spheres in the First and Third Lobes), ca. 1951–54
Brass wire
54 × 11 × 11 inches (137.2 × 27.9 × 27.9 cm)
Private collection
p. 24

Untitled (S.793, Hanging Two Spheres Attached with Chain), ca. 1951–52
Brass wire, brass chain
18 × 7⅝ × 7⅝ inches (45.7 × 19.4 × 19.4 cm)
Private collection
p. 19

Untitled (SF.003, Undulating Parallelograms), ca. 1951–52
Pen and brush and black ink on gouache on board
27 × 27 inches (68.6 × 68.6 cm)
Private collection
p. 63

Untitled (SF.046b, Potato Print, Blue/Orange), 1951–52
Blue and orange ink on paper
14 × 10 inches (35.6 × 25.4 cm)
Private collection, New Jersey, courtesy David Zwirner
p. 65

Untitled (S.030, Hanging Eight Separate Cones Suspended through Their Centers), ca. 1952
Iron wire
76 × 24 × 24 inches (193 × 61 × 61 cm)
Private collection
p. 69

Untitled (S.095, Hanging Single-Lobed, Six-Layered Continuous Form within a Form), ca. 1952
Iron wire
15½ × 17 × 17 inches (39.4 × 43.2 × 43.2 cm)
Private collection
p. 10

Untitled (S.166, Hanging Two Interlocking Cones with a Center Disc), ca. 1952
Brass wire
22 × 21 × 21 inches (55.9 × 53.3 × 53.3 cm)
Private collection
p. 22

Untitled (S.435, Hanging Eight-Lobed, Single-Layered Continuous Tear-Drop Form), 1952
Iron wire
120 × 12 × 12 inches (304.8 × 30.5 × 30.5 cm)
William and Joan Roth Collection
p. 70

Untitled (S.334, Hanging Fifteen-Lobed [Seven Open and Eight Interlocking] Continuous Form), ca. 1953–55
Enameled copper wire
134 × 8 × 8 inches (340.4 × 20.3 × 20.3 cm)
Private collection
p. 57

Untitled (S.042, Hanging Three-Lobed Continuous Form, with a Sphere in the Second Lobe, and an Open Sphere Suspended from the Bottom), 1954
Aluminum and brass wire
90 × 36 × 36 inches (228.6 × 91.4 × 91.4 cm)
Private collection
p. 71

Untitled (S.373, Hanging Six-Lobed, Multilayered Interlocking Continuous Form within a Form), 1954
Enameled and oxidized copper wire
87 × 8 × 8 inches (221 × 20.3 × 20.3 cm)
Black Mountain College Museum + Arts Center Collection; Gift of Lorna Blaine Halper
p. 72

Untitled (S.562, Hanging Sphere with Two Cones that Penetrate the Sphere from Top and Bottom), ca. 1954
Galvanized steel wire and brass wire
28 × 18 × 18 inches (71.1 × 45.7 × 45.7 cm)
The Museum of Fine Arts, Houston; Museum purchase funded by the Caroline Wiess Law Accessions Endowment Fund. 2014.194
p. 73

Untitled (S.026, Hanging Three-Lobed, Continuous Form with Penetrating Cones within Each Lobe), ca. 1955
Enameled copper wire and brass wire
60 × 19 × 19 inches (152.4 × 48.3 × 48.3 cm)
Collection of Holly Johnson and Parker Harris
p. 74

Untitled (S.398, Hanging Eight-Lobed, Four-Part, Discontinuous Surface Form within a Form, with Spheres in the Seventh and Eighth Lobes), ca. 1955
Copper, brass, and iron wire
104½ × 14½ × 14½ inches (265.4 × 36.8 × 36.8 cm)
The Museum of Modern Art, New York. Promised gift of Alice and Tom Tisch, 2016
p. 75

Untitled (S.040, Hanging Eight-and-a-Half Open Hyperbolic Shapes that Penetrate Each Other), ca. 1956
Enameled copper wire and galvanized steel wire
78 × 16 × 16 inches (198.1 × 40.6 × 40.6 cm)
Private collection
p. 23

Untitled (S.089, Hanging Asymmetrical Twelve Interlocking Bubbles), ca. 1957
Galvanized steel, brass, and iron wire
26 × 22 × 17 inches (66 × 55.9 × 43.2 cm)
Private collection
p. 64

Untitled (S.270, Hanging Six-Lobed, Complex Interlocking Continuous Form within a Form with Two Interior Spheres), 1955 (refabricated 1957–58)
Brass and steel wire
63⅞ × 14$\frac{15}{16}$ × 14$\frac{15}{16}$ inches (162.2 × 37.9 × 37.9 cm)
Whitney Museum of American Art, New York; Gift of Howard Lipman, 63.38
p. 21

Untitled (S.453, Hanging Three-Lobed, Three-Layered Continuous Form within a Form), ca. 1957–59
Iron wire
41¼ × 16½ × 16½ inches (104.8 × 41.9 × 41.9 cm)
Private collection, courtesy David Zwirner
p. 77

Untitled (S.113, Hanging Five-Lobed, Multilayered Continuous Form within a Form with Spheres in the First and Third Lobes), ca. 1958
Copper and brass wire
90 × 16½ × 16½ inches (228.6 × 41.9 × 41.9 cm)
Collection of the San José Museum of Art; Gift of the artist, in honor of the San José Museum of Art's 35th Anniversary. 2003.28.02
p. 78

Untitled (S.114, Hanging Six-Lobed Continuous Form within a Form with One Suspended and Two Tied Spheres), ca. 1958
Iron, copper, and brass wire
131 × 22 × 22 inches (332.7 × 55.9 × 55.9 cm)
San Francisco Museum of Modern Art; Phyllis C. Wattis Fund for Major Accessions
p. 79

Untitled (S.155, Hanging Seven-Lobed, Multilayered Interlocking Continuous Form with a Sphere Suspended in the Top and Fifth Lobes), ca. 1958
Copper and brass wire
79 × 15½ × 15½ inches (200.7 × 39.4 × 39.4 cm)
Collection of the San José Museum of Art; Gift of the artist, in honor of the San José Museum of Art's 35th Anniversary. 2003.28.01
p. 99

Untitled (S.433, Hanging Nine Open Hyperbolic Shapes Joined Laterally), ca. 1958
Oxidized copper wire
76 × 15 × 15 inches (193 × 38.1 × 38.1 cm)
William and Joan Roth Collection
p. 83

Bentwood Rocker (MI.176), ca. 1959–63
Pen and black ink on paper
18 × 22¾ inches (45.7 × 57.8 cm)
Black Mountain College Museum + Arts Center Collection. Gift of Rita Newman
p. 107

Untitled (S.036, Hanging Seven-Lobed, Multilayered Interlocking Continuous Form within a Form with Spheres in the First, Sixth, and Seventh Lobes), 1959
Oxidized copper and brass wire
137½ × 17 × 17 inches (349.3 × 43.2 × 43.2 cm)
Collection of the San José Museum of Art; Gift of the artist, with additional support from the Collection Committee, in honor of the San José Museum of Art's 35th Anniversary. 2003.28.04
p. 121

Untitled (S.208, Hanging Three Interlocked, Three-Layered Spheres), 1959–60
Enameled copper wire
48 × 22 × 22 inches (121.9 × 55.9 × 55.9 cm)
Private collection
p. 81

Untitled (S.659, Hanging Single Section, Reversible Open Window Form), ca. 1959
Nickel-plated copper wire
37½ × 25 × 25 inches (95.3 × 63.5 × 63.5 cm)
Private collection, courtesy David Zwirner
p. 23

Untitled (AB.004, Waves), late 1950s–early 1961
Pen and black ink on tracing paper
23¾ × 19 inches (60.3 × 48.3 cm)
Private collection
p. 85

Untitled (SF.030, Blue Triangles on Brown), ca. late 1950s
Watercolor and tempera paint on matboard
30 × 28 inches (76.2 × 71.1 cm)
Private collection
p. 86

Untitled (SF.031, Red Meander on Pink), ca. late 1950s
Tempera paint on matboard
28 × 30 inches (71.1 × 76.2 cm)
Private collection
p. 87

Untitled (S.065, Hanging Seven-Lobed, Multilayered Continuous Form within a Form with Spheres in the Second, Third, Fourth, and Sixth Lobes), ca. 1960–63
Oxidized copper and brass wire
94 × 17½ × 17½ inches (238.8× 44.5 × 44.5 cm)
Private collection
p. 90

Untitled (PF.1015, Horse's Tail), 1961
Pen and black ink on rice paper mounted on board
35 × 23 inches (88.9 × 58.4 cm)
Private collection
p. 101

Untitled (S.046 a, b, c & d, Hanging Group of Four, Two-Lobed Forms), 1961
Collection of Diana Nelson and John Atwater
p. 93

S.046a (has a sphere in the top lobe)
Oxidized copper wire and brass wire
60 × 17 × 17 inches (152.4 × 43.2 × 43.2 cm)

S.046b (has no internal spheres)
Brass wire
21 × 12 × 12 inches (53.3 × 30.5 × 30.5 cm)

S.046c (has a single sphere in the bottom lobe)
Oxidized copper wire and brass wire
32 × 13 × 13 inches (81.3 × 33 × 33 cm)

S.046d (has two spheres in the top lobe)
Copper wire and brass wire
41 × 16 × 16 inches (104.1 × 40.6 × 40.6 cm)

Untitled (S.266, Hanging Seven-Lobed, Multilayered Interlocking Continuous Form within a Form), 1961
Brass and copper wire
115 × 22 × 22 inches (292.1 × 55.9 × 55.9 cm)
Snyder Family Living Trust
p. 94

Untitled (S.035, Hanging Six-Lobed, Multilayered Interlocking Continuous Form within a Form with Spheres in the Second, Fifth, and Sixth Lobes), ca. 1962
Brass and copper wire
88 × 15½ × 15½ inches (223.5 × 39.4 × 39.4 cm)
Collection of the San José Museum of Art; Gift of the artist, in honor of the San José Museum of Art's 35th Anniversary
p. 95

Untitled (S.041, Hanging Four Layers of Hourglass Forms Surrounding a Bud-Shaped Center with an Intersecting Disk in Top), ca. 1962
Galvanized steel and iron wire
29 × 31 × 31 inches (73.7 × 78.7 × 78.7 cm)
Private collection
p. 127

Untitled (S.184, Hanging Tied-Wire, Single-Stem, Multi-Branched Form Based on Nature), ca. 1962
Galvanized steel wire
30 × 40 × 40 inches (76.2 × 101.6 × 101.6 cm)
Collection of Diana Nelson and John Atwater
p. 112

Untitled (S.445, Hanging Single Section, Open Windows Form), ca. 1962
Copper wire
56 × 19 × 19 inches (142.2 × 48.3 × 48.3 cm)
Collection of Mrs. Philip A. Hassel
p. 82

Untitled (S.021, Hanging Electroplated Tied-Wire, Center-Tied, Spherical Multi-Branched Form Based on Nature), ca. 1963
Electroplated copper wire
10¼ × 10¼ × 11 inches (26 × 26 × 27.9 cm)
Private collection
p. 29

Untitled (S.059, Wall-Mounted Electroplated Tied-Wire, Center-Tied, Four-Branched Form Based on Nature), ca. 1963
Electroplated copper wire
7⅝ × 8 × 4 inches (19.4 × 20.3 × 10.2 cm)
Private collection
p. 113

Untitled (S.132, Freestanding Electroplated Tied-Wire, Organic Form Based on Nature), ca. 1963
Electroplated copper wire
6½ × 8½ × 8½ inches (16.5 × 21.6 × 21.6 cm)
Private collection
p. 116

Untitled (SD.263, Tied-Wire Sculpture Drawing with Six-Branch Center and Drops at the Ends), ca. 1963–69
Pen and black ink on Japanese paper
6 × 17¾ inches (15.2 × 45.1 cm)
Fine Arts Museums of San Francisco; Gift of Mr. and Mrs. Edgar Sinton, Hillsborough
p. 108

Untitled (S.229, Hanging Tied-Wire, Double-Sided, Open-Center, Multi-Branched Form Based on Nature), 1964
Oxidized copper wire
20 × 20 × 7½ inches (50.8 × 50.8 × 19.1 cm)
Private collection
p. 111

Untitled (S.136, Freestanding Electroplated Tied-Wire, Open-Center, Twelve-Branched Organic Form Based on Nature), 1965
Electroplated copper wire
4½ × 9¼ × 9¼ inches (11.4 × 23.5 × 23.5 cm)
Private collection
p. 115

Untitled (S.557, Wall-Mounted Tied-Wire, Closed-Center, Twelve-Petaled Form Based on Nature), ca. 1965–70
Bronze wire
38 × 38 × 12 inches (96.5 × 96.5 × 30.5 cm)
Crystal Bridges Museum of American Art, Bentonville, Arkansas, 2011.39
p. 27

Untitled (SD.067, Tied-Wire Sculpture Drawing with Five-Pointed Star in Center and Asymmetrical Branches), after 1965
Pen and black ink on paper
6 × 6 inches (15.2 × 15.2 cm)
Fine Arts Museums of San Francisco; Gift of the artist
p. 109

Untitled (SD.139, Tied-Wire Sculpture Drawing with Open Pentagon Center and Branches Enclosed by a Circle), after 1965
Pen and black ink on Japanese paper
36 × 22 inches (91.4 × 55.9 cm)
Fine Arts Museums of San Francisco; Gift of the artist
p. 110

Untitled (S.062, Wall-Mounted Folded Paper Form), ca. 1968–70
Bronze, brown-green patina
14¾ × 4½ × 2½ inches (37.5 × 11.4 × 6.4 cm)
Private collection
p. 119

Untitled (S.634, Hanging Sphere), ca. 1968–72
Brass and copper wire
8½ × 8 × 8 inches (21.6 × 20.3 × 20.3 cm)
Private collection
p. 25

Untitled (S.529, Wall-Mounted Paperfold with Horizontal Stripes), ca. 1970s
Brushed black ink on paper
13¾ × 26½ × 1½ inches (34.9 × 67.3 × 3.8 cm)
Private collection
p. 118

Untitled (S.671, Hanging Tied-Wire, Open-Center, Three-Petaled Form Based on Nature), ca. 1970s
Brass wire
15 × 15 × 8 inches (38.1 × 38.1 × 20.3 cm)
Collection of Chris Houston
p. 103

Wintermass (S.187, Hanging Tied-Wire, Double-Sided, Open-Center, Five-Branched Form Based on Nature), ca. 1974
Stainless steel wire tipped with resin
45 × 46 × 25 inches (114.3 × 116.8 × 63.5 cm)
Private collection
p. 28

Untitled (S.120, Freestanding Reversible Undulating Form), ca. 1975
Bronze, natural verdigris
10 × 18 × 18 inches (25.4 × 45.7 × 45.7 cm)
Private collection
p. 106

Untitled (S.315, Hanging Six-Lobed, Multilayered Interlocking Continuous Form within a Form with Spheres in the Second and Fourth Lobes), ca. 1976
Copper and brass wire
77 × 15 × 15 inches (195.6 × 38.1 × 38.1 cm)
Private collection
p. 120

Untitled (S.020, Hanging Miniature Two Interlocked, Three-Layered Spheres), ca. 1978
Copper wire
16 × 9 × 9 inches (40.6 × 22.9 × 22.9 cm)
Private collection
p. 80

Untitled (S.077, Hanging Miniature Seven-Lobed Continuous Form within a Form), ca. 1978
Copper wire
33 × 5½ × 5½ inches (83.8 × 14 × 14 cm)
Private collection
p. 124

Untitled (S.306, Hanging Miniature Five Interlocking Double Trumpets), ca. 1978
Copper wire
5½ × 5½ × 4 inches (14 × 14 × 10.2 cm)
Private collection
p. 62

Untitled (SD.041, Three Views of Cast Tied-Wire Sculpture S.768 and One of Electroplated S.136), ca. 1978
Pen and black ink on newsprint
20 × 30 inches (50.8 × 76.2 cm)
Fine Arts Museums of San Francisco; Gift of the artist
p. 114

Continuous (S.340, Hanging Miniature Single-Lobed, Three-Layered Continuous Form within a Form), ca. 1981–82
Gold-filled wire
3½ × 4½ × 4½ inches (8.9 × 11.4 × 11.4 cm)
Private collection
p. 125

Cabbage (P.021), 1984
Green ink on coated paper, offset lithograph
9¼ × 9⅜ inches (23.5 × 23.8 cm)
Private collection
p. 117

Untitled (S.043, Hanging Tied-Wire, Cubed Open-Center, Multi-Branched Form Based on Nature), ca. 1994
Bronze wire with green patina
32 × 32 × 32 inches (81.3 × 81.3 × 81.3 cm)
Private collection
p. 96

Untitled (S.130, Freestanding Vessel Form), 1996
Bronze, golden green patina
14 × 13¼ × 13¼ inches (35.6 × 33.7 × 33.7 cm)
Private collection
p. 32

Untitled (S.004, Freestanding Stalagmite Form), 1997
Bronze, golden brown patina
23 × 11 × 11 inches (58.4 × 27.9 × 27.9 cm)
Private collection
p. 55

Untitled (S.292, Hanging Miniature Eight-Lobed, Single-Layered Continuous Form), 2000
Stainless steel wire
33 × 3¾ × 3¾ inches (83.8 × 9.5 × 9.5 cm)
Private collection
p. 123

Selected Bibliography

Monographs

Ruth Asawa. Exh. cat. New York: David Zwirner Books, 2018. Essays by Tiffany Bell and Robert Storr.
Ruth Asawa: A Retrospective View. Exh. cat. San Francisco: San Francisco Museum of Art, 1973. Essay by Gerald Nordland.
Ruth Asawa: Completing the Circle. Exh. cat. Fresno, CA: Fresno Art Museum, 2001.
Ruth Asawa: Line by Line. Exh. cat. New York: Christie's, 2015. Essays by Jonathan Laib and Robert Storr.
Ruth Asawa: Objects and Apparitions. Exh. cat. New York: Christie's, 2013. Essays by Jonathan Laib, Nicholas Fox Weber, and John Yau.
The Sculpture of Ruth Asawa: Contours in the Air. Exh. cat. Edited by Daniell Cornell. San Francisco: Fine Arts Museums of San Francisco; and Berkeley: University of California Press, 2006. Essays by Cornell, Mary Emma Harris, Karin Higa, Jacqueline Hoefer, Emily K. Doman Jennings, John Kreidler, Susan Stauter, and Sally B. Woodbridge; interview with Asawa and Albert Lanier by Paul J. Karlstrom.
Woodbridge, Sally B. *Ruth Asawa's San Francisco Fountain, Hyatt on Union Square*. San Francisco, 1973.

Interviews with the Artist

Interview by Aiko Cuneo. September 24, 2003.
Interview by Mary E. Harris. San Francisco, December 19, 1971.
"Art, Competence, and Citywide Cooperation for San Francisco." Oral history interview with Asawa and Albert Lanier by Harriet Nathan, San Francisco, February 15, March 15, June 28, and October 25, 1974; and January 16, 1976. Regional Oral History Office, Bancroft Library, University of California, Berkeley, 1980.
"Interview with Sculptor Ruth Asawa: Artist Remembers Painful Days of Internment During World War II." *Noe Valley Voice* 13, no. 10 (December 1989/January 1990):20.
Oral history interview by Joanne Iritani, April 7, 2001. Florin Japanese American Citizens League Oral History Project. Transcript available at California State University, Sacramento University Library.
Oral history interview with Asawa and Albert Lanier by Paul Karlstrom and Mark Johnson. San Francisco, June 21 and July 5, 2002. Archives of American Art Oral History program, Smithsonian Institution. Transcript available on the Archives of American Art website.

Articles and Reviews

Anderson, Judith. "A Life Immersed in Art and Affection." *San Francisco Chronicle*, February 8, 1982.
Archer, Sarah. "Maker to Market: Ruth Asawa Reappraised." *Journal of Modern Craft* 8, no. 2 (July 2015): 141–54.
Asawa, Ruth. "Black Mountain College." In *Buckminster Fuller: Anthology for the New Millennium*, 201–204. Edited by Thomas T. K. Zung. New York: St. Martin's Press, 2001.
———. "Making Every Moment Count." In Cathleen Rountree, ed. *On Women Turning 70: Honoring the Voices of Wisdom*, 87–94. San Francisco: Jossey-Bass Publishers, 1999.
Barron, Stephanie, Sheri Bernstein, and Ilene Susan Fort, eds. *Made in California: Art, Image, and Identity, 1900–2000.* Exh. cat. Los Angeles: Los Angeles County Museum of Art; and Berkeley: University of California Press, 2000.
Cooper, Ashton. "Ruth Asawa." *Art + Auction* (October 2013): 141–44.
Duberman, Martin. *Black Mountain: An Exploration in Community*. New York: E. P. Dutton, 1972.
Frankenstein, Alfred. "The Modern Shows the Figure." *San Francisco Chronicle*, August 18, 1963.
———. "Wire Sculpture: A Remarkable Exhibit." *San Francisco Chronicle*, July 5, 1973.
Fried, Alexander. "Refreshing Art of Ruth Asawa." *San Francisco Examiner*, July 2, 1973.
———. "Two Exhibits of Oriental Flavor." *San Francisco Examiner*, May 22, 1960.
Gage, Otis. "Sculpturama." *Arts and Architecture* (February 1955): 4, 8–10, 30.
Gueft, Olga. "For Six Children and Sculpture." *Interiors* 126, no. 12 (July 1967): 96–99.
Hamilton, Mildred. "Ruth Asawa: Headlined Sculptress." *San Francisco Examiner*, March 31, 1968.
Hauseur, Krystal Reiko. "Crafted Abstraction: Three Nisei Artists and the American Studio Craft Movement: Ruth Asawa, Kay Sekimachi, and Toshiko Takaezu." PhD diss., University of California, Irvine, 2011.
———. "The Crafted Abstraction of Ruth Asawa, Kay Sekimachi, and Toshiko Takaezu." Chapter 8 in *American Women Artists, 1935–1970: Gender, Culture, and Politics*. Ed. Helen Langa. London: Routledge, 2016.
Jennings, Emily K. Doman. "Defining the Transparent? The Sculptures of Ruth Asawa." Master's thesis, San Francisco State University, 2006.
Link, Terry. "The Art of Ruth Asawa." *San Francisco* 15, no. 4 (April 1973): 22–25.
Molesworth, Helen, and Ruth Erickson. *Leap Before You Look: Black Mountain College, 1933–1957.* Exh. cat. Boston: Institute of Contemporary Art; and New Haven: Yale University Press, 2015.
Munro, Eleanor C. "Globe within a Cup within a Sphere." *ArtNews* 55 (April 1956): 26.
———. "Ruth Asawa." *ArtNews* 57 (June 1958): 16.
"Eastern Yeast." *Time* 65, no. 2 (January 10, 1955): 54.
"Four Artist-Craftsmen." *Arts and Architecture* (June 1954): 24–25.
Nordland, Gerald. "Los Angeles: Ruth Asawa." *Artforum International* 1, no. 1 (June 1962): 8.
The Oakland Art Museum California Sculptors' Annual Exhibition for 1959. Exh. cat. Oakland, CA: Oakland Art Museum, 1959.
Parker, Tyler. "Ruth Asaw [*sic*]." *ArtNews* 53 (December 1954): 52.
Photographic viewbook. Black Mountain, NC: Black Mountain College, 1949–50.
"Ruth Asawa: A Snare for Shifting Light." *ArtNews* (June 1958): 16.
Selz, Peter. "Ruth Asawa." *Sculpture* 21, no. 9 (November 2002): 67.
Simon, Katie. "A Conversation with Ruth Asawa, Artist." *Artweek* 26, no. 8 (August 1995): 17–18.
Smith, Elizabeth A. T. "'What can be done, what I must learn, what there is to do . . .': Process, Materials, and Narrative in the 1950s." In Paul Schimmel and Jenni Sorkin, eds. *Revolution in the Making: Abstract Sculpture by Women, 1947–2016*, 18–33. Exh. cat. New York: Hauser & Wirth; and Milan: Skira, 2016.
Webster, Mary Hull. "Ruth Asawa at J. J. Brookings Gallery." *Artweek* 26, no. 8 (August 1995): 17.

Contributors

Aruna D'Souza writes about modern and contemporary art, intersectional feminisms and other forms of politics, and how museums shape our views of each other and the world. Her work appears regularly in 4Columns.org, where she is a member of the editorial advisory board; she also has been published in the *Wall Street Journal*, *ArtNews*, *Garage*, *Bookforum*, *Momus*, *Art in America*, and *Art Practical*, among other places. Her book *Whitewalling: Art, Race, and Protest in 3 Acts* was published by Badlands Unlimited in 2018. She is also editor of the forthcoming volume *Making It Modern: A Linda Nochlin Reader*, to be published by Thames & Hudson.

Helen Molesworth was the chief curator at the Museum of Contemporary Art, Los Angeles, from 2014 to 2018, where she organized the large-scale group exhibition *One Day at a Time: Manny Farber and Termite Art*, and co-organized major exhibitions on artists Anna Maria Maiolino and Kerry James Marshall. From 2010 to 2014 she was the Barbara Lee Chief Curator at the Institute of Contemporary Art, Boston, where she assembled one-person exhibitions of artists Steve Locke, Josiah McElheny, Catherine Opie, and Amy Sillman, and the group exhibitions *Leap Before You Look: Black Mountain College 1933–1957*; *Dance/Draw*; and *This Will Have Been: Art, Love & Politics in the 1980s*. While head of the Department of Modern and Contemporary Art at the Harvard Art Museums, she presented an exhibition of photographs by Moyra Davey and *ACT UP NY: Activism, Art, and the AIDS Crisis 1987–1993*. She is the author of numerous catalogue essays, and her writing has appeared in publications such as *Artforum*, *Art Journal*, *Documents*, and *October*. A recipient of the Bard Center for Curatorial Studies Award for Curatorial Excellence (2011), she is currently at work on a book of essays about art and what it does.

Tamara H. Schenkenberg is the curator at the Pulitzer Arts Foundation in St. Louis. Since joining the Pulitzer in 2012, she has curated a wide range of exhibitions including *Fred Sandback: 64 Three-Part Pieces*; *The Ordinary Must Not Be Dull: Claes Oldenburg's Soft Sculptures*; *Medardo Rosso: Experiments in Light and Form*; *Living Proof: Drawing in 19th-Century Japan*; and, most recently, *Mona Hatoum: Terra Infirma*, for which she served as the organizing curator. Prior to joining the Pulitzer, she held curatorial positions at the Saint Louis Art Museum, where she assisted in the planning and research of multiple exhibitions of postwar German art. Schenkenberg was a Fulbright scholar at the Free University of Berlin (2010–11) and holds a PhD in art history from the University of Wisconsin–Madison.

Lenders to the Exhibition

Black Mountain College Museum + Arts Center Collection
Crystal Bridges Museum of American Art, Bentonville, Arkansas
Fine Arts Museums of San Francisco
Chuck and Kathy Harper
Harvard Art Museums/Busch-Reisinger Museum
Mrs. Philip A. Hassel
Chris Houston
Holly Johnson and Parker Harris
Museum of Fine Arts, Houston
Museum of Modern Art, New York
Promised gift of Alice and Tom Tisch
Diana Nelson and John Atwater
Private collection
Private collection, courtesy David Zwirner
Private collection, New Jersey, courtesy David Zwirner
San José Museum of Art
San Francisco Museum of Modern Art
Snyder Family Living Trust
William and Joan Roth Collection
Whitney Museum of American Art, New York

Board of Trustees

Photography Credits

Unless otherwise noted all images copyright Estate of Ruth Asawa, courtesy the Estate of Ruth Asawa and David Zwirner

Photographs by Alise O'Brien Photography are copyright Pulitzer Arts Foundation and Alise O'Brien Photography

Photos by Alise O'Brien Photography, 7–10; photo courtesy the Department of Special Collections, Stanford Libraries, p. 12; © 2021 Imogen Cunningham Trust, p. 13; (top) © 2021 Imogen Cunningham Trust; (bottom) photo by Paul Hassel, p. 14; photo courtesy Imaging Department, © President and Fellows of Harvard College, p. 15; (top) photo by Laurence Cuneo; (bottom) photo by Hudson Cuneo, p. 17; photos by Hudson Cuneo, p. 18; photo by Alise O'Brien Photography, p. 19; photo by Dan Bradica, courtesy David Zwirner, p. 20; photo © Whitney Museum, New York, p. 21; photo © 2015 Christie's Images Limited, p. 22; photos by Laurence Cuneo, p. 23; photo © 2012 Christie's Images Limited, p. 24; photo by Laurence Cuneo, p. 25; photo by Aiko Cuneo, p. 26; photos by Laurence Cuneo, pp. 27–28; photo by Alise O'Brien Photography, © Pulitzer Arts Foundation and Alise O'Brien Photography, p. 29; (left) photos courtesy the Estate of Ruth Asawa; (right) photo by Nat Farbman, p. 30; (top) photo by Laurence Cuneo; (bottom) photo by Aiko Cuneo, p. 31; photo by Laurence Cuneo, p. 32; photo by Alise O'Brien Photography, p. 34; (left) photo by Arnold Newman/Getty Images; (right) courtesy Center for Creative Photography, University of Arizona © 1991 Hans Namuth Estate. Digital Image © The Museum of Modern Art/ Licensed by SCALA / Art Resource, NY, p. 36; © 2021 Imogen Cunningham Trust, p. 37; photo courtesy the Fine Arts Museums of San Francisco, p. 39; © 2021 Rondal Partridge Archive, p. 40; © 2021 Imogen Cunningham Trust, p. 41; © Ladies Home Journal, June 1964, photo by Ernst Beadle, p. 43; © 2021 Imogen Cunningham Trust, p. 44; photo by Paul Hassel, p. 46; © 2021 Imogen Cunningham Trust, p. 47; (top) © 2021 Imogen Cunningham Trust; (bottom) © The Ray Johnson Estate, photo courtesy the Ray Johnson Estate, p. 48; photo by Alise O'Brien Photography, pp. 50–51; photo courtesy Imaging Department, © President and Fellows of Harvard College, p. 53; photo courtesy the Fine Arts Museums of San Francisco, p. 54; photo by Alise O'Brien Photography, p. 55; photo by Dan Bradica, courtesy David Zwirner, p. 56; photo by Laurence Cuneo, p. 57; photo courtesy the Fine Arts Museums of San Francisco, p. 58; photo courtesy Imaging Department, © President and Fellows of Harvard College, p. 59; photo courtesy the Fine Arts Museums of San Francisco, p. 60; photo by Dan Bradica, courtesy David Zwirner, p. 61; photo by Laurence Cuneo, p. 62; photo © 2015 Christie's Images Limited, p. 63; photo by Alise O'Brien Photography, p. 64; photo by Dan Bradica, courtesy David Zwirner, p. 65; photos by Alise O'Brien Photography, pp. 66–67; photo by Dan Bradica, courtesy David Zwirner, p. 69; photo by Laurence Cuneo, p. 70; photo by Alise O'Brien Photography, p. 71; photos by Alise O'Brien Photography, p. 74; photo © 2015 Christie's Images Limited, p. 75; photo by Dan Bradica, courtesy David Zwirner, p. 77; photo by JKA Photography, p. 78; photo by Katherine Du Tiel, San Francisco Museum of Modern Art, p. 79; photo by Alise O'Brien Photography, p. 80; photo by Laurence Cuneo, p. 81; photo by Alise O'Brien Photography, p. 82; photo by Laurence Cuneo, p. 83; photo by James Paonessa, p. 85; photo courtesy the Fine Arts Museums of San Francisco, p. 86; photo © 2013 Christie's Images Limited, p. 87; photos by Alise O'Brien Photography, pp. 88–89; photo by Dan Bradica, courtesy David Zwirner, p. 90; photo by Laurence Cuneo, p. 93; photo by Alise O'Brien Photography, p. 94; photo by JKA Photography, p. 95; photo by Alise O'Brien Photography, p. 96; photo courtesy the Fine Arts Museums of San Francisco, p. 97; photo by JKA Photography, p. 99; photo © 2013 Christie's Images Limited, p. 101; photo by Alise O'Brien Photography, p. 103; photo by Alise O'Brien Photography, p. 105; photo © 2013 Christie's Images Limited, p. 106; photos courtesy the Fine Arts Museums of San Francisco, pp. 108–10; photo by Alise O'Brien Photography, p. 111; photos by Laurence Cuneo, p. 112; photo by Alise O'Brien Photography, p. 113; photo courtesy the Fine Arts Museums of San Francisco, p. 114; photos by Laurence Cuneo, pp. 115–16; photo by James Paonessa, p. 117; photos by Alise O'Brien Photography, pp. 118–19; photo by Laurence Cuneo, p. 120; photo by JKA Photography, p. 121; photo by Dan Bradica, courtesy David Zwirner, p. 123; photo by Hudson Cuneo, p. 124; photo by Dan Bradica, courtesy David Zwirner, p. 125; photo © 2013 Christie's Images Limited, p. 127; photos by Alise O'Brien Photography, pp. 128–29; (left) photo by Laurence Cuneo; (center) photo by Alise O'Brien Photography; (right) photo by Dan Bradica, courtesy David Zwirner, p. 131; (left) photo by Alise O'Brien Photography; (center) photo by Laurence Cuneo; (top right) photo by Alise O'Brien Photography; (bottom right) photo © 2012 Christie's Images Limited, p. 132; (left) photo by Dan Bradica, courtesy David Zwirner; (right) photo © 2015 Christie's Images Limited, p. 133; (top left) photo by Dan Bradica, courtesy David Zwirner; (bottom left) photo © 2015 Christie's Images Limited; (right) photo by Laurence Cuneo, p. 134; (top left) photo by Alise O'Brien Photography; (bottom left) photo by Dan Bradica, courtesy David Zwirner; (center and right) photos by Laurence Cuneo, p. 135; (left) photo by JKA Photography; (center) photo by Dan Bradica, courtesy David Zwirner; (top right) photo by JKA Photography; (bottom right) photo by Laurence Cuneo, p. 136; (bottom right) photo by Laurence Cuneo; (bottom left) photo by Alise O'Brien Photography, p. 137; (left) photo by Laurence Cuneo; (center) photo © 2015 Christie's Images Limited; (right) photo by Laurence Cuneo, p. 138; (left) photo by Laurence Cuneo; (top right) photo © 2013 Christie's Images Limited; (bottom right) photo by Laurence Cuneo, p. 139; photos by Laurence Cuneo, p. 140; photos © 2015 Christie's Images Limited, p. 141; (left) photo by Alise O'Brien Photography; (center and right) photos by Laurence Cuneo, p. 142; (top left) photo by Kerry McFate; (bottom left) photo by Hudson Cuneo; (top right) photo by Alise O'Brien Photography; (center right) photo by Laurence Cuneo; (bottom right) photo by Alise O'Brien Photography, p. 143; photo by Alise O'Brien Photography, p. 145.

Index

Works in the exhibition are indicated by italicized page numbers. Figures in the catalog are indicated by "f" following the page number.